Preface

One threat to effective education is that of indoctrination. This indoctrination can be realized when only one point of view is available to students; it can be effected through a professor, a limited set of experiences, or even a book. This book of readings is designed to counteract the threat of indoctrination. If a student is using *Diagnostic and Remedial Reading* as a text, this book should provide him with information which goes beyond the materials in this or most other texts and may differ with those ideas presented in other texts.

By using this book of readings, the student can argue with and discuss points made by Wilson in *Diagnostic and Remedial Reading* or with those made by other authors. As the student selects ideas which seem logical or which are supported by research, he evaluates and reevaluates his position and, finally, forms his own opinions. By undergoing such procedures, the students moves from being indoctrinated to being educated.

Obviously, ideas other than those presented in this book do exist concerning reading. No text and no book of readings can present all that is to be considered important. However, an awareness of some contrasting points of view do tend to make the student cautious for he realizes the need for continued study, constant reexamination of his position, and, eventually, a high commitment to the scholarly pursuit for knowledge.

The organization of these chapters is identical to the organization of *Diagnostic and Remedial Reading*. The student will find it useful to read these chapters as he reads the chapters in the text. Preceeding each article, the editors have posed questions intended to direct the student to the major purpose for the article's inclusion.

The ultimate purpose of education may well be to make learning a useful, inquiring, pleasant process in which each student emerges in his own unique way. The authors are hopeful that these readings will contribute to such a goal.

RMW
JRG
1972

Readings for Diagnostic and Remedial Reading

Readings for Diagnostic and Remedial Reading

Robert M. Wilson
University of Maryland

James Geyer
Shippensburg State College

CHARLES E. MERRILL PUBLISHING COMPANY
A Bell & Howell Company
Columbus, Ohio 43216

Published by
CHARLES E. MERRILL PUBLISHING COMPANY
A Bell & Howell Company
Columbus, Ohio 43216

International Standard Book Number: 0-675-09060-1

Library of Congress Catalog Card Number: 72-84126

Printed in the United States of America

Contents

1

Working with Problem Readers

Field theory has been presented by Snygg. Who needs theory to support practice? Snygg provides one answer.

A COGNITIVE FIELD THEORY OF LEARNING

Donald Snygg

Most teachers consider psychological theories of learning impractical and use them only when they are needed to justify something the teacher wants to do anyway. This may seem odd to outsiders since teaching is supposedly a profession, that is, an occupation whose members do not conduct themselves by rote and are presumably educated to deal effectively with situations which have never arisen before. Professional work can be done only on the basis of theories of cause and effect which enable the professional worker to predict

From *Learning and Mental Health in the School: 1966 Yearbook,* edited by Walter B. Waetjen and Robert R. Leeper (Washington, D.C.: Association for Supervision and Curriculum Development, 1966), pp. 77-87. Copyright © 1966 by the Association for Supervision and Curriculum Development. Reprinted with permission of the Association for Supervision and Curriculum Development.

what will happen in a given case even though the circumstances and situation are completely new.

Knowledge of what has happened in one situation cannot, without a theory of why it happened, enable us to predict what will happen in any other situation if it is different in the slightest degree. If we cannot predict the results of our acts we cannot choose between alternative courses of action or plan new ones. Without a scientific theory of learning, teachers and administrators have to meet new problems with inappropriate routines that were devised long ago to meet other problems or to base their decisions on folk beliefs about learning which, although thoroughly disproved in the laboratories, still pass for common sense.

Teachers are not the only people with professional licenses who tend to drop into the ways of routine workers. As a result of the great surge of scientific discovery, engineers and physicians are having more and more difficulty keeping up with basic theory and are able to remain real professionals only by restricting themselves to narrow fields of specialization. These specialties can be made comprehensible by a narrow band of theory so limited that a busy practitioner can keep in touch with the significant research that bears upon it.

If teachers have not been forced so far on this path of specialization, it may be because the results of teaching are much harder to find and evaluate than the results of engineering or even medicine. Since the primary social purpose of education is a more effective adulthood, the really significant results of teaching do not occur until years afterward. By that time the casual connection between the adult behavior and any classroom events has been covered over by thousands of other experiences and is impossible to trace. As a result, educational innovations tend to be accepted or rejected, not in terms of their results, which are largely unknown, but in terms of the degree to which they fit the beliefs about human nature and human purpose which happen to be in vogue at that time.

NEED FOR THEORY

Each of us accepts the validity of methods and devices that fit our view of reality; but methods which do not fit our personal concept of human nature and educational purpose or which we do not feel capable of using are regarded as "impractical theory" and rejected. This makes for a static profession because once an educational practice has come into use it tends to acquire a legitimacy of its own.

Teachers who have encountered such a practice from their kindergarten days perceive it as an essential aspect of real teaching. When the practice was new it was accepted because it conformed to the folk belief or the theory of psychology that passed for common sense at the time. Yet once it becomes an accepted part of school practice it no longer needs the sanction of a theory. Instead such a practice comes to serve as a criterion that teachers and parents use for evaluating new educational and psychological theories. Those theories which do not sanction the now hallowed practice are obviously crackbrained, impractical, and for use only in passing examinations and gaining degrees. If this seems exaggerated, consider how the full-arm system of penmanship hangs on in spite of half a century of research on the motor development of children which has negated every assumption on which the full-arm system was based.

If there is now a new interest in theories of learning it is because the tremendous changes in our society have given us the task of preparing children to live in a very different society than we have had in the past. This is a society whose problems we cannot solve and cannot even anticipate. The social and technological changes now sweeping the world are moving so fast that almost any specific fact or procedure taught today will be obsolete before the learner leaves school. As a result, the new subject matter projects take as their objectives the student's discovery of concepts and generalizations and the development of thinking processes, independent learning skills, and creativity. This is not an education solely for an elite class. Within a very few years all routine tasks outside the home will be done by machines, and the adults who have not been helped to attain the conceptual skills and the attitudes of initiative and responsibility required for technical, managerial or professional work will be economically dispossessed, unable to participate in productive work.

We do not know how many people can be brought to the level of intellect, initiative, and responsibility that will be required. Nevertheless, the fact that there is already a shortage of professional and technical workers while several million routine workers are unable to find jobs suggests that we must at once begin our search for a solution to this problem.

This new problem requires new methods. The conventional classroom practices were devised at a time when the chief task of the school was the communication of information and the desired outcome was memorization of this information. The fact that the personal qualities required for professional, technical, and managerial work are found in many of our graduates does not mean that these qualities are implanted by the schools. The fact that these qualities are seldom found in disadvantaged neighborhoods and are frequently found among children from middle- and upper-class homes strongly suggests that these qualities are usually learned in the home and not in school. Also, remembering that the general tone and basic methods of instruction were devised long before psychology had become a field of experimental inquiry, when people harbored a great many beliefs about human motivation and learning that have now been disproved or qualified in important ways, it does not seem likely that we can significantly change the product of our schools by just doing more of what we have been doing all along.

It is true that many teachers, unable to see adequate results from their labors, become discouraged time servers, striving only to "make it look good." However, no one who knows teachers can believe that their failure to achieve results which the schools were not designed to achieve is due to any lack in the personal qualities of our teachers. It seems much more likely that we are failing to achieve the new educational objectives of our society because teachers have to base their campaigns, their strategy, and their tactics of teaching on inaccurate assumptions about human nature and human learning.

When the free, compulsory public schools first assumed the task of teaching unwilling children what they did not want to know, the first psychology laboratory was still far in the future. On a day-to-day basis, the classroom teacher in the early public schools, while the mold of tradition was being set, seems to have dealt with the new problems, just as most teachers do now, in terms of one or the other of two prescientific "common sense" hypotheses about learning, neither of which has stood the test of experimental investigation.

INFLUENCE OF FREQUENCY HYPOTHESIS

The first of these we shall call the habit or frequency hypothesis. Most people who have attempted to analyze the learning process have begun by noticing that learning, particularly schoolroom learning, often does not occur without a great deal of practice. Logic does not insist that since A commonly occurs before B it must be the cause of B, yet this seems to be an easy conclusion to draw. I once knew a cat which, after cleaning the fish out of the neighborhood pond, succumbed to this logical fallacy and spent most of the next winter sitting on a toilet bowl waiting for fish to appear. In time he gave up his delusion that water causes fish. Nevertheless, many teachers, in spite of their frequent observation of practice that has not resulted in perfection or even progress, persist in the delusion that practice, if continued long enough, will eventually result in learning. "Practice makes perfect" is part of the culture and when all else fails teachers can salve their consciences and satisfy the public by devoting more time to drill, assigning more problems in the workbook, or by lengthening the school day or the school year. The only cost of this type of educational reform is the additional money spent for paper, pencils, electricity, and fuel.

Experimental psychologists, like teachers, are children of their culture. As a rule they have started, like the teachers, with the assumption that frequency, repetition, practice, or exercise causes learning—that habits are caused by practicing them. Yet few of them have been able to keep that opinion for long. In 1929 Knight Dunlap demonstrated that one way to break habits was to practice them. He cured typists of their characteristic errors by requiring them to practice the error. He cured children of thumb sucking by requiring them to suck their thumbs. It is reasonable to believe that many children have been cured of piano playing by the same method, and it is quite likely that we have cured quite a few of arithmetic and reading.

Confronted by this situation and by the further observation that much repetition and practice do not result in improvement, a learning theorist must find a "cause" of learning which will either supplement the frequency hypothesis or replace it completely. Looking again into the cultural fund of "common sense" he finds that learning is also believed to be promoted by rewards and punishments.

The Reinforcement Model of Learning

Teachers have traditionally used praise and blame, prizes, marks, gold stars, certificates of merit, smiles, frowns, detention, and, until recently, the rod to promote learning. On the common sense level almost everyone assumes that acts which are punished are less likely to be repeated, that acts which are rewarded are more likely to be repeated. But what is rewarding? Pleasure? And what is punishment? Pain? Perhaps. Yet what is pleasant to one person may be painful to another, a fact well known to most families that have only one TV set. Some pupils work hard for high marks; others try to avoid them. A good conduct award in the fourth grade may cause more misconduct than it prevents. Experiments show that under conditions of high motivation strong rewards and punishments interfere with problem-solving. In some experiments animals given an electric shock every time they made the correct response have learned faster than comparable animals who did not suffer shock.

The conventional methods of teaching—repetition, reward, and punishment—are far from reliable. Practice does not insure perfection. In some cases repetition leads to learning; in others it merely leads to inattention. Rewards and punishments may promote learning or they may interfere with it. The folk theories of learning are very unreliable guides to educational planning.

It is no wonder that many teachers, disappointed in the results of their attempts at professional planning, lose faith in themselves and fall back on a ritual of routine practices copied from the teachers they respect.

In an effort to build a more reliable model of the learning process, present-day S-R psychologists have dropped the terms "reward" and "punishment" in favor of positive and negative "reinforcement." Although many people assume that "reinforcement" is merely a technical name for "reward" and think of the two as synonymous, the shift from reward to reinforcement is a very significant one. Reward theory assumed that "rewards," acting independently, will strengthen the pupil's tendency to perform the act which has been rewarded. "Reinforcement" implies a vaguer theory of causation. Reinforcement is merely defined as whatever strengthens the tendency for a particular response to follow a particular stimulus. That is, a "reinforcement" is identified only by its consequences. In effect, the S-R psychologists, having decided that at this time no one has enough information to tell why reinforcement takes place, have decided to quit worrying about it and to go to other problems. "Reinforcement" is not reward. It is simply the name for a hypothetical process and offers no explanation of the process.[1]

This leaves the teacher who wishes to use reinforcement theory in a bad situation. Without a theory of what causes reinforcement he is unable to make any plans for achieving it. The most anyone can do is to give the practice lip service and go on using the old folk theories of repetition, reward, and punishment as teachers have always done. As a matter of fact a good many psychologists do this, too, but they have one advantage in the laboratory that the teacher does not have in the classroom. The psychologist knows by experience that starving a rat or pigeon down to 75 percent of normal body weight provides a situation in which the presentation of food very frequently results in reinforcement. So, if he wants to, he can forget

---

[1]To be accurate, not all S-R psychologists accept the concept of reinforcement. Guthrie was able to construct an S-R theory which did not use this concept.

that problem and go on to study other aspects of learning. Public sentiment fortunately prevents the application of this empirical discovery to schoolchildren.

Unquestionably the stimulus-response model of learning is by far the easiest model on which to base research. In the past fifty years an overwhelming majority of learning experiments have used the S-R pattern. Indeed this pattern has had such a monopoly on the field that some psychologists call it "learning theory" implying that no other conceptual model is possible. Others concede that other conceptual models for learning are possible and may even be useful but believe that only the S-R can be scientifically legitimate. This, of course, is nonsense.

The only scientific criterion for judging any theory is its usefulness in predicting previously unknown facts and thus making possible new and better practices. By this criterion the S-R model of learning has failed to justify itself. For fifty years it has almost monopolized the facilities of the experimental laboratories and during that time this theory has not led to the invention of a single educational technique which was not already in use and originally derived from the prescientific folk theories of exercise, reward, and punishment. When it has been possible to apply S-R theory to educational practice the results have not validated the model. The early teaching machines were expected to open a new era in education by making possible the immediate reinforcement (by showing when the answer was correct) to the student's response (writing an answer to the stimulus question). A number of research studies have found that their subjects learned just as well when they did not write an answer (make a response) to be reinforced at all but simply read the machine tape, as when they read a book. Generally these students learned more in a given length of time than the students who followed the standard procedure because they did not have to spend time writing. Other experimenters found that some of the best learners in their experiments were the subjects who made the most mistakes and consequently had had the fewest correct responses reinforced.

The reinforcement S-R model of learning cannot serve the needs of education in this century because it is a model for teaching that which is already known. The task of the teacher using reinforcement theory looks, on the face of it, very simple. His task is to set up a situation in which the student will make the desired response and then, without delay, the teacher must see that something happens which will result in that response being reinforced. This does not look hard to an experimental psychologist who has a supply of feed and a hungry pigeon or rat in a box where it has only two possible choices. This task, however, is probably impossible for a teacher who is in a room with thirty children with widely differing interests, abilities, and personal problems. The essential limitation of the model is that the teacher has to decide what words or actions should be reinforced. An act which does not conform to the teacher's idea of what is good, proper, and effective, a problem solution which differs from the solution he would make, cannot be reinforced. In such a situation, conventional, routine behavior is going to be reinforced; creative and inventive behavior is not.

If reinforcement theory could be put into educational practice, it would only serve to teach what is already known, to promote conventional, conforming behavior, to prepare pupils to live in a world exactly like the one in which they are educated. In a world changing as rapidly as the world is changing now, in which we cannot teach our children the answers to their future problems because we cannot even anticipate the problems, an education based on reinforcement theory would be an education for obsolescence. If what is desired is a creative, adaptable citizen, able to deal with problems his teachers could not have envisaged and with problems they were unable to solve, another model for learning must be used.

One of the strong reactions against the reinforcement model for learning has come from the people who have been developing the National Science Foundation projects. They have been confronted with the problem of teaching what Bruner has called the structure or logic of a subject matter area. Although the concept of subject matter structure is not new, most teaching in American schools has conformed to the stimulus-response model of Thorndike's early "prebelonging" theories. Items of information are taught separately and rewarded or, as in Skinner's learning machine, "reinforced" separately. The scientists given responsibility for the NSF projects have insisted that teaching items of information is not the way to teach science. Each area of science, they insist, is made up of a structure of interrelated concepts and conceptual models which gives meaning to the separate facts and thus makes possible the deduction of new ones. Isolated facts, without a theory to unify them, do not tell us what to expect in new situations and consequently do not equip the student for success in any but routine situations where other people have already worked out the answers. If this is true, the first qualification of a teacher should be the ability to practice the science he is teaching. Yet he must also understand a great many things about teaching, including the answers to some questions about how concepts are taught, that people are just beginning to think about.

COGNITIVE FIELD THEORIES OF LEARNING

Psychologically, the concept of subject matter organization fits into a general concept of cognitive organization and motivation which is being developed by a number of psychologists. Ausubel, Combs, Festinger, Heider, Rogers, Snygg, and Taba, and many others have contributed to the general theory. At the present time the work of Piaget is most influential in providing a common ground for definition of problems. While the proponents of the cognitive approach differ from one another in minor ways they have, under the influence of Gestalt psychology, Tolman's cognitive behaviorism, Lewin's field theory, and a number of other sources, come to fairly close agreement on their model of learning. However the particular version which follows is that of the author.

It is assumed that an individual's behavior is always appropriate to his phenomenal field, perceptual field, cognitive field, conceptual field or cognitive structure. Snygg and Combs define the phenomenal field as the universe, including himself, as perceived by the individual at the instant of action and postulate that all his behavior is determined by the appropriate to the field at that instant. If his field changed, he would change his behavior to conform to it. The purpose of education is to promote more effective and realistic behavior. This is done by helping the individual to achieve a more fruitful and realistic concept of himself and of the universe.

The term "field," as used by various writers, implies an organized whole which behaves in such a way as to maintain its organization. Piaget, as interpreted by Taba, believes that "the individual in 'any cognitive encounter with the environment' of necessity organizes the objects and events into his existing cognitive structure, and invests them with the meaning dictated by that system." He perceives each new phenomenon in terms of an already existing conceptual framework, and new phenomena have meaning only to the extent that they can be fitted into the patterns of concepts and relationship that already exist in his mind. Festinger postulates that individuals will always perceive in such a way as to reduce the dissonance in the cognitive field; Snygg that the immediate purpose of all an individual's behavior, including his behavior as a perceiver, is the maintenance or organization of his individual field.

Generally speaking, a learner will accept into his field anything which fits what he already believes but there are two qualifications: a. in order to be perceived or assimilated an object or event must be necessary to the field organization; b. assimilation of an event involves what another person, looking at the event from the point of view of his own perceptual field, would call distortion. Any item's value and meaning are aspects of its function in the perceiver's particular field at that particular time.

If these conclusions are correct, any attempt to make a really significant change in a student's field by verbal means seems fore-doomed to failure. Lectures, reading assignments, and class discussions may give students the raw material for filling in gaps in their perceptual worlds and for rationalizing the preconceptions and prejudices they already have. Such methods by themselves, however, are not at all likely to cause a radical change in any student's concept of reality. We can assume that each external event is perceived, if at all, in such a way as to cause the least possible change in the student's field. The words of a lecturer will only rarely be relevant to the private reality and personal problems of the students he addresses and are very easy to ignore.

The usual plan for overriding this implacable mechanism for protecting the student against the intrusion of dissonant perceptions is to disorganize his field by threats of failure and humiliation in the hope that he will try to remove the threat by learning the required material. The results are frequently far from what teachers and parents intend. All teachers are by now aware of the cheating and the defensive changes in self-concept and personal values that may result among "poor" students. More attention should be given to the problem of the "good" student who learns the required material for examination purposes but keeps it from entering and changing his view of reality by dividing his field into two parts, "reality" and "school," the latter having nothing to do with real life. This is the game that has given the word "academic" its connotation of imprac-tical futility. The bright people who have used this defense and made a success of school without changing their concepts of reality feel more competent in "school" than in "real life." Apparently many such persons become teachers. We often see teachers and children playing the school game together, equally unaware that the concepts they discuss have anything to do with life or action.

Unfortunately for our efforts to write examinations that are easy to mark, the ability of a student to write the verbal definition of a concept does not prove that the student has the concept. A few years ago I had in one of my classes a student from India who was eager to see snow. She had read about snow; she had seen pictures of snow crystals; she had seen snow on the tops of distant peaks in northern India; and she had taught Indian children all about snow. Then one morning in early December she walked out of her dormi-tory to find the air full of fluttering white objects. "Oh!" she ex-claimed. "What kind of insects are these?" The verbal definition is the last stage of development of a concept and the concept will be perceived as part of reality only when it has been discovered by the student as part of the reality of his own experience, in his own perceptual field.

Any concept, no matter how well expressed, can only be accepted if it fits the student's own cognitive field. In conventional terminology he is "ready" for such learning but the trouble is that if he is that ready there is not much change in his field. On the other hand, if the fit is imperfect the law of least change operates with distressing results. If the dissonant statement is heard at all, the most economical way to deal with it, that is to keep the change in the student's field at a minimum, is to accept it as a statement of fact which has no relevance to the real life of the listener. Probably most lecture and reading material is disposed of in this way. Unfortunately for the student, this denial of personal meaning insures that the material will not be available when he needs it later. He may, of course, perceive the statement as pertinent to the school sector of his life, particularly the next class meeting. But since the material is perceived as mainly pertinent to the next recitation, it is not available after that date and has to be reinstated for the examination by cramming. After the examination, as we all know, it is lost forever.

In the sense in which I have been using the term, a concept is defined as "a general meaning, an idea, or a property that can be predicated out of two or more individual terms." Whether he can express it verbally or not, an individual cannot be presumed to have a concept unless he is able to discover and identify new items which fit the concept. Tests for concepts, to be valid, must be performance tests which require applications of the concepts in new situations. Since concepts are cognitive, and since "cognitive" is often mistakenly equated with "verbal," it should be pointed out that when people develop concepts the formulation of a verbal definition has to be the last step in the process, and that it is probably not an essential one. A great many people who have developed their own concepts and who use them with precision have never had the need to put them into words and may not even have the ability to do so.

Can anything be taught by verbal means? Yes, if the words can be used to upset the student's perceptual field or if the student can use them to organize it. Learning takes place when the field is so disorganized that a new perception, which would ordinarily be ignored, is sought out as a means of restoring or enhancing the organization. New ideas are accepted only in situations where their rejection would cause even more change than their acceptance. We postpone the perception of discrepancies as long as possible but once their perception is forced upon us we must go on to a new organization and actively seek a means of achieving it. Piaget calls this extension of the field to fit new demands "accommodation." Taba illustrates it by the example of a child who, having thought of measurement as an operation done with a yardstick, is confronted with the problem of measuring a volume of water and has to enlarge his concept of measurement.

A COGNITIVE FIELD MODEL OF LEARNING

As a pattern for promoting learning from this point of view we can use the following model. It is applicable to both learning and problem solving and is a modification in cognitive field terms of one proposed by Cronbach.

Step 1. Awareness of a need for greater organization (e.g., hunger, anxiety).

Step 2. Search of the phenomenal field for some means of achieving organization (e.g., food, self-assurance). This or some means of approaching it is differentiated in some degree as Goal.

What effect does previous learning have upon the new learner?
Positive or negative? Gagné presents an interesting viewpoint.

SOME NEW VIEWS OF LEARNING AND INSTRUCTION

Robert M. Gagné

Does learning require repetition? What factors
affect recall? How important is diagnostic testing?

A generation ago, learning psychologists based an-
swers to such questions on Thorndikean formula-
tions. In this article, a leading contemporary
educational psychologist discusses the new theories
and explains some of the provocative experiments on
which they are based.

During recent years there has been an increased recognition of, and even emphasis on, the importance of principles of learning in the design of instruction for the schools. This recognition of the central role of learning in school-centered education seems to be accorded whether one thinks of the instruction as being designed by a teacher, by a textbook writer, or by a group of scholars developing a curriculum.

When the findings of research studies of learning are taken into account, one usually finds questions about instruction to be concerned with such matters as these:

1. For student learning to be most effective, how should the learning task be presented? That is, how should it be communicated to the student?
2. When the student undertakes a learning task, what kinds of activity on his part should be required or encouraged?
3. What provisions must be made to insure that what is learned is remembered and is usable in further learning and problem solving?

From *Phi Delta Kappan* 4 (May 1970): 468-72. Reprinted by permission of the journal and the author.

Questions such as these are persistent in education. The answers given today are not exactly the same as those given yesterday, and they are likely to be altered again tomorrow. The major reason for these changes is our continually deepening knowledge of human behavior and of the factors which determine it. One should not, I believe, shun such changes nor adopt a point of view which makes difficult the application of new knowledge to the design of novel procedures for instruction. The opportunities for improvement seem great and the risks small.

STATUS OF LEARNING RESEARCH

As a field of endeavor, research on how human beings learn and remember is in a state of great ferment today. Many changes have taken place, and are still taking place, in the conception of what human learning is and how it occurs. Perhaps the most general description that can be made of these changes is that investigators are shifting from what may be called a connectionist view of learning to an information processing view. From an older view which held that learning is a matter of establishing connections between stimuli and responses, we are moving rapidly to acceptance of a view that stimuli are processed in quite a number of different ways by the human central nervous system, and that understanding learning is a matter of figuring out how these various processes operate. Connecting one neural event with another may still be the most basic component of these processes, but their varied nature makes connection itself too simple a model for learning and remembering.

My purpose here is to outline some of these changes in the conception of human learning and memory, and to show what implications they may have for the design and practice of instruction. I emphasize that I am not proposing a new theory; I am simply speculating on what seems to me to be the direction in which learning theory is heading.

THE OLDER CONCEPTION

The older conception of learning was that it was always basically the same process, whether the learner was learning to say a new word, to tie a shoelace, to multiply fractions, to recount the facts of history, or to solve a problem concerning rotary motion. Edward L. Thorndike held essentially this view. He stated that he had observed people performing learning tasks of varied degrees of complexity and had concluded that learning was invariably subject to the same influences and the same laws.[1] What was this model of learning that was considered to have such broad generalizability?

One prototype is the conditioned response, in which there is a pairing of stimuli, repeated over a series of trials. The two stimuli must be presented together, or nearly together, in time. They are typically associated with an "emotional" response of the human being, such as an eyeblink or a change in the amount of electrical resistance of the skin (the galvanic skin reflex). The size of the conditioned response begins at a low base-line level and progressively increases as more and more repetitions of the two stimuli are given. Such results have been taken to indicate that repetition brings about an increasingly "strong" learned connection—with an increase in strength that is rapid at first and then more slow.

Learning curves with similar characteristics have been obtained from various other kinds of learned activities, such as simple motor skills like dart-throwing and memorization of lists of words or sets of word-pairs.

Remembering: What about the remembering of such learned activities? Is learning retained better as a result of repetition? Is something that is repeated over and over at the time of learning better recalled after the passage of several weeks or months? The curve which describes forgetting is perhaps equally familiar. Forgetting of such things as lists of nonsense syllables is quite rapid in the beginning and after several weeks descends to a point at which only about 20 percent is remembered. A motor task is usually retained a great deal better and after the same amount of time its retention may be as much as 80 percent.

These are the basic facts about remembering. But how is it affected by repetition? Is retention better if the original learning situation has been repeated many times? Evidence is often cited that this is so. Increasing the number of trials of repetition during original learning has the effect of slowing down the "curve of forgetting," i.e., of improving the amount of retention measured at any particular time. Underwood,[2] for example, has stated that "degree of learning" of the task to be recalled is one of the two major factors which

---

[1] E. L. Thorndike, *Human Learning* (New York: Appleton-Century-Crofts, 1931), p. 160.

[2] B. J. Underwood, "Laboratory Studies of Verbal Learning," *Theories of Learning and Instruction, Sixty-third Yearbook,* Part 1, edited by E. R. Hilgard (Chicago: National Society for the Study of Education, 1964), p. 148.

influence forgetting in a substantial manner. The second factor is interfering associations, whose strength is also determined by their degree of learning. It should be pointed out that when Underwood uses the phrase "degree of learning" he refers to amount of practice —in other words, to amount of repetition.

At this point, let me summarize what I believe are the important implications for instruction of what I call the "older" conceptions of learning and memory. The designer of instruction, or the teacher, had to do two major things. First, he had to arrange external conditions of presentation so that the stimulus and response had the proper timing—in other words, so that there was contiguity between the presentation of the stimulus and the occurrence of the response. Second, he had to insure that sufficient repetition occurred. Such repetition was necessary for two reasons: It would increase the strength of the learned connections; the more the repetition, within limits, the better the learning. Also, repetition was needed to insure remembering—the greater the number of repetitions, the better the retention. Presumably, whole generations of instructional materials and teacher procedures have been influenced in a variety of ways by application of these conceptions of learning to the process of instruction.

Questioning Older Conceptions

During recent years, a number of significant experimental studies of learning and memory have been carried out which call into question some of these older conceptions. (Of course there have always been a certain number of individuals—voices in the wilderness— who doubted that these principles had the general applicability claimed for them.) I shall describe only a few of the crucial new studies here to illustrate the perennial questions and their possible answers.

Does learning require repetition? A most provocative study on this question was carried out by Rock[3] as long ago as 1957. It has stimulated many other studies since that time, some pointing out its methodological defects, others supporting its conclusions.[4] The finding of interest is that in learning sets of verbal paired associates, practice does not increase the strength of each learned item; each one is either learned or not learned. To be sure, some are learned on

---

[3] I. Rock, "The Role of Repetition in Associative Learning," *American Journal of Psychology* (June 1957): 186-93.

[4] W. K. Estes, B. L. Hopkins, and E. J. Crothers, "All-or-None and Conservation Effects in the Learning and Retention of Paired Associates," *Journal of Experimental Psychology* (December 1960): 329-39.

the first practice trial, some on the second, some on the third, and so on; but an item once learned is fully learned.

So far as school subjects are concerned, a number of studies have failed to find evidence of the effectiveness of repetition for learning and remembering. This was true in an investigation by Gagné, Mayor, Garstens, and Paradise,[5] in which seventh graders were learning about the addition of integers. One group of children was given four or five times as many practice problems on each of ten subordinate skills as were given to another group, and no difference appeared in their final performance. A further test of this question was made in a study by Jeanne Gibson,[6] who set out to teach third and fourth graders to read decimals from a number line. First, she made sure that subordinate skills (reading a number in decimal form, writing a number in decimal form, locating a decimal number on a number line) were learned thoroughly by each child. One group of students was then given a total of ten practice examples for each subordinate skill, a second group twenty-five for each, and a third none at all. The study thus contrasted the effects of no repetition of learned skills, an intermediate amount of repetition, and a large amount of repetition. This variable was not found to have an effect on performance, both when tested immediately after learning and five weeks later. Those students who practiced repeated examples were not shown to do better, or to remember better, than those who practiced not at all.

Still another study of fairly recent origin is by Reynolds and Glaser,[7] who used an instructional program to teach ten topics in biology. They inserted frames containing half as many repetitions in one case and one-and-a-half times as many repetitions in another as those in a standard program. The repetitions involved definitions of technical terms. When retention of these terms was measured after an interval of three weeks, the investigators were unable to find any difference in recall related to the amount of repetition.

I must insert a caveat here. All of the studies I have mentioned are concerned with the effects of repetition immediately after learning. They do not, however, test the effect of repetition in the form of spaced reviews. Other evidence suggests the importance of such

---

[5] R. M. Gagné, J. R. Mayor, H. L. Garstens, and N. E. Paradise, "Factors in Acquiring Knowledge of a Mathematic Task," *Psychological Monographs* 7 (1962): whole No. 526.

[6] J. R. Gibson, "Transfer Effects of Practice Variety in Principle Learning" (Ph.D. Dissertation, University of California, 1964).

[7] J. H. Reynolds and R. Glaser, "Effects of Repetition and Spaced Review upon Retention of a Complex Learning Task," *Journal of Educational Psychology* (October 1964): 297-308.

reviews; in fact, this kind of treatment was found to exert a significant effect in the Reynolds and Glaser study. Note, though, that this
result may have quite a different explanation than that of "strengthening learned connections."

MODERN CONCEPTIONS OF LEARNING

Many modern learning theorists seem to have come to the conclusion that conceiving learning as a matter of strengthening connections is entirely too simple. Modern conceptions of learning tend to
be highly analytical about the events that take place in learning,
both outside the learner and also inside. The modern point of view
about learning tends to view it as a complex of processes taking place
in the learner's nervous system. This view is often called an "infor-
mation-processing" conception.

One example of an information processing theory is that of
Atkinson and Shiffrin.[8] According to this theory, information is first
registered by the senses and remains in an essentially unaltered
form for a short period of time. It then enters what is called the
short-term store, where it can be retained for thirty seconds or so.
This short-term store has a limited capacity, so that new information
coming into it simply pushes aside what may already be stored there.
But an important process takes place in this short-term memory,
according to Atkinson and Shiffrin. There is a kind of internal reviewing mechanism (a "rehearsal buffer") which organizes and re-
hearses the material even within this short period of time. Then it
is ready to be transferred to long-term store. But when this happens
it is first subjected to a process called coding. In other words, it is not
transferred in raw form but is transformed in some way which will
make it easier to remember at a later time. Still another process is
retrieval, which comes into play at the time the individual attempts
to remember what he has learned.

It is easy to see that a much more sophisticated theory of learning and memory is implied here. It goes far beyond the notion of
gradually increasing the strength of a single connection.

Prerequisites for learning: If repetition or practice is not the major
factor in learning, what is? The answer I am inclined to give is that

---

[8]R. C. Atkinson and R. M. Shiffrin, "Human Memory: A Proposed System and Its
Control Processes," in *The Psychology of Learning and Motivation: Advances in
Research and Theory,* Vol. 2, edited by K. W. Spence and J. T. Spence (New York:
Academic Press, 1968), pp. 89-195.

the most dependable condition for the insurance of learning is the prior learning of prerequisite capabilities. Some people would call these "specific readinesses" for learning; others would call them "enabling conditions." If one wants to insure that a student can learn some specific new activity, the very best guarantee is to be sure he has previously learned the prerequisite capabilities. When this in fact has been accomplished, it seems to me quite likely that he will learn the new skill without repetition.

Let me illustrate this point by reference to a study carried out by Virginia Wiegand.[9] She attempted to identify all the prerequisite capabilities needed for sixth-grade students to learn to formulate a general expression relating the variables in an inclined plane. Without using the exact terminology of physics, let us note that the task was to formulate an expression relating the height of the plane, the weight of the body traversing downwards, and the amount of push imparted to an object at the end of the plane. (Wiegand was not trying to teach physics, but to see if the children could learn to formulate a physical relationship which was quite novel to them.) The expression aimed for was, "Distance pushed times a constant block weight equals height of plane times weight of cart."

Initially, what was wanted was explained carefully to the students; the plane and the cart were demonstrated. Thirty students (out of thirty-one) were found who could not accomplish the task; that is, they did not know how to solve the problem. What was it they didn't know? According to the hypothesis being investigated, they didn't know some prerequisite things. Figure 1 (on page 20) shows what these missing intellectual skills were thought to be.

What Wiegand did was to find out which of these prerequisite skills were present in each student and which were not present. She did this by starting at the top of the hierarchy and working downwards, testing at each point whether the student could do the designated task or not. In some students, only two or three skills were missing; in others, seven or eight. When she had worked down to the point where these subordinate capabilities were present, Wiegand turned around and went the other way. She now made sure that all the prerequisite skills were present, right up to, but not including, the final inclined plane problem.

The question being asked in this study was, "If all the prerequisite skills are present, can the students now solve this physical problem which they were unable to solve previously?" Wiegand's results

[9]V. K. Wiegand, "A Study of Subordinate Skills in Science Problem Solving" (Ph.D. Dissertation, University of California, 1969).

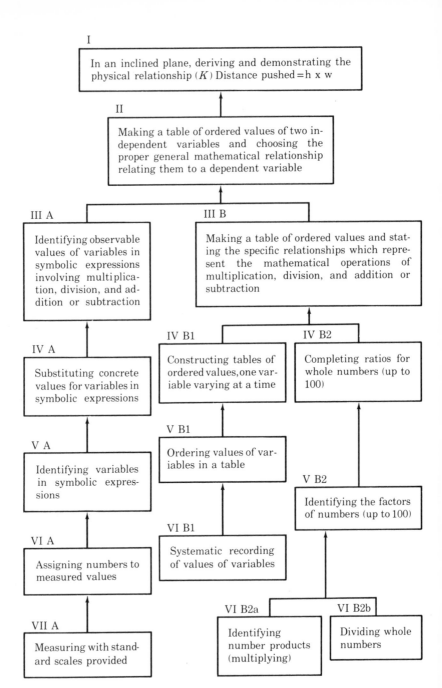

A Hierarchy of Subordinate Intellectual Skills
Applicable to the Problem of Deriving a General
Expression Relating Variables in an Inclined Plane
(Wiegand, 1969).

are quite clear-cut. Having learned the prerequisites, nine out of ten students were able to solve the problem which they were initially unable to solve. They now solved the problem without hesitation and with no practice on the problem itself. On the other hand, for students who did not have a chance to learn the prerequisites, only three of ten solved the problem (and these were students who had no "missing" skills). This is the kind of evidence that makes me emphasize the critical importance of prerequisite intellectual skills. Any particular learning is not at all difficult if one is truly prepared for it.

Coding and remembering: Quite a number of studies appear in the experimental literature pertaining to the effects of coding of information on its retention. I choose as an illustration a study by Bower and Clark.[10] These investigators studied the recall by college students of twelve lists of ten nouns apiece. In learning each list, each student was encouraged to make up a story connecting the nouns. For each student there was a yoked control who was not encouraged to make up a story but who was permitted the same amount of time to learn each list of nouns.

Here is an example of a story which one of the subjects constructed for the words vegetable, instrument, college, nail, fence, basin, merchant, queen, scale, and goat:

> A vegetable can be a useful instrument for a college student. A carrot can be a nail for your fence or basin. But a merchant of the queen would scale that fence and feed the carrot to a goat.

The subjects were asked to recall each list immediately after their study of it. They recalled 99 percent under both conditions. The subjects were later asked to recall all of the lists, after they had learned all twelve. In this case there was an enormous difference. The recall of the narrative group averaged 93 percent, that of the nonnarrative group only 13 percent. In other words, deliberate coding had increased recall by seven times.

Retrieval and remembering: Suppose that learning has indeed occurred; what will insure that whatever has been learned will be remembered? There seems to be at least some absence of evidence that simply practicing or repeating things after they have been learned has the effect of improving retention. What the individual does when he is asked to remember something is to *retrieve* it; that

---

[10]G. H. Bower and M. C. Clark, "Narrative Stories as Mediators for Serial Learning," *Psychonomic Science* (April 1969): 181-82.

is, he brings to bear a process of searching and finding, in his memory, something he is looking for. This process is probably very little understood at present, but there is increasing evidence that it does occur and that it plays a crucial role in remembering.

Some interesting work has been done on the subject of retrieval. In one experiment, Tulving and Pearlstone[11] had groups of high school students learn lists of words of various lengths: twelve words, twenty-four words, or forty-eight words. The words themselves were instances of categories, such as four-footed animals (cow, rat); weapons (bomb, cannon); forms of entertainment (radio, music); professions (lawyer, engineer), and so on. The words were presented one at a time in mixed-up order. Different lists also used one, two, or four words in each category.

Once the lists of words had been learned, recall was measured under two different conditions. In the first, the learners were simply told to write down all the words they could remember. In the second, the category names were used as cues to recall; that is, the learners were asked to write down all the words they remembered which were "forms of entertainment," all which were "four-footed animals," and so on. These extra cues worked wonders on recall. The effect was more marked the greater the number of words that had to be recalled. The differences among those learning forty-eight words was striking, amounting to a twofold increase.

These results show in a rather clear way how powerful is the effect of such extra cues on retrieval of information that has been learned. In this study, the words themselves can be said to have been "equally well learned" in all the groups. What was different between the groups was the aid they were given in retrieving what they had learned. This is only one of the accumulating pieces of evidence that remembering is markedly affected by retrieval at the time of recall, more than it is, perhaps, by events taking place at the time of learning.

IMPLICATIONS FOR INSTRUCTION

The contrasts between older and newer conceptions of learning and memory seem to me quite remarkable. What implications do they have for instruction? If there are indeed newly discovered ways to

---

[11]E. Tulving and Z. Pearlstone, "Availability versus Accessibility of Information in Memory for Words," *Journal of Verbal Learning and Verbal Behavior* (August 1968): 381-91.

affect learning and remembering, how might they be put to use in the classroom and in materials of the curriculum?

First, there is the very fundamental point that each learner approaches each new learning task with a different collection of previously learned prerequisite skills. To be effective, therefore, a learning program for each child must take fully into account what he knows how to do already, and what he doesn't know how to do already. One must find out what prerequisites he has already mastered—not in a general sense, but in a very precise sense for each learner. Does this mean one must do "diagnostic testing"? Yes, that's exactly what it means. To do so, of course, one must first develop the requisite diagnostic tests. By and large, we don't have them.

Second, the most important guide to the learning that needs to be accomplished is the set of prerequisites that the student has not yet mastered. Remember here Wiegand's experiment. When she systematically saw to it that students climbed the hierarchy, skill by skill, this was what was specifically needed to get them to engage in the problem solving they were originally unable to do.

Third, do students need additional practice to insure retention? If by this is meant, "Should they be given many additional examples so that what they have learned will be 'strengthened'?" I think the evidence says it probably won't work this way. Periodic and spaced reviews, however, are another matter, and it seems likely that these have an important role to play in retention. Notice that when a review is given the student has to exercise his strategies of retrieval.

This brings me to the final point, which concerns the processes of coding and retrieval. Probably what should be aimed for here is the learning by students of strategies of coding. These are by no means the same as what are called "mnemonic systems," although it is possible that such systems have a contribution to make in teaching us how coding might be done. For meaningful learning, it appears even more likely that notions like "advance organizers" and "anchoring ideas," as studied by Ausubel,[12] may be particularly powerful.

Similarly, retrieval strategies are also a class of objective that might be valued for instruction. From the evidence we have, I should say that retrieval strategies might very well consist in networks of superordinate categories into which newly learned specific information, or specific intellectual skills, can be placed. Having students learn to retrieve information by a process of search which first lo-

---

[12]D. P. Ausubel, *Educational Psychology: A Cognitive View* (New York: Holt, Rinehart and Winston, 1968).

cates such superordinate networks may be a major way of providing them with the capability of good retention.

Even these two or three aspects of modern learning conceptions, it seems to me, lead to a very different view of what instruction is all about. In the most general sense, instruction becomes not primarily a matter of communicating something that is to be stored. Instead, it is a matter of stimulating the use of capabilities the learner already has at his disposal, and of making sure he has the requisite capabilities for the present learning task, as well as for many more to come.

2

Introduction to Diagnosis

*How does failure affect a child and those who are important to him?
For an interesting discussion, read Auerbach's case for a new approach.*

THE SOCIAL CONTROL OF
LEARNING DISABILITIES

Aaron G. Auerbach

In this paper I shall first discuss three approaches to learning disabilities currently in practice, and then present a new approach to dealing with certain aspects of the problem—the social control of learning disabilities. The systems now in use are described by Bateman (1965):

1. The differential diagnostic approach,
2. The diagnostic-remedial approach, and
3. The teaching technique approach.

The differential diagnostic approach is the traditional medical and psychological model of diagnosis of learning disabled children.

From *Journal of Learning Disabilities* vol. 4, no. 7 (August–September 1971): 26-34. Reprinted by permission of the journal.

The child is seen by a neurologist, a psychologist, sometimes a psychiatrist, a social worker, and an educator. The purpose of such a comprehensive approach is to detect symptoms or signs that may be related to minimal brain dysfunction or neurological impairment. The procedures and tests administered, such as electroencephalograms, pneumoencephalograms, blood tests, other specialized neurological examinations, the Stanford-Binet test, the Wechsler Intelligence Scales for Children, the Illinois Test of Psycholinguistic Abilities, and the traditional casework intake interview require costly professional time and may require costly instrumentation. In this approach, learning disabilities are considered to be the result of neurological impairment and therefore within the prerogative of the medical specialties. The virtue of this method is that it is comprehensive, detailed, and scientific to a fault. However, this high-powered, time-consuming approach is becoming counterproductive: While certain of the diagnostic and treatment facilities will continue to be needed, the present scale of operations is too costly.

The diagnostic-remedial approach is one that does not separate diagnosis and treatment as much as the differential diagnostic approach. Testing is done on a more selective basis. For example, Kephart's Purdue Perceptual-Motor Survey and Marianne Frostig's form perception tests comprise both diagnostic tests and prescriptions for programming; according to these assessment instruments, when a deficit is noted, the next step is already known. Programming for the child follows directly from the assessment, as can be illustrated with a subtest of the Purdue Perceptual-Motor Survey: When a child is not able to hop on alternate feet in a particular rhythmic sequence, the assessment of poor foot coordination leads to direct remedial steps. These could be activities such as swimming in a particular rhythmic pattern with emphasis on leg movements. In order to develop the rhythm of hopping, the child could use the trampoline; as he jumped, he would be up in the air longer than on the ground and would get the feeling of where each foot was in space. Dancing, as a more sophisticated and enjoyable technique, could be used at a later period of treatment. Thus, from simple diagnostic signs, a whole remedial program could be developed in accordance with a predetermined sequence found within the assessment technique. In the Frostig test, if the child cannot keep the pencil between the lines because he has trouble crossing his midline, the remedial approach would be to have him practice on the same Frostig material, positioning him so that eventually he would be able to cross the midline. Both of these assessment instruments tell one how to program on an immediate basis. A weakness of these techniques is that they are not as comprehensive as a differential diagnosis; their strengths are that they are relatively inexpensive, highly practical, and easy to adapt to various kinds of children in various circumstances.

The third approach, the teaching technique approach, focuses less on the symptoms or the "soft" neurological signs of the child with a severe perceptual-motor handicap. Here the beginning point is the specific problems of children exhibiting learning difficulties in a classroom situation. It has the following rationale: In order for any program to be successful, the teacher must be fully involved. The teacher is apprised of various techniques of working with problem children and then it is hoped that she can get through to these children on an immediate basis instead of having to wait for a specialized program to be planned. The virtue of this approach is that it stresses handling problems on the spot. Children are not referred outside the classroom for some special treatment designed to "cure" them, and they are not segregated from the other children in the class. One of the shortcomings of this approach is, of course, that many teachers are not qualified, not trained to handle children with learning problems. Nevertheless, a major approach for the foreseeable future should be to train as many teachers as possible to handle all kinds of children, including children who have special difficulty in learning. Indeed, many special courses and special programs are currently under way to convert regular classroom teachers who are competent and qualified to working with children who have special problems. However, a note of caution should be struck against over-involvement and overcommitment to teacher training as a panacea for all learning disabled children. To say that parts of this problem should not be handled in a medical setting or under specialized remedial approaches, but entirely in a regular teaching situation could possibly be merely shifting the burden of doing what is not being done in other settings to the teacher—away from other knowledgeable professionals and parents.

A new approach, the social control of learning disabilities, is more parent-centered than any of the above three approaches. Controlling the disability to allow the child to grow and develop, rather than controlling the child, is central to this approach. Otherwise, an attack on the disability can easily be misconstrued as an attack on the child's person or self-image. *The approach argues that the child's disability affects mainly his parents and then teachers, school officials, and professionals in such a way that their efforts to help him are thwarted by the same complex of symptoms as those of the child's disability.* By becoming aware of the effects of the child's disability on adults, the adults can band together to establish the social controls around the child.

The following symptoms are generally considered to be major symptoms of learning disabilities: 1. failure, 2. anxiety, 3. hyperactivity, 4. distractibility, 5. rigidity, and 6. emotional lability. By examining each symptom as found in parents, teachers, professionals, and school officials, as well as in the children themselves, an attempt will be made to solve the practical problems of management through recommending specific social controls on the part of adults.

FAILURE

Accompanying the learning disabled child's inability to perform a required task is the child's assumption that he is "no good." Given that assumption about himself, he becomes "wise" and will not attempt a new task because he is afraid of failure. The child has failed so many times that his refusal to try anything new is a symptom of "how really smart he is." The child's "wisdom" is reflected by the parents. Parents who are "wise" to the child know that he will refuse to do a suggested activity. He will be negativistic, stubborn, and difficult. Therefore, why should a "wise" parent waste his time when nothing will work anyway. Thus the parent, like the child, assumes that any new attempts will fail. Rather than try a new approach, the parent, like the child, will not try and will fail. This is the ultimate of the self-fulfilling prophecy.

Similarly, the teacher will often complain she has done all she can but that this child just can't learn. She evokes sympathy from onlookers and professionals with the question, "What's a teacher to do?" She will give up and stop trying to teach the child because so many of the techniques that she has learned in school have been maladaptive for this particular child. The "wise" teacher is one who has been working with these children for many years and believes that if anything could have been done for this child, she would have done it. In support of the teacher, it must be stated that these children are incredibly frustrating to work with. However, a good teacher will work on the sense of failure and frustration that the child has rather than reflect her own failures or frustrations. In effect, the teacher, like the parents, can contract the symptoms of the learning disabled child.

Similarly, the school administrators who say that they would deal with the problem if it existed are essentially setting up a failure situation. The school administrator takes the position that he will not adapt a new program because it cannot be demonstrated that it will succeed. As it is difficult to demonstrate a high probability that a particular new program will succeed, the school administrator will not approve it. Since he will not try a new approach, obviously remedial attempts are at a disadvantage at the start. The school administrator has become a part of the self-fulfilling prophecy.

Professionals such as psychologists, medical doctors, and social workers also contribute unwittingly to the failure syndrome by treating the presenting symptom of the child, parent, or teacher and not the specific cause of the problem. Professionals who have casual contact with learning disabled children and their families often are concerned with the anxiety problems of the children, parents, and teachers rather than with the child's learning problems. Their approach is to utilize the techniques helpful in reducing anxiety that they learned in their professional training. Often they assume that the child and his parents are having an acute anxiety attack not necessarily related to a particular failure situation, and they do not pursue anxieties related to a specific problem, such as failure in school, peer rejection, or parent-management difficulties. Treating individuals as neurotics when their problems are specific and reality-related is not likely to successfully resolve the problems.

ANXIETY

Anxiety reverberates throughout the world of learning disabled children, their parents, their teachers, and the school officials and professionals connected with them. The child, after many failures and increasing anxiety, suddenly "blows up" in school for no apparent reason. At this point the teacher has just about reached the end of her endurance and calls the parents to take the child home. The parents, upset by the frantic phone call, label the teacher incompetent and they call the principal. The principal defends the teacher against the outrageous accusations and anger of the parents and enters a mood of frustration and despair as he explains to the parents how woefully inadequate is the teacher's training in special education. Then they all calm down and console each other by blaming the professional who hasn't done anything to help them cope with the child.

The learning disabled child is often anxious, especially in test situations. This anxiety prevents him from fully using the skills that he does possess. Clinically, he looks more like a child with a severe anxiety attack than a traditional learning disabled child. The anxiety can be seen building up and seems impossible to stop until the child goes to pieces and becomes uncontrollable. He usually has to be held until he calms down. "Blowing up" is not a constructive experience for a learning disabled child, and little seems to be gained from working it out—in contrast to a truly emotionally disturbed child. The preventive action which can avoid crisis situations is simply to watch the child, try to predict when he is about to "blow up," and take steps before this happens. This may sound difficult to do but in practice it is relatively simple. Usually parents can be helpful because they are used to watching the sequence develop and can communicate the state of the child rather well to teachers, school administrators, and professionals.

But many parents, after the daily interminable struggle to get the child to do something, themselves become harassed, anxious, and upset, and then they "blow up." They become irrational, demanding, and, clinically speaking, are in an anxiety state and are barely able to control themselves. When they come in to see the professionals or school officials, they behave much as their children do and then they are treated as though they are neurotic. The treatment of parental anxiety without reference to the total disability does little to help the parents over their own anxiety state or to enable them to deal with the specific cause of their anxiety.

The teacher, like the parents, can become agitated after constant daily dealings with these children. She is often alone, with little support. The isolation of teachers can prevent them from reducing one another's anxiety. Camp counselors too, must sometimes deal with learning disabled children on a daily basis, virtually alone and with little support. Their own anxiety states often build up in direct relationship to the intensity of the anxiety of the children. Both teachers and counselors, because of their daily contact with learning disabled children, can exhibit the same anxiety symptoms as the children. These teachers probably need what might be called a "drop-in center" where they can talk with someone, and they also need further training. They need support, not so much for their own particular problems, but support in helping them cope with the anxieties of the children.

Other school personnel, usually the school principal and the consulting psychologist, can see these outbursts of anxiety. Both these groups are well trained to "handle" crisis situations. Their responses range from genuine sympathy and concern with the plight of the children, parents, and teachers to the condescending "I'll give you a hand" and the babying reassurance, "There, there, it will get better." Just to handle a situation is quite different than to deal effectively with it. The principal or psychologist cannot be faulted for the handling of anxiety situations, but only for their failure to take steps to prevent them from recurring. The best solution to an anxiety state is to deal with the origins and the causes of the anxiety rather than to just hold the person's hand while waiting hopefully for the anxiety state to pass.

HYPERACTIVITY

The four primary characteristics of learning disabled children—namely, hyperactivity, distractibility, rigidity, and emotional lability—influence the adults around them in a way so as to maintain the disability just as do the failure syndrome and anxiety.

Hyperactivity, or hypoactivity, is the characteristic of learning disabled children most often cited in the literature. The children exhibit little regulated activity, little rhythmic capability, and poor coordination. Their activity level is more apt to be at one extreme of the continuum of activity and passivity. The child's inability to sit still and his continuous motion which can be stopped only by severe controls is accompanied by passivity and withdrawal, and by avoidance of specific motor tasks, social involvements, and academic pursuits. The child needs to be pushed either to control his hyperactivity or to overcome his inertia.

This characteristic makes handling the learning disabled child extremely difficult. The sheer activity level required of adults to keep up with this child must be balanced with enough firmness to overcome passivity and avoidance techniques. The parents, however, often imitate this characteristic of hyperactivity or hypoactivity by becoming either totally involved in parent groups—such as the local association for children with learning disabilities, a perceptual-motor program, or a camping situation—or by withdrawing and becoming passive and unapproachable because of their weariness. The burden of organizational work in relationship to parent programs, school liaison functions, or communicating with the public, the professional, or political community seems to fall disproportionately on specific parents of learning disabled children while other parents fade away at critical junctures. The unwillingness of parents to work together, their avoidance of organizational responsibilities, their lack of cooperative behavior, and their shying away from contact with professionals stems not from irresponsibility but rather from great love, from involvement and identification with the child's problem and with the child. The sophisticated parent must learn to disengage himself or herself from the disability while still being heavily engaged in planning programs and treatment for the child.

Similarly, the organizations that teachers find themselves in either tend to demand total commitment to learning disabled children or to permit the teacher to ignore the disability by claiming lack of training. Either hyperactivity or hypoactivity on the part of the teacher is fostered by the concept of the dedicated special education teacher in contrast to the duties of the regular teacher. In truth, the dedicated special teacher of learning disabled children needs relief from the strain of being constantly with these difficult children, just as the teacher in the regular classroom should expect to have outside support when she has these children in her class. Teaching learning disabled children can become an endurance contest for a teacher or even an indicator of masochistic tendencies. The expectations of great achievements to be obtained by ceaseless motion is countered by the plaintive wails of outside observers who say, "But nothing ever happens in special classes. Why don't those teachers do something with those children?"

School officials exhibit the same hyperactivity and hypoactivity. They declare that they need an additional number of special education teachers because they discovered yesterday at 11:45 A.M. that many children were not learning. Of course, had they known about it before, they never would have allowed such a situation to develop. However, now that they are aware of the problem, they are going to work on it until it is totally solved. Then the school officials will never have to deal with it again unless, of course, somebody discovers at 10:40 tomorrow morning that other children are not learning. Both the awareness and the total apparent naiveté of school officials in dealing with the existence of learning disabled children seem to to follow cycles of political pressure. Under pressure, school officials themselves can become either hyperactive or hypoactive. Either they decide to do too much without thinking about it or decide to do nothing because they just can't handle the problem.

Professionals are no different. The recent flurry of activity in "discovering" learning disabilities belies the classical description in the late twenties by such authorities as Strauss and Lehtinen (1947) and Strauss and Kephart (1955). Activity has come in spurts, from the period of the late twenties through the most recent surge of activity we are now experiencing. Until recently, few professionals have specialized in learning disabled children. However, instant experts come forth full blown as funds and programs become available. Many professionals are hypoactive in this area—that is, even if they recognize the problem, they would rather not do anything about it, avoiding contact with the problem because they are busy with other activities—unless they are called in on a crisis basis. Then they either do nothing to cope with the problem of learning disabilities or suddenly become instant experts and become totally immersed in the problems of learning disabled children.

DISTRACTIBILITY

Distractibility, short attention span, or the inability to focus or attend to a specific learning requirement is considered a major characteristic of the learning disabled child. By structuring the child's environment, extraneous input can be kept from interfering with the child's attending behavior. The learning task itself can be stressed and emphasized by multisensory input techniques and everyday drills. Since a major problem of the learning disabled child is keeping him focused upon the required task, a major accomplishment for therapists is getting the child to attend to particular tasks for a longer period of time.

The parents exhibit a form of distractibility in their inability to focus upon the treatment program. Parents frequently interfere with this program at the last minute as their anxiety distracts them. This distractibility often causes failure in programs when victory is within their grasp. Like their children, the parents do not attend to the task at hand. The parents are always looking for new techniques, even if the ones they are using are effective. This constant search for new answers, rather than maintaining a set of activities that has proven successful, is due to both the desire to learn new ways and the hasty and impulsive need to get away from the task at hand because it is so arduous. In sum, a little distractibility for parents can be motivating, but too much can impede progress.

Similarly, if a teacher will stay with a task, she can often succeed in teaching the child a particular content. The child often succeeds in distracting the teacher from the task at hand by verbal manipulation or avoidance mechanisms. The experienced teacher will keep the child at the particular task until he has completed it, bringing closure to the task and permitting the child to then concentrate his efforts on the next item. The teacher will not attempt several activities at once, but will sequence the activities so that the child will focus upon the desired task. The teachers themselves have to avoid being distracted by the whole slew of things that can affect a teacher in a school system, such as anxious parents and irrational demands from other sources.

The attention paid to learning disabilities by professionals and school administrators is mainly a function of factors extraneous to learning disabilities. Rather than attending to the problem on a long-term, continuing basis, professionals and school administrators are continually rediscovering the phenomenon of learning disabilities and deciding to do something about it. In the rush, professionals and school administrators who have previously developed similar programs are often not consulted. The need to constantly be starting a new program effort prevails as a form of administrative distractibility.

RIGIDITY

The term rigidity is a technical one, meaning the inability to shift direction according to the appropriate external stimulus. The rigidity of the child can entice the parents into the same trap of inflexibility. When the child has committed himself to a course of action, his rigidity will not permit him to shift to a more reasonable course of action. For example, if he has decided he won't do his homework or won't do what his mother has just told him to do, no amount of cajoling, wheedling, or reason will budge him from this position. The mother, trying one approach and then another, becomes frustrated and tearful. The scenario ends with a plea to her husband to take a firm stand—that is, to be more rigid than she was.

Such a problem would not arise if the lack of flexibility were seen as a legitimate part of the learning disability syndrome and not as willfullness, stubbornness, or rebellion. The learning disabled child, once he has committed himself to a course of action, is unable to change it easily. However, it is possible for an adult to take advantage of this characteristic by restructuring the immediate environment so that the child will conform to the desires of the parent. The necessity of preparing the environment should not be underestimated. The value of extensive preparation is that both parent and child can avoid the impossible situation of the child's shouting, "I can't, I won't, you can't make me, and I'm not going to." The unwillingness of parents to change their ways because they want a culturally acceptable child is a major source of difficulty. Parents are extremely susceptible to social pressure as to how they should raise their children. Parents often raise their children according to the way their social group thinks children should be raised, while ignoring the characteristics that the child himself possesses. The mother who has succumbed to social pressure to be permissive feels guilty when she has to be assertive to control her child. But different children need to be dealt with in different ways. It is easy for a parent to say this, but it is difficult to follow through when the different ways may not always be socially approved.

The parents often interpret the learning disabled child's rigidity as a personal affront. The child's obstinate behavior is seen as a challenge to their ability as parents. Often, professional advice is sought at this point with the expectation that only the right child-rearing technique or miracle could help the parents out of this impossible situation. Frequently, professionals fall into this trap by offering "solutions" instead of pointing out the real impasse.

Teacher training is by definition rigid. Teachers learn the "right" way to teach. The right way, for many, is the way that they themselves were taught in school. Teachers often do not understand why things are not working out well when they have done everything "properly." They often regard the child's rigidity as a test of will between the teacher and the student, and they attempt to enforce their will upon the child. Up to a certain point the teacher's superior power can produce conformity in the children. It is a tragedy when teachers fall into rigid behavior patterns when they are dealing with rigid children. The teacher needs to exploit the child's rigidity by being flexible and adaptive and creating new situations which permit the child to shift his behavior without having a confrontation with the teacher.

Professionals and school administrators may use the rigidity of the child as a way of "copping out." Their argument is that they are in the business of changing behavior and changing people. Obviously the more flexible and adaptive a person is, the easier it is to change the behavior. Therefore, the argument goes, why waste professional time and talent upon children who are rigid, that is, children who are not likely to change their pattern of behavior. The argument is short-sighted. If the rigidity were seen as part of the syndrome common to learning disabled children, it could be utilized by professionals in a particular way. Programs in classrooms could be restructured and reorganized in such a way that the resolute behavior of learning disabled children could be adaptive rather than maladaptive. For example, a teaching and program approach utilizing the child's rigidity would have him begin by elaborating upon his already existing strengths rather than trying something new. Any new learning would take place upon the base of what the child already knows. In the futile attempt to impose unfamiliar patterns on a learning disabled child, the resistance on the part of the child is an indication of his commitment to existing patterns.

EMOTIONAL LABILITY

The learning disabled child often appears emotionally disturbed or emotionally labile. Adults often misinterpret this as primary emotional disturbance unrelated to learning disabilities. The placement of learning disabled children in classrooms with emotionally disturbed children is a way of telling the learning disabled child that he is not only "dumb" but also "bad." The child's experience of his self-image as a combination of being both "dumb" and "bad" as compared to being "smart" and "good," has an ominous significance for him and should be avoided at all possible costs. As is well known, many learning disabled children have a secondary emotional disturbance because of their inability to learn. To view such a child as primarily emotionally disturbed rather than as learning disabled is essentially to do a poor differential diagnosis. Through accurate diagnosis and assessment, it should be possible to separate these children so that a teacher can concentrate on the emotional disturbance and the learning disabilities as distinct phenomena.

Similarly, parents often exhibit emotional lability and become angry, disturbed, hostile, or threatening for no apparent reason. The question is whether they are genuinely emotionally disturbed or whether their emotional disturbance is related solely to a problem that the child is having at that particular time. If one listens carefully to the mother's explanation of why she is emotionally upset, one can usually determine whether or not she has a severe and prolonged emotional disturbance. Most normal people become concerned and disturbed when they perceive something threatening their child. Actually, not to become emotionally upset under such circumstances would be abnormal. Again, accurate diagnosis is the answer.

One reason that some people become teachers is because of the opportunity to exercise leadership. In the teaching situation, they have much power and control over a group of people at once. It is normal for teachers to regard control over their own emotions as a major virtue, and their ability to control others is well thought of by school officials. But working with learning disabled children may exaggerate the control needs of teachers who fear that they are losing control of these children and become emotionally upset as a result. These teachers often go home from school feeling emotionally exhausted, and this can usually be traced to specific problems with specific children. The teacher who is emotionally upset *most* of the time must be distinguished from the teacher who has just had "a bad day." Knowing that a teacher may have a serious emotional problem, such as a need to control others, is essential to dealing with the teacher's problems with a particular child.

Professionals and school administrators learn early in their experience that they have two options with learning disabled children. Either the learning disability can be dealt with in all its complexity or the situation can be redefined as an excuse to do psychotherapy with the parents and children. School administrators or principals can shift their perception to see both the parents and the children as emotionally disturbed and treat them accordingly. While it is undoubtedly true that many parents of learning disabled children need help, the determination as to the kind of help required must be carefully assessed. Do they need supportive therapy and assistance to help them in handling their child? Or do they need assistance because they themselves have chronic personality problems which affect their children? The effectiveness of parent-education programs, as compared to psychotherapy for parents of learning disabled children, would indicate that parent education is the route for professionals to take with this particular group. School administrators and principals have discovered that more can be accomplished by involving parents in plans to help their learning disabled children than by treating the parents as though they were emotionally disturbed. In general, professionals and administrators have discovered that the parents of these children are no more emotionally disturbed than any randomly selected group of parents. In all instances, accurate diagnosis and assessment of the situation is a prerequisite to determining procedures.

THE SOCIAL CONTROL OF LEARNING DISABILITIES

Each of the six major characteristics of learning disabilities discussed above tends to splinter and alienate one group from the next. Children, parents, teachers, school administrators, and professionals seem continually in a state of conflict, alienation, and hostility with one another, yet they are all concerned with helping the child. It is altogether possible for them to develop a reasonable working relationship without conflict if it can be recognized and accepted that the learning disability itself affects everyone that comes in close contact with the child. Hostility can abate and cooperation can increase when the problem is dealt with objectively rather than on a personal basis. The following suggestions may help reduce the friction among the adults and the child with a learning disability.

A consistent approach is a prerequisite to any successful treatment plan for the learning disabled child. The goals of the treatment program should be set by the parents and the teachers, since they will be working with the children most of the time to implement the program, while school officials and professionals serve as consultants. This is a variation of the medical treatment plan, with nonprofessionals replacing professionals. The traditional medical treatment plan would include physicians, psychologists, social workers, and various educational specialists, and a special counselor to bear the responsibility for carrying out the treatment plan. The approach presented here is that those individuals who have the greatest responsibility for carrying out the treatment plan should have a major voice in the decision as to what the treatment plan should be. It is unwise to have professionals alone determine the treatment plan being carried out as directed are not good. It is better to have a less sophisticated treatment plan that will be followed than a very sophisticated plan that will be ignored.

The persons concerned with designing a suitable treatment plan for learning disabled children should meet in a positive or at least neutral atmosphere conducive to a cooperative relationship. The key to working together is the development of positive or neutral relationships with one another so that all are prepared to meet whatever crisis may arise among these children. It is suggested that the teachers, parents, professionals, and school officials be invited for coffee or a meal without any program or plan. This would give the parents an opportunity to know as human beings the other adults who work with their child and to develop realistic expectations of the teacher. To meet as adults outside the setting of the learning disabilities problem presents the opportunity for developing a structure which will be equipped to counteract the effect that the learning disabled child may have upon them in any crisis situation that may develop. Classifications of individuals as "good" or "evil" often garnered from superficial acquaintance during a crisis situation can be avoided. Adults concerned with learning disabled children often describe one another as being "on our side" or "against our side." For example, the professionals are often seen as good or evil depending on whether they support the parents. Further, if a professional recommends a treatment procedure that is successful for a particular child, he is a hero, while if something he suggests is not effective, then he is a worthless fellow. The "hero-bum" dichotomy isn't real for baseball, let alone the complex game we call learning disabilities. In truth, all the adults are on one side, the side of the child, and only the learning disability is on the other side. Moderation must be fostered for all the adults surrounding the learning disabled child if an effective treatment plan is to be agreed upon and if it is to succeed.

REFERENCES

Bateman, Barbara. *An Educator's View of a Diagnostic Approach to Learning Disorders.* In *Learning Disorders,* vol. 1, edited by J. Hellmuth. Seattle, Washington: Special Child Publications, 1965.

Kephart, N. C. *The Slow Learner in the Classroom,* 2d ed. Columbus, Ohio: Charles E. Merrill Publishing Co., 1971.

Strauss, A. A., and Kephart, N. C. *Psychopathology and Education in the Brain-injured Child,* vol. 2. New York: Grune and Stratton, 1955.

Strauss, A. A., and Lehtinen, Laura. *Psychopathology and Education in the Brain-injured Child,* vol. 1. New York: Grune and Stratton, 1947.

How do respect and love—even for those who have been labeled delinquent—effect future progress? Rice has some ideas worth serious consideration.

EDUCO-THERAPY: A NEW APPROACH TO DELINQUENT BEHAVIOR*

Ruth Dianne Rice

The most salient aspects of several different theories from education and psychology were considered and carefully worked into a treatment program to meet the needs of ten delinquent girls who were appraised by a group of several evaluators as having learning disabilities and/or behavior disturbances. This very intensive, in-depth intervention occupied their total life space for three months. Most of the behavioral changes were documented by subjective evaluations made by the institutional and project staff. Educational improvements in reading performance and intellectual functioning are substantiated by post-test scores.

The incidence of learning disabilities in school-age children has been cited from three to forty percent. Because the delinquent child is so often a child who is an underachiever, who can't read, who can't relate in terms of language skills, and who leaves school early to find success elsewhere, it would seem reasonable to assume that an even higher incidence of learning disabilities would be found among children in schools of correction. A survey of the court records for the causes of incarceration of girls aged eleven to sixteen in a Tennessee State institution for correction revealed that over sixty percent had been judged delinquent because of school-related problems: for the reasons of "truancy" or "home-school unable to control."

*This project, No. 67-01, was supported under Title I funds, through the State Board of Education in the State of Tennessee.

From *Journal of Learning Disabilities* vol. 3, no. 1 (January 1970): 18-25. Reprinted by permission of the journal.

Now, if the delinquent behavior occurred subsequent to the learning disability, then treatment should focus both on remediating the educational deficits and on modifying the maladaptive behavior. An experimental pilot project is reported on here, in which the treatment model, designed by the writer and labeled "Educotherapy," is an eclectic, gestalt approach utilizing the disciplines of both psychology and education in an intensive treatment program.

The treatment program was in three phases or progressive levels, each designed to meet a basic, developing need. There were three overriding objectives:

1. To attempt behavior modification through conditioning and reinforcement,
2. To institute remedial education procedures, and
3. To stimulate improvement of self-concept and social integration through an enriched cultural-social-personal improvement program.

SUBJECTS

An initial survey using the Gates Reading Survey Test, Form MI, indicated that ninety percent of the 110 girls confined to the institution were functioning two to seven years below grade level.

Further testing and evaluation was done. The educational evaluation was determined by a battery of tests which included the Peabody Picture Vocabulary Test, Form A; Primary Mental Abilities Test, Level 2-6; Spache Diagnostic Reading Scale; a Telebinocular test; and a test for hearing using the audiometer. The psychological evaluation included the WISC, the Children's Form of the Rosenzweig Picture-Frustration Study, the Vineland Social Maturity test, the Peabody Child Interview test, and the Bender-Gestalt. Medical examinations were given when indicated.

Using below-norm scores as criteria, the results of these educational and psychological tests were evaluated by the group of examiners. Sixty-eight percent of the total population of 110 girls were determined to have a specific educational or learning disability and/or a behavior disorder which was felt to be related to a learning disability. It seems likely that much of the disruptive behavior that brought the girl into the institution was a consequence of the failure, frustration, and anxiety she had experienced as a result of learning problems.

A screening committee comprised of this writer, a research assistant, and the remedial reading teacher interviewed twenty-five girls chosen at random from the seventy-five who had been evaluated initially as having specific learning and/or behavior disorders. Ten subjects, ages eleven to fifteen, were selected by the committee as being representative of those with severe behavioral and educational deficits. None of the subjects felt she had profited from the treatment provided by the institution.

The treatment model was designed following a careful study of the girls' delinquent behavior, their characteristics, and basic needs. Briefly, these characteristics can be described as follows:

1. Placing a great value on oral pleasures—such as thumb sucking, gum chewing, eating.
2. Being unable to postpone pleasure or gratification.
3. Having little control over impulses.
4. Having a low self-concept; being unable to feel good about things she did that were socially acceptable.
5. Being unable to understand humor—unable to take a joke.
6. Reading poorly or not at all.
7. Having rarely or never a satisfying relationship with an adult.
8. Having rarely experienced success—either in school or at home. She sees herself as a failure.

There was no impairment of vision and hearing functioning as determined by the initial survey. Evaluative testing results for the subjects are given in Table 1. Two instruments were used in post-testing. The scores and gains made on these two tests—for reading performance and intellectual functioning are shown in Tables 2 and 3.

Three of the subjects were second- or third-time offenders. The reasons given for incarceration of the ten subjects were "home-school unable to control" or "habitual truancy," with the exception of one subject who was incarcerated for murder. She, too, had had unsuccessful school experiences. All the subjects stated that they "hated" school; eight stated that they "hated" school and teachers.

Eight subjects were Negro, two were Caucasian. Their backgrounds were both rural and urban. Two of the girls were almost constant thumb suckers; one was a nightly bed-wetter.

PROCEDURE

A three-phase, intensive program of differential treatment provided remedial education and behavior shaping through a contingency

TABLE 1

Scores of Various Pre-Tests Given to Aid in Describing Subjects

Tests	Subjects	A	B	C	D	E	F	G	H	I	J
	Age	13-11	13-4	11-4	14-1	15-2	14-0	14-3	15-1	15-0	14-1
Primary Mental Abilities-Test. Level 2-6. Quotient Scores	Verbal Meaning	50	52	79	66	73	56	59	88	68	95
	Number Facility	74	68	67	75	74	69	77	79	64	81
	Spatial Relations	82	82	87	98	94	88	82	98	94	105
	Reasoning	88	88	89	78	79	78	74	78	88	94
	Perceptual Speed	92	88	97	80	76	74	82	88	90	90
	Total I.Q. Score	70	69	77	72	72	66	69	82	73	91
Peabody Picture Vocabulary Test. (Form A)	Mental Age Score	8-0	8-11	10-2	10-2	9-2	8-11	8-11	11-4	1-2	13-7
	Intelligence Quotient	70	72	76	76	72	71	71	83	76	92
Spache Diagnostic Reading Scales	Word Recognition (Grade level)	4.5	6.0	3.8	3.3	3.8	3.8	3.3	4.5	4.5	7.5
	Instructional Level "	4.5	6.0	3.8	3.3	3.8	3.8	3.0	4.5	4.5	7.5
	Independent Level "	4.5	6.0	3.8	3.3	3.8	3.8	3.3	4.5	4.5	8.0
	Phonics Test: (No. correct)										
	Consonants	all	all	all	all	all	all	all	all	all	all
	Vowel sounds	3	2	5	3	2	1	1	4	3	5
	Consonant Blends	14	11	14	12	14	10	12	13	14	15
	Common Syllables	32	30	31	30	32	28	32	30	31	33
	Blending	50%	50%	50%	60%	40%	20%	30%	50%	50%	80%
	Letter Sounds	all	all	all	all	all	all	all	all	all	all
Telebinocular	Information Summarized	normal	normal	normal	normal	normal	normal	normal	normal	normal	normal
Audiometer	Information Summarized	normal	normal	normal	normal	normal	normal	normal	normal	normal	normal
	Vineland Social Maturity Scale (Social-age Values)	9.7	8.0	8.1	10.3	11.3	10.9	8.1	10.9	11.0	10.8

Rosenzweig P-F Study Test:

Most of the subjects generally had high conformity scores, depressed extra-punitive scores, and elevated intropunitive scores.

Peabody Child Interview Test:

All the subjects indicated a strong dislike for school and related activities; negative feelings were expressed toward parents or parent substitutes (4 of the 10 subjects were illegitimate). There usually a "don't have any" or "I don't know" response to questions about interests, hobbies, etc.

Bender-Gestalt:

With the exception of Subject "J", all protocals showed difficulty with angulation, symmetry, fragmentation, and separations. A clinical psychological interpretation of the protocals would infer inadequate personality developmental formation or perhaps organicity.

43

reinforcement system. To provide stronger self-concepts and more social integration, an enriched cultural-social-personal improvement program was instituted as part of the daily schedule. The treatment focus changed in each phase, but the philosophy remained constant. The overriding rationale held each girl worthy of respect and love. The treatment philosophy stated that each girl should 1. experience success in school (particularly in reading), 2. learn modes of behavior that are socially acceptable, 3. have her self-concept enhanced, and 4. should learn to assume the responsibility of the consequences of her behavior.

TABLE 2

Gates Reading Survey Tests

Grade-Level		Scores		
		Pretest	Post-test	
Subject	Age	Form M1	Form M2	Gain
A	13	4.5	4.5	0
B	13	6.4	6.6	2 months
C	11	3.7	4.4	7 months
D	14	3.4	4.1	7 months
E	15	3.7	3.9	2 months
F	14	3.8	4.9	1 year 1 month
G	14	2.9	3.9	1 year
H	15	4.0	4.1	1 month
I	15	4.1	4.7	6 months
J	14	7.3	8.3	1 year

There was sufficient evidence that in the delinquent subculture and the correctional institution milieu the systems are geared to reinforce maladaptive behavior. A preliminary study of the influence of the peer group and the staff in shaping and controlling maladaptive behavior in the institution was made prior to beginning the project. To reduce staff and peer reinforcement of aberrant behavior during the project, the ten subjects were housed in a separate wing in one of the dormitories and placed under the care of project personnel. The project staff consisted of the writer, who directed the treatment program and who lived, for the most part, in the institution during the three-month project; a part-time research assistant; a part-time remedial reading teacher; and three employees of the institution: a teacher and two residential supervisors who had volunteered to participate and who received in-service training as the program progressed.

TREATMENT PROGRAM: PHASE I

The treatment program in Phase I placed emphasis on providing the subjects with oral and emotional gratification. Effort was made to elicit the girls' confidence and trust in the staff. A behavior repertoire and a reinforcement hierarchy were observed and noted for each subject. A contingency system of social and oral reinforcement was begun. As the subject exhibited an approximation of desirable behavior, social reinforcement was provided with praise, affection, and individual attention. It was noted that the girls had a strong need for placing something in their mouths. Thus, extrinsic oral reinforcers were used in the form of chewing gum, candy, and food. Communication skills were developed. The girls were encouraged to give verbal expression of their feelings, to talk, sing, hum, and yell.

Body contact provided further conditioning and reinforcement; praise was accompanied by an affectionate pat, or a hug, or a kiss. The institutional staff had been reluctant to engage in body contact in any form either from the staff or among the girls would encourage and promote homosexuality. The consequent policy stated that any girl who engaged in a form of physical contact, even the touching of hands, would receive severe punishment. The attitude of the staff had not changed sufficiently to permit them to engage sincerely in this aspect of the treatment program until the final month of the project. There was not one incident of behavior that approached homosexuality during the entire treatment program. This freedom of body contact provided opportunities for the girls to explore their feelings of sexuality and femininity, and the discussions initiated suggestions for more healthy sexual relationships.

Other freedoms that had never been granted by the institution were permitted. Room doors were left unlocked, and privacy was given in the toilet and bathing areas. The girls were permitted to walk unsupervised on the grounds, and marching single file was no longer required when entering and leaving the buildings.

An evening gathering was held, continuing through all phases of the treatment program for the purpose of permitting the girls to talk freely about themselves. Each girl was encouraged to set a daily behavior or attitude goal for herself. The goals were posted on a bulletin board, and each girl could decide whether she had met her own goal. As more positive peer relationships developed, the girls aided each other in achieving their goals. After the evening gathering each girl was tucked into bed and bid good-night. More physical affection, such as one might give an infant or young child—kissing, caressing, hugging, patting, singing to—was given if the staff felt the girl indicated a need. It was during this intimate experience with an adult that the development of a sense of humor was attempted. A joke or a humorous incident that had occurred during the day was mentioned. It was felt that the girls should experience some joy and gaiety each day.

When it was assumed that negative reinforcement was necessary, it was in the form of ignoring the deviant behavior, or, in extreme cases, a restriction of privileges. In all cases restrictions were lifted at the end of the day. A girl could begin each new day with a clean slate and new hopes. This was a drastic change from the previous procedure where punishment periods often ranged from two to six weeks in duration.

PHASE II

Because of the time limitation, incorporation of Phase II principles was begun in three weeks. It would be better for phase length to be determined on the basis of the individual subject's needs. The more emotionally deprived and "damaged" the subject, the longer Phase I should be continued.

A full-day instruction schedule began in Phase II. Classes in remedial language and reading development were held all morning. Instruction in personal improvement and social graces was provided in the afternoon. In Phase II an economic system using tokens was introduced. Tokens of colored construction paper were given to reinforce appropriate behavior. At first all tokens were of one denomination; later, denominations of 1, 5, 10, and 25 were adopted.

A commissary was set up where a variety of items, such as gum, candy, cosmetics, and clothing, could be purchased with tokens. In Phase I, gum and candy were used as reinforcement agents. In Phase II, the girls were required to "purchase" these items with tokens.

Reinforcement schedules were revised with the advent of academic stimuli. Incentive and motivation were elicited in the classroom by establishing a reading base and the reward system of tokens. The Science Research Associates Reading Laboratories were used to establish a level of reading performance. A reading "base" was determined by taking a percentage average from a reading session in the SRA booklet. Each ten percent performance under base earned one token; base and each one percent performance over base earned two tokens; and each number of lessons worked in the booklet earned one token. A new reading base was established as each girl progressed to a different color or level in the SRA Reading

Series. Tokens had to be earned in the reading class before the subject was eligible to earn them elsewhere.

The SRA reading time was limited to two one-half hour periods unless the girl requested additional reading time. The balance of the morning was utilized in building reading skills—building word recognition through phonetic and structural analysis; building comprehension; building listening and auditory discrimination skills through audio-active tape recorders; and giving individualized remedial reading aid in the specific deficits indicated by each girl's performance. Attending and participating behaviors in these activities were also rewarded with tokens.

Because much of their hyperactive and acting-out behavior seemed to occur with classroom activities which required verbal response or individual participation in front of the class, these kinds of methods were eliminated. The conventional-type teaching with classroom participation seemed to elicit the aversive behaviors we were trying to extinguish. The subjects did not appear to have the self-control to actively or verbally participate in a class discussion without inappropriate behavior.

The staff felt that the best responses were obtained at the audio-tape center, with the SRA Reading Laboratory kits, and with teacher instruction to groups of three. Activities were varied and were not more than thirty minutes in duration. There was a five-minute break at the end of each hour.

When the girls began to experience success in reading and language skills, they began to look forward to going to school. There was more cooperative and participating behavior in the classroom, and conversation after school was frequently about some class-related topic. Other subjective indications of improvement were noted. Their attitude toward the classroom teacher changed from being silent, suspicious, and wary to friendliness and openness; it became a privilege to be asked to be her assistant in preparing class materials or in other classroom duties. This was in great contrast to their previous behavior when they were fearful and angry toward teachers, schools, and academic learning.

Tokens could be earned for "appropriate" behavior outside the classroom. The behaviors deemed by the staff as being "appropriate" were: keeping bedrooms clean, having acceptable table manners, having a clean and neat appearance, being courteous, observing institutional rules, and so on. Helpful, friendly, and affectionate behaviors were also rewarded with tokens.

The class in personal improvement and social graces provided instruction and demonstration in hair styling and care, make-up, selection and care of clothing, and instruction for a more graceful body carriage. Table etiquette, and etiquette at parties, dances, and other social functions were discussed. These classes also provided opportunities for the girls to discuss sexual behavior on dates and in relating to males. With their tokens, the girls could "buy" participation in field trips, movies, dances, swimming, outdoor outings, concerts, shopping, and beauty salon trips. The girls responded by achieving a more attractive personal appearance, as rated by their peers and project personnel. Their improvement in body posture, their verbal responses when conversing with each other and with other people, and their less hostile expressions made the staff feel that the subjects were experiencing new feelings of confidence and personal worth.

PHASE III

At the beginning of the third month, Phase III was incorporated into the treatment program. Remedial education with token reinforcement still remained the focus of treatment. The basic reinforcers, tokens and affection in the form of body contact or praise, continued to be used. However, there was a lessening of physical contact and affection from the staff as the girls began to receive social and emotional gratification from each other and from a strengthening of their self-concepts. The reinforcement schedule was revised again. Greater academic achievement and longer periods of appropriate behavior were necessary for token reinforcement. More emphasis was gradually placed on intrinsic rewards, and the girls were encouraged to develop values and moral judgments. They were given more opportunities to make decisions and assume responsibility. Each girl was given the responsibility for getting to designated places on time. If she was late for class, she forfeited part of the opportunity to earn tokens. During this phase of the program, meals had to be paid for with tokens. If a girl had not earned tokens, she was not permitted in the dining room. Concern and interest for one another was manifested when a girl who had no tokens was given tokens by other girls so that she could join them for a meal.

During Phase III the girls were given opportunities to work and earn extra tokens. When the project began, the girls had been eliminated from the routine institutional assignments to laundry, kitchen, or cleaning details. Now they could volunteer for work assignments and were paid in tokens.

More and more opportunities were provided for off-campus excursions. Toward the end of the project, the girls could exchange their tokens for a visit to their own home. Heretofore, except in the event of a death in the family, no girl had ever been permitted to go home for a visit.

RESULTS AND DISCUSSION

Improvement was evidenced in the language and reading performance of nine subjects on a post-test of the Gates Reading Survey Test (see Table 2). Gains ranged from two months to thirteen months in grade level. Full scale scores on the post-test of the WISC were raised from one to seventeen points (Table 3). The positive relationship of reading score increases to IQ increases in some of the cases could be anticipated in view of results found in other similar studies. Still, considerable speculation could be made about the fact that the greatest rises in reading (double or more the expected) were accompanied by the greatest rises in IQ.

TABLE 3

Gains Made in Performance on the WISC

Subjects	Age	Verbal IQ Pre-test	Verbal IQ Post-test	Verbal IQ Gains	Performance IQ Pre-test	Performance IQ Post-test	Performance IQ Gains	Full-Scale IQ Pre-test	Full-Scale IQ Post-test	Full-Scale IQ Gains
A	13	89	90	1	103	103	0	75	76	1
B	13	69	74	5	83	83	0	73	76	3
C	11	77	86	9	101	107	6	87	96	9
D	14	67	69	2	85	85	0	73	74	1
E	15	89	91	2	87	89	2	87	89	2
F	14	69	81	12	69	80	11	66	79	13
G	14	75	81	6	72	99	27	71	88	17
H	15	90	90	0	108	108	0	99	99	0
I	15	72	75	3	78	79	1	72	75	3
J	14	100	101	1	114	114	0	107	108	1

There were improvements in personal appearance and acquisition of social etiquette that made the subjects more socially acceptable. These improvements, noted in the staff reports, were better personal appearance, a more helping attitude toward each other, a more positive attitude toward school and teachers, improved table manners, more polite and considerate choice of speech, and a general improvement in relating to other people. It was the subjective evaluation of the staff that self-concepts and feelings of personal worth in the subjects were strengthened. It was noted that many of the other inmates began to adopt the behavior of the subjects and there were frequent requests to be included in the experimental group.

The staff noted less hostile and aversive behaviors and a more positive cohesiveness among the ten subjects, demonstrated by their expressing more feelings of joy and a more calm and friendly attitude. There was less abusive language, destructive behavior, and fighting. They assisted each other in not breaking rules and in sharing tokens, and demonstrated concern for each other by helping one another attain their attitude or behavior goals. One girl's behavior goal was to modulate and lower her excessively loud and coarse voice. During the last month of treatment, the other girls would suggest in soft tones that she lower her voice, rather than scream back as they had formerly done. It was felt that the aversive gang or peer influence, which so often determines delinquent behavior, had changed somewhat to encouragement of socially adaptive behavior. And, on the basis of these improvements, at the end of the treatment period, the superintendent of the institution recommended that three of the experimental subjects be released from the institution.

CONCLUSION AND SUMMARY

A treatment model called "Educo-therapy" was designed to remedy the learning deficits and maladaptive behaviors of ten delinquent girls and was used in an experimental pilot project for three months. The treatment model used in the program involved facets of several different theories and procedures. The underlying basic philosophy of educo-therapy held that each girl was worthy of respect and love. The treatment philosophy stated that each girl should:

1. Experience success in school (particularly in reading),
2. Learn modes of behavior that are socially acceptable,
3. Have her self-concept enhanced, and
4. Learn to assume the responsibility of the consequences of her behavior.

The goals of the treatment program were phased in three progressive levels, each designed to meet basic, developing needs. The objective was: behavior modification through conditioning and reinforcement, with resulting educational improvements and improvement of self-concept and social integration.

It was predicted that if a child could experience success in learning and find gratification and reinforcement in academic achievement, many of his maladaptive behaviors, which were most in evidence within the classroom, would be remedied. One of the deficiencies in this study was the lack of comprehensive post-testing, due to insufficient funding and lack of available personnel at the termination of the study. However, in a subjective evaluation by the conservative institutional staff enthusiastic support was given to the belief that educo-therapy shaped academic learning into the behavioral repertoire and provided an effective means of coping with disruptive emotional behavior. A modified version of the pilot project treatment program has been incorporated into the regular program of this institution.

It should be pointed out that the total time and environmental space of each subject was involved in this intensive, three-month treatment program. In terms of institutional economics, it is the writer's opinion that this in-depth, concentrated approach to education remediation and behavior therapy is more economically feasible than long-term incarceration without the treatment program.

REFERENCES

Bachman, S. "Learning Theory and Child Psychology: Therapeutic Possibilities." *Journal of Child Psychology and Psychiatry* 3 (1962): 149-63.

Bandura, A., and Walters, R. H. *Social Learning and Personality Development.* New York: Holt, Rinehart and Winston, 1963.

Bateman, B. "Learning disabilities—An Overview." *Journal of School Psychology* 8 (Spring 1965): 1-12.

_____. "Learning disabilities—Yesterday, Today, and Tomorrow." *Exceptional Child* 31 (December 1964): 166-67.

_____. "Learning Disorders." *Review of Educational Research* 36 (February 1966): 93-119.

Blain, D. "Unhealthy Emotional Development and Its Relation to School Learning." *California Journal of Elementary Education* 31 (1962): 25-29.

Broadwin, I. T. "A Contribution to the Study of Truancy." *American Journal of Orthopsychiatry* 2 (1932): 253-59.

Buehler, R. E.; Patterson, F. R.; and Furniss, J. M. "The Reinforcement of Behavior in Institutional Settings." *Behavioral Research and Therapy* 4 (1966): 157-67.

Chall, J. *Learning to Read: The Great Debate.* New York: McGraw-Hill, 1966.

Eysenck, H. J. "Learning Theory and Behavior Therapy." *Journal of Mental Science* 105 (1959): 61-175.

Fernald, G. M. *Remedial Techniques in Basic School Subjects.* New York: McGraw-Hill, 1943.

Ferster, C. B., and Skinner, B. F. *Schedules of Reinforcement.* New York: Appleton-Century-Crofts, 1957.

Frierson, E. C., and Barbe, W. *Educating Children with Learning Disabilities: Selected Readings.* New York: Appleton-Century-Crofts, 1967.

Gewirtz, J. L., and Baer, D. M. "The Effect of Brief Social Deprivation on Behaviors for a Social Reinforcer." *Journal of Abnormal and Social Psychology* 56 (1958): 49-56.

Glasser, W. *Reality Therapy: A New Approach to Psychiatry.* New York: Harper and Row, 1965.

Hall, C. S., and Lindzey, G. *Theories of Personality.* New York: John Wiley, 1957.

Hellmuth, J., editor. *The Special Child in Century 21.* Seattle, Washington: Special Child Publications, 1966.

Hersov, I. A. "Persistent Non-Attendance at School." *Journal of Child Psychology and Psychiatry* 1 (1960): 130-36.

Kephart, N. C. *The Slow Learner in the Classroom,* 2d ed. Columbus, Ohio: Charles E. Merrill Publishing Co., 1971.

Krasner, L., and Ullman, L. P. *Research in Behavior Modification.* New York: Holt, Rinehart and Winston, 1965.

Leventhal, T., and Sills, M. "Self-Image in School Phobia." *American Journal of Orthopsychiatry* 34 (1964): 685-95.

Money, J., editor. *The Disabled Reader.* Baltimore, Maryland: Johns Hopkins Press, 1966.

Patterson, G. R. "The Peer Group as Delinquency Reinforcement Agent." Unpublished research report, Child Research Laboratory. Eugene: University of Oregon.

Skinner, B. F. "Why Teachers Fail." *Saturday Review* 16 (October 1965): 80.

Sulzer, E. S. "Behavior Modification in Adult Psychiatric Patients." *Journal of Counseling Psychology* 9 (1962): 271-76.

Tyerman, M. J. "A Research into Truancy." *British Journal of Educational Psychology* 28 (1958): 217-25.

Ullman, L. P., and Krasner, L. *Case Studies in Behavior Modification.* New York: Holt, Rinehart and Winston, 1966.

White, R. W. "Motivation Reconsidered: The Concept of Competence." *Psychological Review* 66 (1959): 297-334.

How does one attempt to develop explanations for the performance of bright as compared to dull children? Krippner presents several explanations.

ETIOLOGICAL FACTORS IN READING DISABILITY OF THE ACADEMICALLY TALENTED IN COMPARISON TO PUPILS OF AVERAGE AND SLOW-LEARNING ABILITY

Stanley Krippner

Etiological factors in reading disability for a high intelligence group were compared to those in average and low intelligence groups. All subjects were elementary and secondary pupils ranging from 7-1 to 15-10 in age. The twenty-six high intelligence subjects ranged from 113 to 128 in WISC IQ. The 146 subjects of average intelligence ranged from 88 to 112 in IQ. The thirty-four low intelligence subjects ranged from 70 to 87 in IQ. The subjects were administered several diagnostic tests to determine the etiology of their reading disabilities. When the etiological factors were divided into organic and functional categories, it was noted that the high intelligence group's disabilities were significantly more often functional in origin than those of the other two groups.

In the education of gifted and talented children, the mastery of basic reading skills is essential. Gowan and Scheibel (5), however, have estimated that most gifted children are hidden remedial reading candidates. Wheeler and Wheeler (19) have stated that "the most seriously retarded readers in our

From *The Journal of Educational Research* vol. 61, no. 6 (February 1968): 275-79. Reprinted by permission of the journal.

53

schools are the mentally superior students" while
Strang (15) has noted that the gifted child who reads
only at his grade level is actually a remedial reading
case. Witty (20), Torrance (17), and Goodman (4)
have expressed similar opinions concerning "creative" pupils.

The etiological factors associated with reading
problems among the gifted are similar to those
affecting average and slow-learning pupils. Disorders may be present in the peripheral nervous system (especially in seeing and hearing), in the central
nervous system, or in the endocrine system (1, 9, 14,
18). These disorders are usually referred to as "organic" in nature. In addition, there may be "functional" disorders—those arising from social,
emotional, educational, or cultural handicaps (13,
16).

The purpose of this study was to determine
whether organic or functional etiology was more
characteristic of highly intelligent disabled readers
as compared to pupils representing other intelligence levels.

PROCEDURE

For the purposes of this study, the concept of reading disability
proposed by Bond and Tinker (1) was utilized. The Bond-Tinker
formula computes a pupil's expected reading grade (ERG) by multi-
plying the number of years a child has been in school by his IQ
(divided by 100) and adding 1.0 (because his grade placement was 1.0
when he entered school). Although the IQ is not an adequate criterion of giftedness, it was felt that the goals of the study would be best
served by using it both for the Bond-Tinker formula and as a cut-off
point in delimiting the three mental ability groups.

Each pupil's observed reading grade (ORG) was estimated by
taking the mean of his grade equivalent on the six reading tests of
the Durrell Analysis of Reading Difficulty. These tests included oral
reading rate, silent reading rate, word recognition, word analysis,
visual memory, and phonics. The pupil's ERG was computed by
using the Bond-Tinker formula, and the degree of reading disability
was established by subtracting each pupil's ORG from his ERG. The
only pupils used in this study were those with a reading disability
of one year or more.

Each pupil's diagnostic test data were utilized to arrive at the major cause of his disability. Contributing etiological factors were determined by the same procedure which included diagnostic testing and interviewing, clinical observation, the examination of medical reports, school records, parent conferences, developmental histories, and clinical observations. The final diagnostic statement was made by one of several graduate clinicians working at the Kent State University Child Study Center under the supervision of the author of this report. An attempt was made to lean heavily on objective test scores, so as to prevent subjective judgment from becoming a biasing factor.

During the 1961–1962, 1962–1963, and 1963–1964 academic years, a total of twenty-six disabled readers with WISC IQ's of 113 or above were seen at the Kent State University Child Study Center. During the same period of time, 146 disabled readers were seen with WISC IQ's between 88 and 112; thirty-four poor readers were seen with WISC IQ's of 87 and below. It was decided to refer to these youngsters as "academically talented," "average," and "slow-learning" and to make comparisons among the three groups as to the etiology of their reading problems.

Fifteen etiological categories were established as well as criteria for assigning pupils to those categories. The categorization of *impaired seeing acuity* was made on the basis of a report from an ophthalmologist or optometrist. If the impairment in visual acuity had not been corrected when reading instruction began, this element was cited as an etiological factor. In much the same way, the pupil was placed in the *impaired hearing acuity* category if this problem had not been identified by an audiologist before reading instruction was inaugurated. A pure-tone audiometric screening test and the Keystone Visual Survey were administered.

Visual skills were negatively affected in all cases where seeing acuity was impaired. Many pupils displayed *poor visual skills* who had no eye disease and who did not need corrective lenses. These children typically had problems with the visual discrimination of letters, visual memory, visual closure, and visual-motor coordination. Pupils were classified as having poor visual skills if they were one year or more disabled on the visual memory section of the Durrell Analysis or if their performance on the Perceptual Forms Test (*11*) was below 60. Additional visual problems were also noted on the WISC on such subtests as Coding, Mazes, and Picture Completion and on the Frostig Developmental Test of Visual Perception. Because the latter test was not available when these pupils were diagnosed initially, the only ones who were administered the test were those coming to the Center for supplementary or follow-up testing in 1964.

Pupils were assigned to the category of *poor auditory skills* if they made an unsatisfactory score, for their age, on the Wepman Auditory Discrimination Test. Poor auditory skills were also identified by the Roswell-Chall Auditory Blending Test, the Illinois Test of Psycholinguistic Abilities, and the WISC Digit Span subtest. Pupils with defective auditory skills could not discriminate between two similar phonemes, could not blend individual phonemes together into a simple word, and could not recall material presented auditorially.

As the young child grows and develops, listening and speaking typically precede reading and writing. Reading instruction assumes a certain level of speaking ability, vocabulary development, and articulation preciseness. In some cases, therefore, poor articulation can be a causal factor in reading disability. At the Center, each pupil was administered the Montgomery Look-and-Say Articulation Test (*10*). If one or more major speech sounds were defective, and if those sounds were characteristically mastered by the majority of youngsters of that mental age, the pupil was considered to have a *speech defect.*

Brain injury was suspected among pupils whose scores on the Graham and Kendall Memory-for-Design Test (*6*) fell outside the normal limits. In many cases, this suspicion was confirmed by electroencephalographic examination. In others, neurological diagnosis was not possible because of financial factors. In the latter cases, a tentative diagnosis of brain injury was made on the birth history, developmental history, clinical observation, and additional data.

Rabinovitch (*13*) has described *disturbed neurological organization* in terms of a "developmental lag" between the maturation of verbal capacities displaying a slower development. As a result, these children display reading disabilities coupled with a difference of fifteen or more IQ points between their WISC Verbal Scale scores and their WISC Performance Scale scores. Other symptoms described by Rabinovitch include disturbed body image, poor revisualization, poor reauditorization, difficulties in conceptual thinking, confusion in dealing with time, confusion in dealing with numbers, and confusion in dealing with directions. Those pupils placed in this category by Center clinicians had a WISC Performance IQ that was at least fifteen points higher than their WISC Verbal IQ. In addition, their behavior indicated problems in at least five out of the seven characteristic areas described by Rabinovitch. Frank brain injury was not found to characterize these children, either by Rabinovitch or (with two exceptions) by Center clinicians. As a result, they are often referred to as suffering from "developmental dyslexia" as opposed to "posttraumatic dyslexia," in which damage to the central nervous system, rather than a developmental problem, exists.

Directionality confusion was diagnosed by the Harris Tests of Lateral Dominance. If a pupil had poor left-to-right progression in reading, if he often confused "d" and "b," and if his performance on the Harris Tests was also unsatisfactory, the pupil was placed in this category.

In the case of certain pupils, *endocrinal malfunctioning* was felt to be an etiological factor. In each case, there was a medical report that endocrinal malfunction existed (or did exist when reading instruction began).

Pupils were diagnosed as *socially immature* for their chronological age if they scored below 90 on the Vineland Social Maturity Scale.

All pupils were administered the Purcell Incomplete Sentences (*12*) and either the Mental Health Analysis or the California Test of Personality. On the basis of these measures, as well as clinical observation and outside reports, the Center clinicians made judgments as to whether emotional disturbance was an etiological factor. A breakdown into the categories of *neurotic, psychotic,* and *sociopathic* tendencies was made on the basis of projective test data. No pupil was ever placed in more than one of the above categories, even though it was sometimes felt that an interaction of two or three conditions existed. Almost all children with reading disabilities have some degree of emotional disturbance, generally as a result of their academic frustration. In making their judgments, therefore, the clinicians attempted to classify those pupils as disturbed only if the emotional disturbances were the *cause* of the reading disability rather than the *result* of it.

Unfavorable educational experiences were found to be an etiological factor among many pupils seen at the Center. The placement of a pupil in this category was dependent on such subjective data as parental interviews, school reports, and the types of errors made by the pupil on reading tests.

As a fee was required for an appointment at the Child Study Center, very few culturally disadvantaged pupils were seen during the course of this study. However, a pupil was categorized as *culturally deprived* if his fee had been paid by a social agency. The influence of his disadvantaged condition was subjectively estimated on the basis of reports and interviews.

Rarely is one etiological factor responsible for a reading problem. The clinicians, therefore, cited both the *major* etiological factor and the *contributing* factors in their reports. Isolating the major factor was extremely subjective in many instances and the multifactor causation of reading disabilities became apparent to the clinicians involved in this study.

RESULTS

The mean WISC IQ of the academically talented group was 117.2, with a range from 113 to 128. The average group's mean IQ was 100.5, with a range from 88 to 112. The slow-learning group had a mean IQ of 80.2, with a range from 70 to 87.

The mean reading disability of the academically talented pupils was 2.1 years. The mean reading disability of the average pupils was 2.0 years; the slow-learning pupils had a mean disability of 2.0 years.

The mean age of the academically talented was 11-8, with a range from 7-6 to 14-0. The average group's mean age was 10-8, with a range from 7-1 to 15-10. The mean age of the slow learners was 10-8, with a range from 7-5 to 15-0.

Of the academically talented group, 88.5 percent were boys. Of the average group, 89.0 percent were boys, and of the slow-learning group, 74.2 percent were boys. Of the total group, 87.4 percent were boys.

Chi-square analysis was done on the major etiological factors divided into organic and functional categories. The organic factors included impaired seeing and hearing acuity, poor visual and auditory skills, speech defects, brain injury, disturbed neurological organization, directional confusion, and endocrinal malfunctioning. The functional factors included social immaturity, unfavorable educational experiences, cultural deprivation, and neurotic, psychotic, and sociopathic tendencies. The division was somewhat arbitrary as etiological boundaries are not clear-cut and a great deal of overlap exists. The results of this classification are shown in Table 1.

A non-significant Chi-square of 0.1 was obtained when the average and slow-learning groups were compared in reference to organic versus functional major etiology. A Chi-square of 4.3, significant at the .05 level, was obtained when the average and academically talented groups were compared. A similarly significant Chi-square of 5.2 was obtained when the slow-learning and academically talented groups were compared. In other words, the academically talented group demonstrated significantly *less* organic etiology as a major factor and significantly *more* functional etiology as a major factor than either the average or slow-learning group.

TABLE 1

Major and Total Contributing Etiological Factors in the Reading Disabilities of Three Clinical Groups of Pupils Divided by WISC IQs Into Academically Talented (N = 26), Average (N = 146), and Slow-Learning (N = 34)

	Major Etiological Factors						Total Contributing Etiological Factors					
	Talented		Average		Slow-Learning		Talented		Average		Slow-Learning	
	f	%	f	%	f	%	f	%	f	%	f	%
Organic												
Impaired Seeing Acuity	0	0.0	14	9.6	2	5.9	5	19.2	41	28.1	18	52.9
Impaired Hearing Acuity	0	0.0	1	0.7	1	3.0	1	3.8	13	8.9	5	14.7
Poor Visual Skills	2	7.7	19	13.0	5	14.7	14	53.8	91	62.3	30	88.2
Poor Auditory Skills	0	0.0	1	0.7	1	3.0	2	7.7	52	35.6	24	70.6
Speech Defects	0	0.0	0	0.0	0	0.0	2	7.7	27	18.5	10	29.5
Brain Injury	3	11.5	25	17.1	13	38.2	4	15.4	30	20.5	14	41.2
Disturbed Neurological Organization	6	23.1	27	18.5	1	3.0	7	26.9	30	20.5	2	5.9
Directional Confusion	1	3.8	9	6.2	1	3.0	10	38.5	38	26.0	23	67.6
Endocrinal Malfunctioning	0	0.0	5	3.4	0	0.0	1	3.8	17	11.6	6	17.6
Functional												
Social Immaturity	0	0.0	3	2.1	1	3.0	7	26.9	25	17.1	14	41.2
Neurotic Tendencies	9	34.6	25	17.1	2	5.9	17	65.4	50	34.2	15	44.1
Psychotic Tendencies	1	3.8	2	1.4	2	5.9	1	3.8	3	2.1	3	8.8
Sociopathic Tendencies	2	7.7	6	4.1	1	3.0	3	11.5	8	5.5	1	3.0
Unfavorable Educational Experiences	2	7.7	8	5.5	3	8.8	15	57.7	83	56.8	14	41.2
Cultural Deprivation	0	0.0	1	0.7	1	3.0	0	0.0	9	6.2	5	14.7

DISCUSSION

This study demonstrates the existence of neurological problems among some disabled readers of high intelligence. Often a program of perceptual training, dominance establishment, and/or motor coordination improvement is needed before remedial reading will be helpful. Many pupils seen at the Center had received two or three years of remedial tutoring without positive results. A deeper understanding of the disability was gained through diagnostic testing. Tutoring in reading is a process of sinking shafts into sand if the basic physiological foundations for learning do not exist. Satisfactory auditory discrimination must be present before a child can memorize whole words. A child must know the difference between his right and his left hand before he can master the difference between such words as "was" and "saw."

Once the basis of perception and symbol-making have been established, the academically talented child who is a poor reader shares many of the same remedial needs as other children with neurological inadequacies. He needs to improve his visual discrimination of letters and to improve his ability to blend phonemes into words. Rabinovitch (13) suggests training in directional orientation, phonics, and tactile-kinesthetic tracing. His learning needs constant reinforcement as this training is often slow and unsteady. There are many word recognition skills—sight cues, phonic cues, context, structural analysis—and those best suited for each remedial reader should be emphasized.

The customary skills in abstract thinking and conceptualization which most academically talented children possess cannot be relied on if emotional disturbance, brain injury, or disturbed neurological organization is present. These factors, alone or in combination, may hamper the process of abstraction; as a result, concrete experiences and tangible materials are often called for. Field trips may provide a meaningful basis for symbol-making. Tactile-kinesthetic approaches to words (involving tracing, touching, and framing) may be needed to supplement visual and auditory approaches. Comprehension skills must be built slowly; once again, a variety of reinforcement techniques may be needed.

The reading process is probably the most complex task the child is called upon to master. It should be no surprise that a variety of factors can interfere with the mastery of this process. Pupils falling into different categories of disability should receive different treatment (3). Furthermore, the remedial clinician should start with the child where he is and proceed up the educational hierarchy until the symbol-making process is mastered (*7, 14*). Furthermore, attention must be paid to the fact that children of different intelligence levels demonstrate different modes of problem-solving (*2, 8*). Therefore, three critical variables to be considered are level of intelligence, degree of disability, and etiology of disability.

Diagnosis has little value unless it is the first step in remediation. Reading disabilities of the academically talented demand as close attention to the individual aspects of the problem as do the disabilities of the average and the slow-learning. The fact that a pupil has relatively high general intelligence does not mean that he will overcome his reading problem automatically.

Remedial techniques for the academically talented demand an adaptation to their specific problem areas with an inclusion of intellectually stimulating content whenever possible. This is especially valuable when unfavorable educational experiences have been the major etiological factor in the reading disability. Counseling of parents and teachers is often called for as the bright disabled reader suffering from emotional disturbances seeks to improve his reading skills while simultaneously working out new ways of relating to himself, to his peers, and to adult figures. His giftedness demands a stimulating, challenging, educational environment while his emotional difficulty necessitates a structured, controled pacing of new challenges. If the neurotic, psychotic, or sociopathic tendencies afflicting the disabled reader prove to be deep-seated, remedial reading must be preceded by family counseling and psychotherapy.

REFERENCES

1. Bond, G. L., and Tinker, M. *Reading Difficulties, Their Diagnosis and Correction.* New York: Appleton-Century-Crofts, 1957.

2. Borg, W. "Study Habits and Methods of Superior, Average, and Slow Pupils in Ability-Grouped and Random-Grouped Classrooms." Paper read at the annual meeting of the American Psychological Association, 1964.

3. De Hirsch, K. "The Categories of Learning Difficulties in Adolescents." *American Journal of Orthopsychiatry* 33 (1963): 87-91.

4. Goodman, P. *Growing Up Absurd.* New York: Random House, 1960.

5. Gowan, J. C., and Scheibel, R. W. "The Improvement of Reading in Gifted Children." *Educational and Administrative Supervision* 46 (1960): 35-40.

6. Graham, F. K., and Kendall, B. S. "Memory-for-Designs Test: Revised General Manual." *Perceptual and Motor Skills* 11 (1960): 147-88.

7. Hewett, F. M. "A Hierarchy of Educational Tasks for Children with Learning Disorders." *Exceptional Children* 31 (1964): 207-14.

8. Klausmeier, H. J., and Loughlin, L. J. "Behaviors during Problem-Solving among Children of Low, Average, and High Intelligence." *Journal of Educational Psychology* 52 (1961): 148-52.

9. Mayne, D. "The Intelligent Retarded Reader." *Journal of Developmental Reading* 7 (1963): 62-66.

10. Montgomery, J. *The Look-and-Say Articulation Test.* Chicago: King, 1961.

11. *Perceptual Forms and Incomplete Copy Forms, Teacher's Test Manual.* Winter Haven, Florida: Lions Publication Committee, 1963.

12. Purcell, J. W. *The Purcell Incomplete Sentences.* Kent, Ohio: Kent State University Child Study Center, 1961.

13. Rabinovitch, R. "Reading and Learning Disabilities." In *American Handbook of Psychiatry,* edited by S. Arieti, pp. 857-69. New York: Basic Books, 1959.

14. Sonnenberg, C., and Glass, G. C. "Reading and Speech: An Incidence and Treatment Study." *Reading Teacher* 19 (1965): 197-201.

15. Strang, R. "Gifted Children Need Help in Reading." *Reading Teacher* 6 (1953): 23-27.

16. Strang, R. "Mental Hygiene of Gifted Children." In *The Gifted Child,* edited by P. Witty, pp. 131-62. Boston: D. C. Heath and Co., 1951.

17. Torrance, E. P. *Guiding Creative Talent.* Englewood Cliffs, New Jersey: Prentice-Hall, 1962.

18. Wepman, J. "Auditory Discrimination, Speech, and Reading." *Elementary School Journal* 40 (1960): 325-33.

19. Wheeler, L. R., and Wheeler, V. D. "Relationship between Reading Ability and Intelligence among University Freshmen." *Journal of Educational Psychology* 50 (1949): 230-31.

3

Noneducational Diagnosis

Summaries of research often lead students to studies of importance. In this review, what does the testing of visual perception mean for educators? Leed's review is imperative reading.

SUMMARY OF RESEARCH ABSTRACTS—FROSTIG DEVELOPMENTAL TEST OF VISUAL PERCEPTION

Donald S. Leeds

Considerable research relative to the relationship of visual perceptual abilities in reading has been conducted since the early studies of Gates (4). In subsequent studies (3, 5, 6) the authors reported that reading might require a minimum perceptual ability. Kendall (8) reported a zero correlation between reading achievement and the ability to reproduce shapes of varying complexity from memory for children between ages six and one-half to eight years. Davidson (1), MacLatchy (9), Goins (7), and Frostig et al. (2) report a definite

From *The Journal of the Reading Specialist* vol. 9, no. 3 (March 1970): 125-37. Reprinted by permission of the journal.

relationship between reading achievement and visual perception. The research studies cited in this article primarily deal with the Frostig Developmental Test of Visual Perception (DTVP).

Frostig and her colleagues found that difficulties in visual perception were, by far, the primary problems in learning for many children who were diagnosed as having minimal brain damage. The authors reported that children who had difficulty in writing seemed to be handicapped in hand-eye coordination and that children who were not able to recognize words often had a figure-ground perceptual disturbance. Poor form constancy was attributed to children whose difficulty lies in recognizing a letter when written in different sizes or colors. Reversals or rotations were a result of children with problems in perceiving positions in space. Difficulty in spacial relationships was indicated by interchanging the order of the letters.

In 1958, Frostig and her colleagues developed the prototype of the test which is currently available. The 1963 edition (2a), revised and standardized on more than 2100 children in nursery and public schools, is designed, according to the authors, to measure five abilities which they believe are specifically related to the child's ability to learn. As these five abilities are developed, so is the child's ability to learn. The five abilities are: 1. eye-motor coordination; 2. figure-ground relationship; 3. form constancy; 4. position in space; and 5. spacial relations, each ability developing relatively independently of the others.

1. Davidson, H. "An Experimental Study of Bright, Average, and Dull Children at the Four-Year Mental Level." *Genetic Psychology Monographs* 9 (1931): 119-289.

2. Frostig, M.; Lefever, D. W.; and Whittlesey, J. R. B. "A Developmental Test of Visual Perception for Evaluating Normal and Neurologically Handicapped Children." *Perceptual and Motor Skills* 12 (1961): 383-89.

2a. Frostig, M.; Maslow, P.; Lefever, D. W.; and Whittlesey, J. R. B. "The Marianne Frostig Developmental Test of Visual Perception." *Perceptual and Motor Skills* 19 (1964): 463-99.

3. Gates, Arthur I. "Basic Principles in Reading Readiness Testing." *Teachers College Record* 40 (1939): 495-506.

4. _____. "The Psychology of Reading and Spelling with Special Reference to Disability." New York: Columbia University Teachers College, 1922.

5. _____. "A Study of the Role of the Visual Perception, Intelligence, and Associative Processes in Reading and Spelling." *Journal of Educational Psychology* 18 (1926): 433-45.

6. Gates, Arthur I., and Bond, Guy L. "Reading Readiness: A Study of Factors Determining Success and Failure in Beginning Reading." *Teachers College Record* 37 (1936): 679-86.

7. Goins, Joan T. *Visual Perceptual Abilities and Early Reading Progress.* Chicago: Supplementary Educational Monographs, University of Chicago Press, 1958.

8. Kendall, B. S. "A Note on the Relation of Retardation in Reading to Performance on a Memory for Designs Test." *Journal of Educational Psychology* 29 (1948): 370-73.

9. MacLatchy, J., "Bexley Reading Study." *Educational Research Bulletin* 25 (1946): 141-68.

Allen, Robert M.; Dickman, Isadore; and Haupt, Thomas D. "A Pilot Study of the Effectiveness of the Frostig-Horne Program with Educable Retardates," *Exceptional Children* 33 (September 1966): 41-42.

The authors hypothesized that educable retardates can improve certain visual perceptual skills with this specialized intensive training program. The skills to be improved are: eye-motor coordination, figure-ground discrimination, figure constancy, position in space, and spacial relations.

An experimental group ($N = 10$) and a control group ($N = 6$) were randomly selected and administered the DTVP. The experimental group received one semester of training. It was determined, at the end of the training period, that a large test-retest increase for Tests 2, 3, and 5 (figure-ground, figure constancy, and spacial relations) existed. The difference between the two administrations for the eye-motor coordination and position in space tests (Tests 1 and 4) produced no significant differences. An analysis of variance of the test-retest raw score differences between the experimental and control groups was reported to be reliably different.

The authors concluded that the use of the program indicates special training can improve the educable retardate's skills in making figure-ground discrimination, appreciating figure constancy, and dealing with spacial relations. In general, special training yielded immediate discernible improvement in three of the five testable visual perceptual skills.

Alley, Gordan; Spencer, James; and Angell, Roland. "Reading Readiness and the Frostig Training Program," *Exceptional Children* 35 (September 1968): 68.

The author tested the hypothesis that the Frostig program was an effective method in developing reading readiness of culturally deprived children. The sample for the experiment consisted of 108 kindergarten children with unselected mental ability.

Two groups were formed with the experimental group receiving twenty-five minutes of training daily for an eight-month period (October 1—June 1). The training program involved sensori-motor and visual perceptual exercises as outlined in the teacher's guide accompanying the Frostig Program for Development of Visual Perception (Frostig and Horne, Follett Publishing Co., 1964). The Metropolitan Reading Readiness Test and the DTVP were administered at the end of the experimental period.

Although all eight variable mean scores (MRRT) were in the predicted direction, five scores significantly differentiated the groups (word meaning, numbers, and total subtest scores: .05; matching: .01; listening: .001). Eleven of the thirteen Frostig variable means favored the experimental group with the eye-motor coordination subtest mean difference statistically significant at the .05 level.

Significant differences in favor of the experimental group found on the reading readiness test, after eight months, support the authors' hypothesis that the Frostig program is beneficial in a reading readiness program for culturally deprived kindergarten children. The influence of personality, interest, and classroom management of teachers as possible variables was not controlled.

Frostig, Marianne; Lefever, Welty; and Whittlesey, John. "Disturbances in Visual Perception," *Journal of Educational Research* 57 (November 1963): 160-62.

Between preschool and second grade, two psychological functions have become very prominent in detecting early symptoms of developmental disturbances which may result later in a variety of disorders ranging from intellectual deficits to reading difficulties and poor social adjustment. These psychological functions are language and visual perception, with the latter generally regarded as the more sensitive indicator of the status of central developmental process.

A survey of the child's perceptual functions will enable the psychologist, educator, or physician to pinpoint abnormalities during preschool and early school years. The Stanford-Binet, although loaded with perceptual tests, doesn't differentiate among the various perceptual factors. This research aims to make information available by constructing a test of visual perception for which developmental norms have been developed.

A population of 1800 preschool and school children were used as the base sample. A smaller sample (seventy-one) from the Marianne Frostig School of Educational Therapy was also included. Each child in this select sample was either known or suspected of having a neurological handicap and had difficulty in academic learning.

The overall findings suggest that a large proportion of the children who show either learning difficulties and/or poor classroom adjustment at the preschool and lower grades levels are handicapped by disabilities in visual perception. A test was designed to identify such children as early as possible and to diagnose their particular visual disabilities. Thus, appropriate medical, psychological, and educational intervention is made possible at an early age.

Fortenberry, Warren D., Ed.D. *An Investigation of the Effectiveness of the Frostig Developmental Test of Visual Perception for Word Recognition of Culturally Disadvantaged First Grade Students.* (Hattiesburg: University of Southern Mississippi, 1968). (DA 29:3765A).

This study was undertaken to determine the effectiveness of visual perceptual training upon word recognition and subsequent reading achievement of culturally disadvantaged first-grade students from families whose annual income was $3,000 or less and whose parents had eight or less years of schooling.

For twelve weeks, the experimental groups were given the Frostig program in addition to the regular reading readiness program. The control group benefited from the readiness program, only, as outlined in the teacher's manual of the basal series. Initially, the following tests were administered to each of the subjects: Metropolitan Reading Readiness Test, the Goodenough Drawing Test, the Keystone Visual Survey Test, the Puretone Audiometer Test and the DTVP. The Gates Primary Reading Tests, alternate forms, were administered at the end of twelve weeks (Form 1), eighteen weeks (Form 2), and twenty-four weeks (Form 3).

An analysis of covariance of the data revealed the only significant difference between means (.01) was in word recognition at the eighteen-week period. No difference was found at either the twelve- or the twenty-four-week period. A significant difference between means of the experimental and control groups (.05) with respect to the total reading score was found at the eighteen-week testing (Form 2). Both groups showed significant gains on both total reading score and word recognition.

Hueftle, M. Keene, Ed.D. *A Factor Analytic Study of the Frostig Developmental Test of Visual Perception, the Illinois Test of Psycholinguistic Abilities and the Wechsler Intelligence Scale for Children.* (Greeley: Colorado State College, 1967). (DA29:2139B)

The writer attempted to determine those common and unique factors assessed by five DTVP subtests, nine ITPA subtests and twelve WISC subtests. (Information pertinent to the Frostig and ITPA tests will be presented. The WISC results will be noted when they bear upon either of the two other tests. For more complete information, the reader is referred to either the abstract, noted above, or the original source.)

Fifty-two first graders, drawn from a stratified sample based on paternal educational levels comprised the sample for the research. Each of the three measures were administered individually with a time lapse of nine months between the administration of the WISC and the ITPA and DTVP. Intercorrelations of all twenty-six subtests and total scores were obtained. Each battery was separately and then simultaneously subjected to principal axes factor analysis followed by varimex rotation. Factors with an eigen value greater than .01 were rotated.

Ten correlations between total standard scores of three tests support the idea that the DTVP and ITPA are assessing intelligence as measured by the WISC to a moderate degree. The intercorrelations seem to be almost exclusively to the WISC Performance Scale.

Factor analysis of the DTVP suggests that, at best, two factors [are] being tapped. Factor 1 appears to be eye-hand coordination combined with personality characteristics and ability to understand and remember test directions. Factor 2 seems to involve the recognition and recall of geometric shapes, eye-hand skill, and the ability to understand and remember directions.

Factor analysis of the ITPA reveals one quasi-unique factor and three common factors. The nature of the quasi-factor is unclear. Factor 1 appears to involve visual recognition and association of stimuli, many of which appear culturally loaded and conceptually abstract. Factor 2 seems to assess short-term auditory memory. Factor 3 appears to involve auditory and visual sequential memory. Also, all three of the ITPA common factors apparently are assessing aspects of children's behavior not intended.

The rotated factor analysis of the twenty-six variables resulted in one quasi-unique and eight common factors. Factor 2 is visual-hand in nature and is loaded appreciably with ITPA variables. Factor 3 is also heavily loaded with ITPA and appears to be auditory-visual in nature. Factor 5 is dominated by DTVP variables and seems to be a uniting of two DTVP factors seen in independent analyses. Factors 7 and 8 are loaded with variables from all three tests, but the nature of the factors is unclear. Factor 9 appears to show a strong similarity to the ITPA quasi-unique factor and a likeness to Cohen's Freedom from Distractability (WISC).

Olsen, Arthur V. "The Relation of Achievement Test Scores and Specific Reading Abilities to the Frostig Developmental Test of Visual Perception," *Perceptual and Motor Skills* 22 (1966): 179-84.

The author attempted to determine: 1. the predictive value of the DTVP for general achievement in second grade, 2. the relationship between the Frostig test and specific reading abilities (as measured by: paragraph comprehension; word recognition; learning sounds in words; visual memory using reversible words in context and synthesizing words in context).

Seventy-one second grade children, twenty-nine female and forty-two males, were given a battery of tests. These tests consisted of: DTVP; California Achievement Test: Lower Level, Form W; California Test of Mental Maturity: short form; Gates Advanced Primary Reading Test: Advanced Word Recognition (AWR), Form 1 and Advanced Paragraph Reading (APR), Form 2; Hearing Sounds in Words and Visual Memory of Words (Durrell) and two tests constructed for the research: recognition of reversible words in context and word synthesis tests.

The findings relative to Frostig's hypotheses concerning the DTVP and specific abilities were:

1. No significant difference found between performance on the figure-ground test (DTVP) and advanced word recognition; a significant difference (.01) was found between the figure-ground test and the California vocabulary subtest performance. The Gates AWR is probably a better measure for the purpose of the study since it is a picture-word association test and is designed to sample the ability to read words representative of primary vocabulary. The vocabulary test (CAT) consists of four subtests: word form, word recognition in response to pronounced words; matching the key word with the opposite and a picture-word association test. Frostig's suggestion that a significant relation-

ship exists between poor word recognition and figure-ground perception is not supported by the findings of this study. 2. The Frostig subtest, Form Constancy has little predictive value. 3. The correlation between Frostig's subtest, Position in Space, and reversible words in context is .386 (.01) which supports Frostig's notion that children who reverse or rotate words have difficulty in perceiving position in space.

Ohrmacht, Fred W., and Olsen, Arthur V. "A Canonical Analysis of Reading Readiness and the Frostig Developmental Test of Visual Perception," *Educational and Psychological Measurement* 28 (1968): 479-84.

A study to explore the communality among several measures of reading readiness and the DTVP. It seems likely that several measures of the DTVP can, generally, be expected to exhibit low to moderate correlations with reading achievement in lower elementary grades. Most reading readiness tests currently in use include one or more measures designed to assess visual perceptual ability. The question raised is one of the amount of redundancy existing among the measures of reading readiness and the DTVP.

Two hundred and thirty-two first graders from three semirural north Georgia communities comprised the experimental population. The mean verbal I.Q. for the sample was 92.4 (s.d. = 15.0). The three measures used were: Metropolitan Reading Readiness Analysis (MRRA), Gates Reading Readiness Analysis (GRRA), and DTVP. A matrix of correlations among the subtests of the three measuring instruments is presented in the article, as well as the canonical vector weights for the three criterion tests.

The authors concluded that the MRRA and GRRA possess an underlying common perceptual function which reflects a substantial amount of information yielded by the DTVP. Other studies suggest that information unique to the DTVP appears to yield little that is useful in predicting reading achievement.

Corah, Norman, and Powell, Barbara J. "A Factor Analytic Study of the Frostig Developmental Test of Visual Perception," *Perceptual and Motor Skills* 16 (February 1963): 59-63.

Frostig, et al. (3) stated that the five areas of functioning as represented by the Frostig test are presumed to be relatively distinct from one another. In addition, the authors stated that children with learning difficulties obtained lower total scores and greater subtest scatter (range) than did normal children. No tests of significance were reported to substantiate these statements. They concluded that the greater degree of subtest scatter of the children with learning handicaps "suggest that distinct functions of visual perception can be disturbed independently and in varying degrees" (p. 392). This was the basis for a recommendation that retraining in specific areas of deficit diagnosed by the test be initiated. It might be just as cogently argued that those subjects with lower total scores and greater subtest scatter have their scores based on fewer test items and, consequently, that the increased scatter is a function of decreased reliability. This study was designed to determine what common factors existed among scores and to determine what proportion of the subtest variance was specific.

Forty children, nineteen girls and twenty-one boys, ranging in age from 50 to 76 months with a mean age of 63.2 were used. The Full-Range Picture Vocabulary Test-Form B (1) yielded an IQ range of 79 to 139 with a mean IQ of 106.32. The tests used in the evaluation were DTVP (Eye Motor Coordination; Figure-Ground; Form Constancy; Position in Space; Space Relations and Perceptual Quotient [PQ]; a sum of the subtest scores); Full-Range Picture Vocabulary Test; Ghent Overlapping Geometric Figures Test (a measure of form discrimination) (4); and a form constancy task adapted from Ardis and Fraser (2).

Eleven variables were intercorrelated. A factor analysis of 45 correlations (ten variables, PQ omitted because it is a combination of scores) yielded twelve significant correlations at .01, six correlations at .05, and three correlations at the .10 level. Four factors were extracted from the ten variables and were found to account for 73 percent of the total variance and 70 percent of the total variance of the Frostig test scores. The results of the analysis suggest that two major factors would account for most of the variance: general intelligence and developmental changes in perception. While scatter analysis of the Frostig subtests is of dubious value, the Perceptual Quotient from this test may be a useful measure of perceptual development. Further efforts might be concentrated on eliciting specific correlates of this measure.

1. Ammons, R. B., and Ammons, H. S. *Full-Range Picture Vocabulary Test.* Missoula, Montana: Psychological Test Specialists, 1948.

2. Ardis, J. A., and Fraser, E. "Personality and Perception: The Constancy Effect and Introversion." *British Journal of Psychology* 48 (1957): 48-54.

3. Frostig, M.; Lefever, D. W.; and Whittlesey, J. R. B. "A Developmental Test of Visual Perception for Evaluating Normal and Neurologically Handicapped Children." *Perceptual and Motor Skills* 12 (1961): 383-94.

4. Ghent, L. "Perception of Overlapping and Embedded Figures by Children of Different Ages." *American Journal of Psychology* 69 (1956): 575-87.

Fullwood, Harry Lee. "A Follow-Up Study of Children Selected by the Frostig Developmental Test of Visual Perception in Relation to their Success or Failure in Reading and Arithmetic at the end of the Second Grade." (Norman: University of Oklahoma, 1968). (DA29:2035A).

A follow-up of the children selected by Ferguson in her study (see Ferguson abstract) to determine the success or failure in reading and arithmetic at the end of second grade. The two groups originally constituted, and matched on the basis of the S-B, Form L-M, age, race and prior kindergarten training were separated on the basis of the DTVP for instructional purposes. Approximately 80 percent of the original sample was located and used in this study.

A statistical analysis of reading and arithmetic achievement levels revealed that students with PQ's above 90 performed significantly better than those whose PQ's were below 90 at the end of the second grade. The results indicated that the two groups appear to achieve in a similar manner from first to second grade.

Ferguson, Nelda U. "The Frostig—An Instrument for Predicting Total Academic Readiness and Reading and Arithmetical Achievement in First Grade." (Norman: University of Oklahoma, 1967). (DA28:2090A).

An investigation of the predictive value of the Frostig Developmental Test of Visual Perception as a measure of total academic readiness at beginning first grade and as a predictor of academic achievement in first grade reading and arithmetic.

Two groups, matched as to age, sex, race, IQ and prior kindergarten training were formed. Subjects in group 1 had scores on the perceptual quotient total (PQ) above 90 and those in group 2 had PQ's below 90. The subjects were tested and identified initially. During the week of May 15–20 (of the first year of school), teachers were asked to indicate the arithmetic and reading grade levels of each student.

Group 1 was significantly better on the initial measure, the Metropolitan Reading Readiness test as well as the end of the year reading and arithmetic measures. The author concluded that individuals with a PQ 90 would not be expected to be working up to first grade level at the end of first grade. A PQ below 90, also, indicates poor total academic readiness for grade one. [*See Fullwood abstract* for Jacobs, James N., "An Evaluation of the Frostig Visual Perception Training Program." *Educational Leadership* 25 (June, 1968): 332-40].

In an attempt to determine whether children respond with higher scores on the DTVP after completion of the perceptual training program, three schools were selected, each with two kindergarten, first and second grade classes, affording the researcher eighteen classes with approximately 500 students. Experimental and control groups were set up and the program was evaluated in September (before training) and again in June (following training). The Frostig test was administered to the experimental group initially, whereas the Metropolitan Reading Readiness Test was administered to both groups initially. An analysis of covariance was used to deal with the problem of lack of similarity between the experimental and control groups.

The experimental group had lower *initial* average scores with higher final average scores. The pre-test means, for the experimental group, among the three age-grade levels were highly similar. In the control groups, the pre-test scores did not increase from pre-kindergarten to kindergarten but remained essentially the same from pre-kindergarten through first grade. Observation indicated that skills do not develop normally among the types of pupils in this experiment. The author suggests that special stimulation, such as that produced by the Frostig program, is needed to develop the perceptual skills necessary. The largest gains occurred among the older rather than the younger children. No significant differences were found when reading readiness scores were adjusted.

Jacobs, James N.; Wirthlin, Lenore D.; and Miller, Charles B. "A Follow-Up Evaluation of the Frostig Visual Perception Training Program." *Educational Leadership* 26 (November 1968): 169-75.

In the experiment, cited above, the author found that the largest gains were registered by first graders. Cancelling out initial differences in Frostig scores resulted in no significant differences in the end-of-the-year reading readiness scores among kindergarten subjects in the Frostig/non-Frostig groups. Subtest analyses revealed practically all the differences in the Frostig total test scores, noted, were due to one subject: Form Constancy.

The present study is a replication, to the degree possible, of the former study and follow-up of the children in the earlier study to determine the predictive validity of the Frostig tests as well as to study cumulative effects of the Frostig program upon future reading achievement. The pupils in the earlier research attended five different schools and were "intact" classes. For most comparisons (statistical), control groups were drawn from the same schools in which the experimental classes were located. These pupils were considered "disadvantaged."

The difference in testing schedule for the two experiments was:

	Initial	*Replication*
Frostig	beginning and end of year	end of year
Metropolitan Achievement	beginning and end of year	end of year
Stanford: Primary 1	xxxxxxxxxxxx	end of Grade 2
Gates-McGinitie	May (first grade only)	xxxxxxx

Four questions, raised and answered by the authors, were:

1. Do Frostig program children achieve better than the control group when compared on the DTVP? The pupils trained with the Frostig program in pre-kindergarten and first grade showed higher levels of visual perceptual performance on the DTVP than did the control group.
2. Do kindergarten "Frostig" trained children achieve higher on the Metropolitan Reading Readiness test at the end of kindergarten years than did the control group? No statistically significant difference was found. The predictive validity of the Frostig and Metropolitan Readiness tests were quite low using standardized tests in reading as criteria.
3. What is the predictive value of the Frostig compared with the Metropolitan Reading Readiness test? The Metropolitan Reading Readiness test seems to be a better predictor of reading achievement than the Frostig. The Frostig program pupils had no particular advantage as far as future reading achievement was concerned when compared with the control group.
4. Do the Frostig trained children achieve better on reading tests than the control groups? No significant differences in the achievement between the groups was found at the end of Grade 1. A two year exposure to the Frostig program yields higher Frostig results than a one year exposure which is, in turn, higher than no exposure.

SUMMARY

Interest in the relationship between visual perceptual abilities and reading has been investigated during the past fifty years. Research is in agreement that the reading process involves some perceptual skills. However, general agreement is not evident as to the type of perceptual skill nor the degree of relationship between a specific skill and its role in reading performance.

Recent attention has been given to the Frostig Developmental Test of Visual Perception and the Frostig program designed to assist in strengthening those weaknesses revealed by the DTVP. Research has been reported on the diagnostic value on the DTVP and the accompanying program.

Jacobs (1968), Jacobs, Wirthlin, Miller (1968), Fortenberry (1968) reported an improvement in one or more perceptual skills as a result of utilizing the Frostig program. Olsen (1966) reported a significant relationship between one perceptual skill and a problem revealed in select cases in reading disability (reversals). Ferguson (1967) reported that children with a perceptual quotient below 90 were not reading at grade level at the end of the first year. Fullwood (1968) following up Ferguson's study concurred with the earlier research.

Whereas the research cited indicates some diagnostic value for the Frostig test and certainly value in the program which is designed to correct weaknesses found by the DTVP, the research is too meager to do more than "raise" questions about the specific perceptual skills involved in reading and the value of programs designed to improve the diagnosed weaknesses. Among the questions which the writer has raised is, "Of what value, to reading, is the ability to draw a line from left to right between two lines without touching the borders?" (See Chart 1 below for Summary of Purposes and Conclusions concerning the Frostig Developmental Test of Visual Perception and Frostig Training Program.)

CHART 1

Frostig Developmental Test of Visual Perception and
Frostig Training Program

Summary of Purposes and Conclusions				
Authors	*Year*	*Purpose*	*Sample*	*Conclusions*
Allen, Dickman Haupt	1966	Effectiveness of Frostig-Horne Program	Educable Retardates	Special training improved skills in making figure-ground discrimination, in appreciating figure constancy in dealing with spacial relations

CHART 1 (*continued*)

Authors	Year	Purpose	Sample	Conclusion
Alley, Spencer Angell	1968	Frostig Program as an effective method of developing reading readiness of culturally deprived children	108 unselected kindergarten children	Results substantiated hypothesis that the program was beneficial to culturally deprived children
Jacobs	1968	Evaluation of the Visual Perception Training Program	500 subjects K-2	Frostig program aided in developing necessary perceptual skills
Jacobs, Wirthlin Miller	1968	1. Follow-up Jacob's research (1968) 2. Determine validity of Frostig tests 3. Study cumulative effects of Frostig program upon future reading achievement	500 subjects K-2 (same as above)	Experimental group, using the program, achieved higher level of visual perception. No significant differences on Metropolitan Reading Readiness Test or on reading tests at the end of grade 1. MRRT seemed to be a better predictor of reading achievement than the Frostig
Fortenberry	1968	Effectiveness of visual training upon word recognition and reading achievement of culturally disadvantaged	First graders	Tests were administered at the end of 12, 18 and 24 weeks. Significant differences obtained at the 18 week evaluation (word recognition means and total reading score)
Frostig, Lefever Whittlesey	1963	Basic study relative to the DTVP	1971 pre-school and school children	Large proportion of children with learning difficulties and/or poor classroom adjustment are handicapped in visual perception
Ferguson	1967	Predictive value of DTVP with respect to first grade reading, arithmetic and total academic readiness	First graders PQ above 90 and PQ below 90	Group with PQ below 90 not expected to be working up to grade level at end of first year
Fullwood	1968	Follow-up of Ferguson study	Approximately 80% of Ferguson sample	Groups appear to achieve in a similar manner from first to second grade
Olsen	1966	Relationship of achievement test scores, specific reading abilities and DTVP	71 second grade subjects: 29 (F) 42 (M)	Idea that figure-ground perception and poor word recognition related not supported; Form constancy has little predictive value; Position in Space and reversible words in context significant (.01)
Ohrmacht, Olsen	1968	Statistical study of several reading readiness measures and DTVP	232 first grade subjects	Metropolitan and Gates Reading Readiness Analyses possess underlying common perceptual function reflecting substantial amount of information yielded by DTVP
Corah, Powell	1963	Factor analysis of DTVP	40 subjects 19 (F) 21 (M)	Perceptual quotient may be useful as a measure of perceptual development. Factors accounting for 70 percent variance: general intelligence and developmental changes in perception
Hueftle	1967	Factor analysis of DTVP, ITPA and WISC	52 first graders	Two factors appear to be tapped: 1. Eye-hand coordination with personality characteristics and ability to understand and remember test directions 2. Recognition and recall of geometric shapes, eye-hand skill and ability to understand and remember directions

Of utmost importance is the possible use of subtest scores in reading diagnosis. What are the possibilities of WISC subscores? Deal presents an interesting review from a selection of authorities.

A SUMMARY OF RESEARCH CONCERNING PATTERNS OF WISC SUBTEST SCORES OF RETARDED READERS

Margaret Deal

The following abstracts and summary purports to summarize the pertinent studies carried out since 1945 to discern a pattern of performance on scores of the *Wechsler Intelligence Scale for Children* which typifies the retarded reader. The abstracts included here represent an exhaustive search of the published reports on this topic. Additional unpublished studies are known to have been carried out but their results were not available for examination and inclusion in this summary.

> Altus, Grace T. "A WISC Profile for Retarded Readers." *Journal of Consulting Psychology* vol. 20, no. 2, (April 1956): 155-156.

Purpose: Sought to determine whether children reading two years or more below expected level disclosed distinctive test patterns on the Wechsler Intelligence Scale for Children. Twenty-five children, with grade placement from three to eight, from twelve schools of Santa Barbara County, California, met the criteria.

Conclusion: Found Coding and Arithmetic subtests to be significantly lower than Vocabulary, Digit Span, Picture Completion, Object Assembly and Picture Arrangement. Findings were not conclusive because of the small number of cases, but tended to support trends found earlier by Altus with adult poor readers. No significant difference was found between the Verbal IQ and Performance IQ.

> Burks, Harold F., and Bruce, Paul. "The Characteristics of Poor and Good Readers as Disclosed by the Wechsler Intelligence

From *The Journal of the Reading Specialist* vol. 4, no. 4 (May 1965): 101-11. Reprinted by permission of the journal.

Scale for Children." *Journal of Educational Psychology* 46 (December 1955): 488-93.

Purpose: To test the hypothesis that poor readers may be relatively weak in those parts of intelligence tests which resemble vital characteristics inherent in written language. If a pattern of abilities for poor readers can be found, the resulting profile should have implications for curriculum modification. Population consisted of eleven good readers and thirty-one poor readers (one or more years below grade level), who ranged in grade placements from the third through the eighth grades. Tests used were Wide Range Achievement Test and the WISC.

Conclusion: Poor readers were significantly low in Information, Arithmetic, and Coding subtests, but significantly high on Picture Arrangement, Block Design, and Comprehension subtests. Good readers were significantly high on Similarities subtest. Hypothesis was made that poor readers, as a group, approach learning situations in a more concrete manner because of inability to handle abstractions. Since the reading process inherently consists of making abstractions, these children are handicapped.

Coleman, James C., and Rasof, Beatrice. "Intellectual Factors in Learning Disorders." *Perceptual and Motor Skills* 16 (February 1963): 139-52.

Purpose: To determine whether underachievers show a distinctive pattern of intellectual abilities as reflected on WISC scores. Subjects were 126 underachievers and 20 overachievers with an age range between 7-5 and 16. Tests used were the California Achievement Test or Stanford Achievement Test and WISC.

Conclusion: Low scores were reported on Information, Arithmetic, Vocabulary, Digit Span, and Coding. High scores on Comprehension, Picture Completion, and Block Design. The underachievers were significantly higher than the mean scores on the performance scale. Severe underachievers made significantly lower scores on Digit Symbol. The underachievers scored significantly low on the subtests heavily loaded with school-type learning, concentration and memory factors, but high on those of perceptual organization and incidental learning.

Flanary, Woodrow. "A Study of the Possible Use of the Wechsler-Bellevue Scale in Diagnosis of Reading Difficulties of Adolescent Youth." Abstract of Ed.D. Thesis, University of Virginia, 1953. (V. 14, 1045.)

Purpose: To discern a pattern of performance on scores of the Wechsler-Bellevue which typifies the retarded reader. The subjects were ninety retarded readers and twenty normal readers between the ages of twelve and sixteen. The retarded readers ranged in intelligence from mentally defective to superior, with forty-five of them in the average range; the normal readers ranged from average to very superior.

Conclusion: Found Information, Comprehension, Digit Span, Arithmetic, Similarities, Vocabulary, Picture Arrangement, and Digit Symbol to be the subtests most clearly differentiating the retarded reader from the normal reader. The retarded readers have poor memory functions, conceptual (abstract) thinking ability, short attention span, weak powers of concentration, meager vocabulary, poor planning ability and slow psychomotor speed.

> Graham, Ellis. "Wechsler-Bellevue and WISC Scattergrams of Unsuccessful Readers." *Journal of Consulting Psychology* 16 (1953): 268-71.

Purpose: To compare Wechsler-Bellevue and WISC scattergrams for unsuccessful readers with a pattern reported by Harper for adolescent psychopaths. Subjects were ninety-six unsuccessful readers whose Wechsler-Bellevue and/or WISC profiles were taken from the files of the Psychological Services for Children at the University of Denver. Thirty-one met the criteria as follows: between the ages of 8-0 and 16-11; either the verbal or performance IQ was 90 or more; and were 25 percent or more below their mean reading grade level on the Wide Range Achievement Test and had attended either public or parochial school for the expected number of years.

Conclusion: Found Arithmetic, Digit Span, Information, Digit Symbol, and Vocabulary averaged below the mean, and Object Assembly, Picture Completion, Picture Arrangement, Block Design, Comprehension, and Similarities above the mean. Digit Symbol was usually the lowest performance score; Comprehension and Similarities the high verbal scores. The scattergrams of both groups corresponded closely. Both groups did less well in areas resembling school learning (Arithmetic, Vocabulary, and Coding). The score for Similarities was statistically higher.

> Gurvitz, Milton S. "The Wechsler-Bellevue and the Diagnosis of Psychopathic Personality." *Journal of Clinical Psychology* 6 (October 1950): 397-401.

Purpose: To discover whether there was a psychometric pattern for adult white male psychopathic personalities on the Wechsler-

Bellevue test. The personnel consisted of three groups of eighty-four subjects: a psychopathic prison group, a control group of inmates, and a group outside of prison. Age was restricted to those between nineteen and thirty, and intelligence range was from 80 to 120. Groups were equated for age, education, IQ, economic status, race, and sex. Quotient and subtest distribution were tested for normality of distribution with a minority proving to be normally distributed. The significant difference between groups on the various subtest and quotient values were computed.

Conclusion: No characteristic pattern for psychopathic personalities was found. The patterns proposed by Levi, Wechsler and Schafer were not found to be applicable to adults.

> Hirst, Lynne Shellberg. "The Usefulness of a Two-Way Analysis of WISC Sub-Tests in the Diagnosis of Remedial Reading Problems." *Journal of Experimental Education* 29 (1960): 153-60.

Purpose: 1. To explore the usefulness of a two-way analysis of WISC subtests to facilitate a more accurate appraisal of intellectual functioning in regard to reading retardation, and, 2. to note any distinctive pattern of WISC subtest scores that are characteristic of severely and mildly retarded readers. WISC profiles and other information necessary were taken from the files of the University of Wisconsin's Reading Clinic. The total sample of thirty ranged in age from 8-0 to 13-6, with full scale IQs above 89, and whose reading level was six months or more below that expected from their mental age. Tests used were Chicago Silent Reading Tests, Form 2 and/or Gates Advanced Primary Reading Test.

Conclusion: Both groups were high in Picture Completion and Picture Arrangement, and low in Arithmetic, Coding, and Digit Span. In one subtest, Object Assembly, the severely retarded group rated significantly high. Severely retarded were significantly high on Picture Completion, Object Assembly, and Picture Arrangement; significantly low with lower Digit Span, Vocabulary, and Similarities scores than the mildly retarded. In the mildly retarded group Picture Completion and Picture Arrangement were high. Coding and Arithmetic low.

> Kallos, George L.; Grabow, John M.; and Guarion, Eugene A. "The WISC Profile of Disabled Readers." *Personnel and Guidance Journal* (February 1961): 476-78.

Purpose: Sought to analyze the WISC profiles of a specified sample of poor readers and to compare the findings with those reported earlier by Altus. Sample was composed of thirty-seven boys, aged 9-0 to 14-0, with Full Scale IQ scores of 90-109, chosen from 300 children tested at Michigan State University Reading Center during a two-and-one half year period. Each was reading at least two years below his age-grade expectation.

Conclusion: Found no statistically significant difference between Verbal and Performance IQs. Block Design was significantly higher than six other subtests, and Information, Coding, and Arithmetic were significantly lower than at least two other subtests. The profile resulting from this study and from Altus' study differed most noticeably in the area of Arithmetic, Vocabulary, Picture Completion, and Block Design.

> Muir, Margaret, "The WISC Test Pattern of Children with Severe Reading Disabilities." *Reading Horizons* (Winter 1962): 67-73.

Purpose: Sought to show retarded readers will show a distinctive test pattern associated with the subtest scores on the WISC and that retarded readers will be relatively weak in immediate and long-term memory of processes and information. Sample consisted of 50 WISC profiles from the files of Michigan State University Reading Center of retarded readers (two or more years between expected and actual reading levels as measured by standardized tests). Tests used were Gates Advanced Primary Reading Test or the Gates Reading Survey and the WISC.

Conclusion: Found high subtest scores are Comprehension, Picture Completion, Object Assembly, and Block Design; low are Arithmetic, Coding, Information, and Vocabulary with Coding and Arithmetic significantly below the mean; Picture Completion and Object Assembly significantly above the mean. Burks and Bruce, Graham, Altus, Hirst and Muir indicate Information, Arithmetic, and Coding are significantly below the mean. Hirst, Altus, and Muir report Picture Completion and Object Assembly are significantly above the mean.

> Neville, Donald. "A Comparison of the WISC Patterns of Male Retarded and Nonretarded Readers." *Journal of Educational Research* 54 (1961): 195-97.

Purpose: To compare subtest patterns of WISC of male retarded readers (two or more years below grade level) with those of nonretarded readers (at or above grade level). Subjects were thirty-five pairs matched as follows: 1. total WISC IQ within one point; 2.

grade level, 3. sex. Records were taken from the files of those attending the University of Florida Reading Laboratory and Clinic in the years 1957-58. Tests were the Florida Reading Scales (individually administered test) and WISC.

Conclusion: The results indicated that the retarded readers were significantly low in Information, Arithmetic, and Digit Span, and significantly high in Picture Arrangement and Block Design. It was noted that the low scores seemed to be related to scholastic types of tasks and limited ability to concentrate while the high scores were somewhat removed from formal types of learning. The author does not feel that poor readers are inherently less endowed in some areas, but that they fail to develop in them because of their lack of reading abilities.

Paterra, Mary Elizabeth, "A Study of Thirty-three WISC Scattergrams of Retarded Readers." *Elementary English* vol. 40, no. 4 (April 1963): 394-99.

Purpose: Sought to distinguish any similarities among abilities and disabilities as revealed by WISC to discover implications for teaching of reading to retarded readers. WISC profile of thirty-three retarded readers referred because reading level was below expected level for mental age, average or above intelligence, children of white, American born, English speaking. Compiled and examined eleven mean scaled score scattergrams.

Conclusion: Scattergrams show Comprehension, Similarities, and Picture Completion significantly higher than Information, Arithmetic, Vocabulary, Picture Arrangement, Block Design, and Object Assembly. Arithmetic and Vocabulary were significantly below Comprehension, Similarities, Picture Completion and Coding. The author interprets this result to mean that reading should be improved through verbal reasoning rather than "independent vocabulary study, depending on memorization."

Rapaport, David. "Menninger Clinic Study." *Diagnostic Psychological Testing,* Volume 1. Chicago: Yearbook Publishers, 1945.

Purpose: To determine the pattern of scatter of scores on the Wechsler-Bellevue denoting clinical syndromes. Study was made on the Wechsler-Bellevue profiles of 217 psychiatric cases and 54 controls (motor policemen). Subjects were *not* equated as to age, sex, education, socio-economic level, urban or rural. He and his Menninger clinic colleagues used three main measures of scatter.

Conclusion: Classified nineteen clinical syndromes. Criticisms were many, and findings were rough indicators for a group, but not for individual diagnosis. The findings led Rapaport to conclude that scatter tends to be greater the more serious the form of maladjustment. The most valuable contributions of the study were in the qualitative distributions of the Wechsler-Bellevue subtests and in the hypothesis made regarding the possible psychological processes involved in these performances.

Sawyer, Rita. "A Study of Discrimination by the Subtests of the Wechsler Intelligence Scale for Children between Mildly Disabled and Severely Disabled Readers Diagnosed at the Syracuse Reading Center, September, 1958 to June, 1963." Unpublished Ph.D. dissertation, Syracuse University, 1964.

Purpose: To investigate the extent to which subtests of the WISC would discriminate between a group classified as mildly disabled in reading as contrasted with a group classified as severely disabled. Random sample of 180 disabled readers diagnosed between September, 1958 and June, 1963, at Syracuse Reading Center, IQ between 90 and 119, CA between 8-0 and 15-5, and then stratified according to three age levels. Severely disabled had instructional level less than half the reading expectancy grade score; mildly disabled at least half the progress expected.

Conclusion: Found that Completion, Arithmetic, Vocabulary, Digit Span, Picture Completion, and Object Assembly contribute heavily to reading success; Comprehension, Digit Span, Picture Completion, and Object Assembly are considerable value for group membership. Arithmetic, Digit Span, Comprehension, Object Assembly, Picture Completion, and Vocabulary are discriminative for the total group in descending order; Digit Span, Arithmetic, Vocabulary, Picture Completion, Object Assembly, and Comprehension for males in descending order. The subtests discriminate between mildly and severely disabled readers in both the total group and the males of the sample. The discrimination between two reading disability groups at different age levels declined as CA increased and was accepted at age levels 8-0 to 10-5 and 10-6 to 12-11. Severely disabled had a significantly higher mean performance IQ than verbal IQ. Two cross-validations were carried out concerning the discriminant functions for 1. eleven variables and 2. seven variables and the prediction of probable group membership found highly efficient.

Stroud, James; Bloomers, Paul; and Lauber, Margaret. "Correlation Analysis of WISC and Achievement Tests." *Journal of Educational Psychology* 47 (1957): 18-26.

Purpose: To determine the various combination of subtests on the WISC that might be used to predict performance in reading, arithmetic and spelling. Subjects were 775 youngsters from Grades 3 through 6, all presumed to be in academic difficulty. Sample group was average and had a mean IQ in the Dull Normal range.

Conclusion: Six tests which contributed heavily to predicting achievement in reading and spelling were Arithmetic, Digit Span, Vocabulary, Block Design, Object Assembly, and Coding. Correlation on Arithmetic, Vocabulary, Block Design, and Object Assembly were nearly as high as when all eleven subtests were used.

SUMMARY

During the last half century various causes of children's reading disabilities have been expounded. Mental test performance remains the one best predictor of reading achievement,[1] outside of reading itself. Individual tests of intelligence are considered preferable measures of capacity in the case of disabled readers.[2]

The studies of Rapaport and his colleagues in the early 1940s at the Menninger Clinic found patterns of subtest scores on the *Wechsler-Bellevue* that were rough indicators for a group, but not for individual diagnosis, for the classification of nineteen clinical syndromes. The most valuable contributions of the study were in the qualitative distributions of the *Wechsler-Bellevue* subtests and in the hypothesis made regarding the possible psychological processes involved in these performances. In his doctoral dissertation and subsequent studies (1949–50), Gurvitz attempted to discriminate and diagnose by means of the patterning of the *Wechsler-Bellevue.*

Since the standardization of the *Wechsler Intelligence Scale for Children* in 1949, a few studies have tried to discover a specific pattern of the WISC subtest scores associated with the retarded reader. In many of these studies the results and conclusions are

---

[1]Irving Anderson and Walter Dearborn, *The Psychology of Teaching Reading* (New York: Ronald Press, 1952), p. 10.

[2]Guy Bond and Miles Tinker, *Reading Disabilities: Their Diagnosis and Correction* (New York: Appleton-Century-Crofts, 1957), p. 75.

difficult to interpret and evaluate. In most of the studies the inferences have been based on data collected on a small number of subjects. Ways of determining retardation in reading have been varied. Some of the ways used in determining the amount of retardation were: from the expected grade placement level, from the expected level as determined by the results of the WISC, from the level as determined by mental age, and percentage below expected grade level as determined by standardized tests. Some investigators have used one or more years of reading retardation while others have used two or more years of retardation. The means of determining instructional level have included: referral for underachievement, standardized test results, and informal reading inventories. Age range has been from 7-5 to 16-11, with only Hirst and Sawyer making any attempts to narrow the age range.

Table 1 is an attempt to put the important data from the twelve studies in a form where their similarities and differences may be seen more readily. Three of the studies were concerned primarily with the subtests differentiating the retarded reader from the normal reader, the mildly retarded from the severely retarded, or contributing heavily to reading success. The remaining studies report the WISC subtest scores of retarded readers falling above or below the mean scaled score.

The subtests of Arithmetic, Vocabulary, and Digit Span were found by all three investigators (Table 2) to be contributing heavily to reading success. Comprehension, Object Assembly, and Coding were found by two of the three studies to be also contributing heavily to reading success.

In an analysis of the findings of the studies listed in Table 3, a low Arithmetic subtest score was found by all nine investigators to be indicative of retarded readers. Low Information, Coding, and Vocabulary were found by eight, seven, and five investigators respectively; high Picture Completion, Comprehension, and Picture Arrangement by six, five, and five investigators respectively. Four investigators found Block Design and Object Assembly to be high and Picture Completion low.

To facilitate reading Tables 2 and 3

I	Information	DS	Digit Span
C	Comprehension	PC	Picture Completion
A	Arithmetic	PA	Picture Arrangement
S	Similarities	BD	Block Design
V	Vocabulary	OA	Object Assembly

TABLE 1

Data From Twelve Studies of WISC Subtest Patterns of Retarded Readers

Study	N	Retardation	Gr. Pl.	High	Low	Tests Used	Other Information
1. Altus	25 Ret. Readers	Two or more yrs. below exp. level	3-8	Voc. DS, PC, OA, PA	I, Arith, Coding	Stand.	No sig. dif. between v and p IQ
2. Burks and Bruce	11 good 31 poor	One or more yrs. below grade pl.	3-8	PA, BD, C	I, Arith, Coding	Wide Range Ach.	Poor readers more concrete in learning
					Good readers no weak scores		
3. Coleman	126 underach. 20 overach.	Underachievers sig. higher than mean score on performance.	Age 7-5 to 16-0	C, PC, BD	I, Arith, DS, Coding	Calif. Ach. Stanford	Underach. score sig. low on subtests heavily loaded with school type learning, concentration and memory factors, but high on percept. org. and incidental learning.
4. Flanary	90 Ret. 20 normal	Ret. IQ range from dull nor. to sup.	Age 12-16	I, C, DS, Arith. & DS subtests differentiating r r from n	Sim, V, PA	W-B	R.R. have poor memory functions, conceptual (abstract) thinking abilities, short attention span, weak powers of concentration, meager voc, poor planning and a low psycho-motor speed.
5. Graham	31	25% or more below R.Gr. level	Age 8-0 to 16-11	Sim, Comp.	Arith, Voc, Coding, I, DS	W-B/WISC Wide Range Ach.	Did less well in sch. type of learning. Pattern similar to adol. psychopaths.
6. Hirst	30	Mild Severely	Age 8-13-5	Both PC, PA, SR also OA	Arith, DS, Coding Voc, Sim.	W-B, WISC	Two way analysis of WISC subtests

	N	Criteria	Group/Age	High	Low	Test	Comments
7. Kallos	37	Two gr. below age-grade level	Age 9-14	PA, OA, PC No sig. diff. between V. and P. IQ	I, Arith, Coding	Word Recog.	Suggest ret. devel. of visual-motor skills (Coding) may be primary cause of read. diff.
8. Muir	50	Two or more yrs. between exp. and actual read. level	Age 8-16	C, PC, OA, BD	Arith, I, Coding, Voc.	Gates Ad. Prim. or Survey	Inadequate ass. between vis. symbol and auditory stimulus. Learn better in structured situation.
9. Neville	35 ret. 35 normal	Referral	Matched pairs Lower V than P	PA, BD	Arith, I, DS	Florida Read. Scales	Low score related to sch. type learning and limited ability to concentrate. Hi scores somewhat removed from formal type learning.
10. Paterra	33	Not exp. level for MA	Age 6-5 to 14-6	C, S, PC	I, PA, BD, OA, A, Voc.	WISC	Strengths and weaknesses of various subtest score vary with age.
11. Sawyer	180	Mild Severe	Age 8-0 to 15-5	C, A, V, DS, PC, OA contribute IRI heavily to reading success.	C, DS, PC, OA for group		P IQ sig. greater V IQ for severely disabled 7 var. disc. nearly as well as 11.
12. Stroud	Sample group from 775		Gr. 3-6 Overage, Dull Normal	A, DS, V, BD, OA, Coding contributed heavily to predicting reading achievement.		WISC	Almost as high corr. on 4 (A, V, BD, OA) as when all 11 subtests were used.

TABLE 2

Subtest Scores of WISC Reported by Three Investigators
as Contributing Heavily to Reading Success

	I	C	A	S	V	DS	PC	PA	BD	CA	Coding
Flanary	X	X	X	X	X	X		X			X
Stroud			X		X	X			X	X	X
Sawyer		X	X		X	X	X			X	
Total	1	2	3	1	3	3	1	1	1	2	2

TABLE 3

Subtest Scores of WISC for Retarded Readers as
Reported by Nine Investigators

High	I	C	A	S	V	DS	PC	PA	BD	CA	Coding
Altus					X	X	X	X		X	
Burks and Bruce		X						X	X		
Coleman		X					X		X		
Graham		X		X							
Hirst							X	X		X	
Kallos							X	X		X	
Muir		X					X	X		X	
Neville								X	X		
Paterra		X		X			X				
Total High	0	5	0	2	1	1	6	5	4	4	0

Low	I	C	A	S	V	DS	PC	PA	BD	CA	Coding
Altus	X		X								X
Burks and Bruce	X		X								X
Coleman	X		X		X	X					X
Graham	X		X		X	X					X
Hirst			X	X	X	X					X
Kallos	X		X								X
Muir	X		X		X						X
Neville	X		X			X					
Paterra	X		X		X			X	X	X	
Total Low	8	0	9	1	5	4	0	1	1	1	7

Three of the studies (Altus, Kallos, Muir) found no significant difference between the Verbal IQ and Performance IQ. Neville reported a significant difference between Verbal IQ and Performance IQ with Performance IQ the higher. Coleman reported that underachievers were significantly higher than the mean score on performance and Sawyer reported a significant difference in Verbal IQ and

Performance IQ when only the severely disabled were considered, but when the entire population of the study was considered, the difference between Verbal and Performance IQ was not significant.

Sawyer and Paterra, who divided their population into age groups to consider the various factors, concluded that the strengths and weaknesses of the various subtest scores vary with the age level.

Coleman concludes that the retarded reader scores significantly low on subtests heavily loaded with school type learning, concentration, and memory factors, but high on perceptual organization, social and immediate learning. Flanary describes retarded readers as having poor memory functions, conceptual (abstract) thinking abilities, short attention span, weak powers of concentration, meager vocabulary, poor planning ability and slow psychomotor speed.

4

Classroom Diagnosis

The usefulness of informal testing is often proclaimed. But how does one interpret the results? Powell suggests some interesting interpretations.

THE VALIDITY OF THE INSTRUCTIONAL READING LEVEL

William R. Powell

The real value of the informal reading inventory (IRI) lies not so much in its identification of the instructional reading level—and, by interpolation, the independent and frustration levels—rather, its real value is that it affords the possibility of evaluating reading behavior in depth. Furthermore, it has the potential for training prospective teachers about reading behavior, a potential unequaled by other types of learning opportunities. For purposes of training teachers, the process becomes the product.

From *Diagnostic Viewpoints in Reading* (1971): 121-33. Reprinted by permission of William R. Powell and the International Reading Association.

The strength of the IRI is not as a test instrument but as a strategy for studying the behavior of the learner in a reading situation and as a basis for instant diagnosis in the teaching environment.

When we speak of instructional level, we are referring to a teacher task; when we speak of performance, we are referring to the learner's behavior; and when we speak of difficulty of material, we are referring to the characteristics of the media. For maximum learning, all three have to match: performance level (child), instructional level (teacher), and passage difficulty (material). The instruction should be provided by the teacher at the performance level of the child that will allow for the exclusion of interfering or disruptive reading behaviors.

BACKGROUND

Statements and comments on the informal reading inventory are not new. Indeed, many papers on this general topic have been presented. But in the past few years, the nature of the discussion has shifted from one of description and exposition to one of inquiry and critical analysis. This altered perspective now is focusing on the critical issues—generating critical questions in an open forum about the concept, criteria, application, and empirical basis of the IRI, which has become a part of the fabric of reading instruction since its structured formulation by Betts (2) nearly thirty years ago.

A major product derived from the use of the IRI is the identification of three distinct reading levels—independent, instructional, and frustration. For instructional purposes, the assumption has been that each literate individual, regardless of maturity, has three such levels. Supposedly, these would be in hierarchical order in relationship to the difficulty of the materials, with the independent reading level being the lowest, or easiest, of the three. The other two levels, instructional and frustration, follow in ascending order as the readability of the material increases. Each reading level is alleged to have specific instructional implications for the classroom teacher. While the existence of three different reading levels for literate persons is a powerful concept, it would have to be considered presently as a functionally useful but unvalidated construct.

Because the use of an IRI embodies most of the elements of the instructional environment, this process offers potential beyond the important task of making a match between children and suitable materials. There is the opportunity for teachers to gain diagnostic insights, from the simple indication of level to the complex evaluation of reading behavior. The latent power of this process is just beginning to be tapped as a means of expanding the conceptual framework of individuals in teacher education programs.

PURPOSE AND LIMITATIONS

Contrary to the possible implications of the title of the paper, I shall explore some of the facets and perceptions beyond the limited range of the instructional level. I trust the fact that I do not expand broadly into other related dimensions of the IRI will not be taken as a lack of sensitivity to the probable issues there. Components such as comprehension, rate, and symptoms of difficulty all play their interacting parts in affecting the total reading performance.

Rather than elaborate on the descriptive elements of the informal reading inventory, I am going to assume that you are somewhat familiar with its characteristics, construction, and administration, as well as with at least one scoring scheme used for the interpretation of levels. For those who wish to pursue information about the fundamental constituents of the IRI, I would refer you to Betts (2), Johnson and Kress (10), and Zintz (18).

The purpose of this paper is to present a critical inquiry about the product of the informal reading inventory and about some of the elements used in the process of determining that product. To achieve this purpose I propose to review recent developments on this topic briefly and to raise three particular questions. The first two deal with the process of the IRI, and the last deals with its product:

1. What is a suitable criterion level for word recognition in identifying the instructional reading level?
2. Is it appropriate to apply one set of performance standards uniformly across all grade levels?
3. Could it be that the major product of the IRI, i.e., the identification of three distinct reading levels, is a misinterpretation?

RECENT INQUIRIES

Without much doubt, the most widely used predetermined standards for evaluating reading performance on the IRI are those originally suggested by Betts (2). His criteria follow:

TABLE 1

Level	Word Recognition (%)	Comprehension (%)	Symptoms of Difficulty
Independent	99	90	none
Instructional	95	75	none
Frustration	90	50	some

Through the years, several individuals have expressed reservations and concern about the original criteria, but few have suggested other standards of performance that differed markedly.* In 1968, at the IRA convention in Boston, I broke the "silence of doubt" and openly challenged the existing sets of criteria (12). My investigation suggested that the original criteria simply are not consistent with

TABLE 2

Revised Scoring Criteria for the Informal Reading
Inventory (IRI)

Passages 1−2	Word Recognition		
	Independent	*Instructional*	*Frustration*
	1/99−1/50	1/49−1/8	1/7 (and below)
	Comprehension		
	100%−90%	89%−70%	69% or less
Passages 3−5	Word Recognition		
	Independent	*Instructional*	*Frustration*
	1/99−1/50	1/49−1/13	1/12 (and below)
	Comprehension		
	100%−90%	89%−70%	69% or less
Passages 6+	Word Recognition		
	Independent	*Instructional*	*Frustration*
	1/99−1/50	1/49−1/18	1/17 (and below)
	Comprehension		
	100%−90%	89%−70%	69% or less

*Smith (15) is a notable exception to this statement. Since 1959, she has proposed a lower percentage for correct pronunciation. Smith suggests an 80 to 85 percent accuracy range. Spache (16) has also offered an opinion that the Betts standards are arbitrarily too high.

the actual reading behavior for the instructional reading level are too stringent, even for the proficient readers. The alternate criteria that I found to be more consistent with children's actual performances are presented in Table 2.

TABLE 3

Word Recognition Error Ratios by Eight Sets of Criteria

Criteria Levels	Powell	Spache	Durrell	Gilmore	Gray	Gates McKillop	Betts-Killgallon	Cooper
P		1/4	1/3	1/3	1/7		1/20	1/50
1^2	1/6	1/5		1/5	1/8		1/20	1/50
2^1		1/8	1/8	1/6	1/11		1/20	1/50
2^2	1/8	1/7	1/9.			1/2	1/20	1/50
3^1		1/10		1/8	1/11		1/20	1/50
3^2	1/11	1/13	1/12			1/3	1/20	1/50
4	1/13	1/15	1/13	1/11	1/10	1/4	1/20	1/25
5	1/12	1/16	1/16	1/13	1/11	1/6	1/20	1/25
6	1/17	1/16	1/18	1/14	1/9	1/6	1/20	1/25
7		1/16	1/17	1/18	1/10	1/6	1/20	
8		1/18		1/20	1/9	1/6	1/20	

At the IRA convention in Kansas City, one full symposium program was devoted to the validity of the IRI. These presentations have subsequently been published (8). Particularly noteworthy out of that symposium collection was a paper by Beldin (1). He systematically traced the historical development of the informal reading inventory and pointed out some of the issues regarding the process of this instrument.

In November 1969 at the NCTE convention in Washington, D.C., Dunkeld and I (13) presented further comparative data concerning the validity of the criteria. We compared sets of criteria from eight sources, five of which were derived from commonly used oral reading tests. These data are presented in Table 3. Attention should be called to the similarity of the criteria in the first four columns. Also, please note that only one of the word-recognition error ratios (on the Gilmore at the eighth grade) reached the predetermined standards originally set by Betts.

REFERENCES TO TESTS IN TABLE 3

Durrell, Donald D. *Durrell Analysis of Reading Difficulty.* New York: Harcourt, Brace and World, 1955.

Gates, Arthur I., and McKillop, Anna S. *Gates-McKillop Reading Diagnostic Tests.* New York: Bureau of Publications, Teachers College, Columbia University, 1962.

Gilmore, John V. *Gilmore Oral Reading Test.* New York: Harcourt, Brace and World, 1968.

Gray, William S. *Gray Oral Reading Tests,* edited by H. M. Robinson. Indianapolis: Bobbs-Merrill, 1963.

Spache, George D. *Diagnostic Reading Scales.* Monterey, California: California Test Bureau, 1963.

QUESTIONS AND ISSUES

What is a suitable criterion level for word recognition in identifying the instructional reading level? We have enough evidence to suggest what is an unsuitable criterion but not enough yet to say with assurance what is suitable. It definitely would appear that the original criterion of 95 percent correct pronunciation (word recognition) —that is, one error in every twenty running words—is too high for all age-grade levels.

The way two occurrences relate tends to support this conclusion. Studies have been conducted to evaluate other concurrent events using the original criteria, such as investigations comparing grade placement scores derived from standardized reading measures with levels obtained from the informal reading inventory. In general, such studies have consistently indicated that scores from standardized tests vary at least from one to three years *above* a reported instructional reading level, as determined by the *IRI.** While one study did clearly caution that generalizing from standardized scores to the instructional reading level was tenuous at best, a significant gap did exist between the two types of assessment for a large number of the children studied (6). Undoubtedly, the nature of the assessment process between the two types of instruments could be expected to produce a difference between scores. Nevertheless, the degree of difference has been viewed with some suspicion as being greater than what should be expected for proficient readers.

---

*The studies by Killgallon (11), Daniels (5), Williams (17), Sipay (14), Davis (6), and Brown (3) all support the contention that standard tests tend to overestimate the instructional level. All studies except the one by Sipay used the Betts criteria with slight modification. For example, Williams adjusted the minimum acceptance in comprehension at the instructional level from 75 to 70 percent. Sipay, however, used the criteria suggested by Cooper (4) (see Table 3). Since these criteria are even more rigorous than those developed by Betts, the same pattern was found.

Now, suppose we apply this information to the model generally used for determining reading disability. The model typically used is the degree of difference between the subject's estimated capacity and actual reading achievement, as determined by scores from a standardized test. If the difference between capacity and achievement equals or exceeds a predetermined cut-off point, then the child is said to be disabled. If we apply the difference between standardized reading achievement measures and the instructional reading level and then add the discrepancy between estimated capacity scores and the reading achievement scores, an interesting phenomenon occurs. For most children of average ability with at least average reading achievement scores, their instructional reading level is not likely to be within the acceptable lower limits of their estimated capacity. Suppose the estimated capacity and reading achievement match perfectly; even then, the difference between their reading performance, as estimated by standardized tests, and their instructional reading level, as measured by the IRI, would be great enough to cause the instructional reading level to be outside the usually acceptable limits of normal reading behavior. Is this outcome at all suitable? If the criteria for determining the instructional reading level were representative of children's actual reading performance, would the discrepancies noted diminish? It would seem logical to assume that for youngsters of average ability and achievement, the instructional level should be within the tolerable limits of their estimated capacity.

Is it appropriate to apply one set of performance standards uniformly across all grade levels? Here, we need to divide our attention between the quantitative and the qualitative. The quantitative dimension refers to the numerical count of the errors or miscues used in computing the percent correct figure or the word recognition error ratio. The qualitative aspect of the issue refers to the types of errors or miscues that are permitted for computational purposes.

The data in Table 3 would not support an assumption that the same quantitative ratio or percentage figure can apply uniformly across all grade levels. Apparently, there is a differential function in oral reading miscues from grade level to grade level.

My earlier investigation, resulting in new criteria, implied that the change in the word recognition error ratio was due to the age/grade of the child. While the maturity of the reader certainly would be a factor in such a shift of error ratio, I now believe that the important factor is not the age/grade relationship but the difficulty level of the passage.

The implications of this conclusion were made only too clear to me by a written comment from one of my graduate students.

> If we now decide to use the criteria for passage levels rather than the child's level in school, is our decision to do so founded on the evidence in your study? For the average child's reading grade, it won't make much difference, but what about the sixth grader referred to the clinic experiencing difficulty in reading. On which basis do we judge his performance, on say first and second grade passage? There is a big difference between 1/8 and 1/18.* '

All available data, nevertheless, seem to indicate that there is an inverse relationship between the difficulty, or readability, level of a passage and the number of word recognition errors tolerated by a reader. That is, the easier the material, the higher the percent of miscues that can be permitted by the reader while still maintaining an acceptable understanding level of the material read. Conversely, the more complex the written language, the fewer the number of deviations that can be so tolerated and still realize an acceptable comprehension level.

The key word in such a discussion as the one in the preceding paragraph is *tolerate* (1). What is meant by *tolerate?* It is the level of error difficulty or deviation from the expected response that is not detrimental to total reading performance. The tolerance level allows for a compensation or adjustment of the reader within *his* range of functioning. As error intolerance increases, the material and instruction must be adjusted downward; and as error intolerance decreases, the adjustment should increase.

Before leaving the quantitative dimension of this issue, I would like to offer a point of curiosity. What relationship exists, if any, between the percent of word recognition deviations and sentence length? As the material increases in complexity and difficulty, the sentence length will also increase. Is there an inverse relationship between sentence length and error tolerance? Or is deep structure or some other linguistic factor the important variable, not sentence length?

Quantitatively, uniformity across passage levels would not appear to be appropriate either. The type of errors that significantly affect a reader's tolerance level are not uniform from level to level. That is to say that the types of significant errors between an average second grader and an average sixth grader are different, and should be. This observation is based on a doctoral study by Dunkeld (7)

---

*Comment by Patricia Stoll as contained in an intraoffice memo to the author.

currently near completion at the University of Illinois. It also coincides with the types of findings by Goodman (9) in her study of oral reading miscues. She states, "It became evident that the type of miscues which beginning readers made change qualitatively as they become more proficient readers." Therefore, certain types of miscues in the reading of a passage of second grade difficulty might not be scored as errors at that level but might be used for determining error ratios at the fourth grade difficulty level, and vice versa.

An apparent problem concerning the qualitative value placed on errors depends on the definition and classification used in processing those errors. There is little agreement among authorities on what constitutes a substitution, a mispronunciation, etc. The lack of agreement is not only in the basic definition but also in the implications. Certainly, if error types are to have relevance and provide cues for instruction, then a reasonable degree of common interpretation will have to be established.

Could it be that the major product of the IRI, i.e., the identification of three distinct reading levels, is a misinterpretation? To search for truth, one has to be willing to risk the ultimate. To critically analyze the process and product of the IRI, one has to consider that the ultimate answer may be negative—that indeed the IRI has no actual validity and that we who work with it are making something out of it that it is not. But that finding would offer positive direction for other types of options.

Research evidence to support the construct of an instructional reading level is minimal and incomplete, as it is for the frustration reading level. This statement does not mean that we do not believe such levels exist. It simply means we do not yet have the data to support our beliefs.

One of the traditional beliefs regarding reading levels is that they form a hierarchical sequence—independent, instructional, and frustration, in that order. Spache challenges that opinion by reversing the position of the instructional and independent reading levels. He orders the levels this way: instructional, independent, and frustration.

There is absolutely no empirical data for defining the rank order nor the limits of the independent reading level. It has been assumed to be beyond the upper limits of the instructional level; therefore, Spache's reversal of the rank order may well be correct. How would we know which sequence is correct?

Since everyone is guessing about the location of the independent reading level, I might as well offer a conjecture on the subject. My impression is that the independent reading level is not static. (It "floats.") It may not always be located above or below the instructional reading level. The leverage to the reader is the interest value of the ideas and concepts. The greater the interest, the higher the passage difficulty can be for the independent reading level of a particular pupil. Conceivably, interest could cause this level to be quite variable, and it may be equal to or above the instructional level in specific types of materials. It is possible that for brief, transitory, high-intensity periods, the interest value could project the independent reading level into the usual frustration zone (defined as beyond the lower limits of the instructional level). But until we have some data with which to define the limits of the independent level, your guess is as good as the three just given.

Another option may be that we are applying the right labels to the wrong agent. What we are really concerned with is the degree of mastery. The child does not have an *instructional* level; he only has a *performance* level. To obtain the desired performance level, adjustment has to be made in criterion levels, the learning time, or the linguistic complexity of the written language. The selection of the adjustment variables is a teacher task and, therefore, an instructional one. When we speak of performance, we are referring to the learner's behavior; and when we speak of difficulty of material, we are referring to the characteristics of the media.

For maximum learning, all three have to match: performance level (child), instructional level (teacher); and passage difficulty (material). The instruction should be provided *by the teacher* at the performance level *of the child* that will allow for the exclusion of interfering or disruptive reading behaviors.

CONCLUDING STATEMENT

The value of the IRI lies not in its identification of what has been called the instructional level (and the other levels by interpolation) because there are probably more effective and efficient methods of accomplishing such tasks. The use of cloze procedure is one alternative already available that has a considerable body of research data to support it. The real value of the IRI is that it affords the possibility of *evaluating reading behavior in depth*. Furthermore, it has the potential for training prospective teachers about reading behavior, a potential unequaled by other types of learning opportunities. For purposes of training teachers, the process becomes the product.

The strength of the IRI is not as a test instrument but as a strategy for studying the behavior of the learner in a reading situation and as a basis for instant diagnosis in the teaching environment.

REFERENCES

1. Beldin, H. O. "Informal Reading Testing: Historical Review and Review of the Research." In *Reading Difficulties: Diagnosis, Correction, and Remediation,* edited by William K. Durr, pp. 67-84. Newark, Delaware: International Reading Association, 1970.

2. Betts, Emmett A. *Foundations of Reading Instruction.* New York: American Book Company, 1946.

3. Brown, Sandra R. "A Comparison of Five Widely Used Standardized Reading Test Scores and an Informal Reading Inventory for a Selected Group of Elementary Children." Unpublished doctoral dissertation, University of Georgia, 1963.

4. Cooper, J. Louis, "The Effect of Adjustment of Basal Reading Materials on Reading Achievement." Unpublished doctoral dissertation, Boston University, 1952.

5. Daniels, John E. "The Effectiveness of Various Procedures in Reading Level Placement." *Elementary English* 39 (October 1962): 590-600.

6. Davis, Sister M. Catherine Elizabeth. "The Relative Effectiveness of Certain Evaluative Criteria for Determining Reading Levels." Unpublished doctoral dissertation, Temple University, 1964.

7. Dunkeld, Colin G. "The Validity of the Informal Reading Inventory for the Designation of Instructional Reading Levels: A Study of the Relationships between Children's Gains in Reading Achievement and the Difficulty of Instructional Materials." Unpublished doctoral dissertation, University of Illinois, 1970.

8. Durr, William K., editor. *Reading Difficulties: Diagnosis, Correction, and Remediation.* Newark, Delaware: International Reading Association, 1970.

9. Goodman, Yetta. "Studies of Reading Miscues." Translated remarks made in Symposium II, *Applications of Psycholinguistics to Key Problems in Reading.* Kansas City: International Reading Association Convention, 1969.

10. Johnson, Marjorie Seddon, and Kress, Roy A. *Informal Reading Inventories.* Reading Aids Series. Newark, Delaware: International Reading Association, 1965.

11. Killgallon, Patsy A. "A Study of Relationships among Certain Pupil Adjustments in Reading Situations." Unpublished doctoral dissertation, Pennsylvania State University, 1942.

12. Powell, William R. "Reappraising the Criteria for Interpreting Informal Inventories." In *Reading Diagnosis and Evaluation,* 1968 Proceedings, Volume 13, Part 4, edited by Dorothy L. DeBoer, pp. 100-09. Newark, Delaware: International Reading Association, 1970.

13. Powell, William R., and Dunkeld, Colin G. "Validity of the IRI Reading Levels." *Elementary English* 48, 6 (October 1971): 637-42.

14. Sipay, Edward R. "A Comparison of Standardized Reading Achievement Test Scores and Functional Reading Levels." Unpublished doctoral dissertation, University of Connecticut, 1961. (See also *Reading Teacher* 17 (January 1964): 265-68.)

15. Smith, Nila Banton. *Graded Selections for Informal Reading: Diagnosis for Grades 1 through 3.* New York: New York University Press, 1959.

16. Spache, George D. *Reading in the Elementary School.* Boston: Allyn and Bacon, 1964.

17. Williams, Joan. "A Comparison of Standardized Reading Test Scores and Informal Reading Inventory Scores." Unpublished doctoral dissertation, Southern Illinois University, 1963.

18. Zintz, Miles V. *The Reading Process: The Teacher and the Learner.* Dubuque, Iowa: William C. Brown Company, 1970.

Oral reading is often suggested for the diagnosis of reading problems. But what is an error? Goodman presents interesting linguistic interpretations.

A LINGUISTIC STUDY OF CUES AND MISCUES IN READING

Kenneth S. Goodman

This is a report of the conclusions to date of a descriptive study of the oral reading of first-, second-, and third-grade children. It is a study in applied linguistics since linguistic knowledge and insights into language and language learning were used.

ASSUMPTIONS

In this study, reading has been defined as the active reconstruction of a message from written language. Reading must involve some level of comprehension. Nothing short of this comprehension is reading. I have assumed that all reading behavior is caused. It is cued or miscued during the child's interaction with written language. Research on reading must begin at this point of interaction. Reading is a psycholinguistic process. Linguistic science has identified the cue systems within language. The child learning to read his native language has already internalized these cue systems to the point where he is responding to them without being consciously aware of the process. To understand how children learn to read, we must learn how the individual experiences and abilities of children affect their ability to use language cues. We must also become aware of the differences and similarities between understanding oral language which uses sounds as symbol-units and written language which depends on graphic symbols.

From *Elementary English* (October 1965): 639-43. Copyright © 1965 by the National Council of Teachers of English. Reprinted by permission of the publisher and the author.

CUE SYSTEMS IN READING

Here is a partial list of the systems operating to cue and miscue the reader as he interacts with written material. Within words there are:

Letter-sound relationships
Shape (or word configuration)
Known "little words" in bigger words
Whole known words
Recurrent spelling patterns.

In the flow of language there are:

Patterns of words (or function order)
Inflection and inflectional agreement (examples: The boy runs. The boys run.)
Function words such as noun markers (the, a, that, one, etc.)
Intonation (which is poorly represented in writing by punctuation)
The referential meaning of prior and subsequent language elements and whole utterances.

Cues external to language and the reader include:

Pictures
Prompting by teacher or peers
Concrete objects
Skill charts.

Cues within the reader include:

His language facility with the dialect of his subculture
His dialect (his own personal version of the language)
His experiential background (the reader responds to cues in terms of his own real or vicarious experiences)
His conceptual background and ability (a reader can't read what he can't understand)
Those reading attack skills and learning strategies he has acquired or been taught.

PROCEDURES

The subjects of this study were 100 children in Grades 1, 2, and 3 who attend the same school in an industrial suburb of Detroit. Every second child on an alphabetic list of all children in these grades was included. There were an equal number of boys and girls from each room.

From reading materials, a sequence of stories was selected from a reading series not used in the school. With the publisher's permission the stories were dittoed on work sheets. A word list from each story was also duplicated.

An assistant called each subject individually out of the classroom. The subject was given a word list for a story at about his grade level. If the child missed many words, he was given a list for an earlier story. If he missed few or none he was given a more advanced story. Each child eventually had a word list of comparable difficulty. The number of words which each child missed on the lists, then, was a controlled variable.

Next the child was asked to read orally from the book the story on which his word list was based. The assistant noted all the child's oral reading behavior on the work sheets as the child read. The assistant refrained from any behavior which might cue the reader. Finally, each subject was to close his book and retell the story as best he could. He was not given advance notice that he would be asked to do this. The reading and retelling of the story was taped. Comparison between the structure of the language in the book and in the retold stories is underway utilizing the system of the Loban and Strickland studies.[1] It is not complete and will not be reported here.

WORDS IN LISTS AND IN STORIES

One concern of the research was the relative ability of children to recognize words in the lists and read the words in the stories. The expectation was that children would read many words in stories which they could not recognize in lists. I reasoned that, in lists, children had only cues *within* printed words while in stories they had the additional cues in the flow of language. I was not disappointed.

As is shown in Table 1, the children in this study were able to read many words in context which they couldn't read from lists. Average first graders could read almost two out of three words in the story which they missed on the list. The average second grader missed only one-fourth of the words in the story which he failed to recognize on the list. Third graders were able to get, in the stories, all but 18 percent of the words which they did not know in the list.

As Table 2 shows, except for a small group of first graders and a very few second and third graders, all the children in this study could read correctly in the story at least half of the words that they could not recognize on the lists. Sixty-nine percent of first-grade children could "get" two-thirds or more of their list errors right in reading the story. Sixty-six percent of the second graders could read three-fourths or more of their errors in the story. The comparable

TABLE 1

Average Words Missed in List and in Story

	List Average	Also Missed in Story		
		Average	Percent	Ratio
Grade 1	9.5	3.4	38%	2.8:1
Grade 2	20.1	5.1	25%	3.9:1
Grade 3	18.8	3.4	18%	5.5:1

TABLE 2

Ability to Read Words in Context Which Were Missed
on List

	Less Than 1/2	More Than 1/2	More Than 2/3	More Than 3/4	More Than 4/5	N
Grade 1	11%	89%	69%	49%	26%	35
Grade 2	3%	97%	81%	66%	50%	32
Grade 3	6%	94%	91%	76%	67%	33

*Cumulative percents of subjects

TABLE 3

Total Errors and Substitution Errors on Lists

	List Errors	Included Substitutions		
	Average	Average	Percent	Ratio
Grade 1	9.5	4.9	52%	1.9:1
Grade 2	20.1	11.5	57%	1.7:1
Grade 3	18.1	14.3	79%	1.3:1

group of third graders could get better than four out of five. The children in successive grades in this study were increasingly efficient in using cue systems outside of words.

At the same time, as Table 3 shows, children in successive grades were making greater attempts to use word attack skills, here defined as responses to *cue systems within words*. About half of the listed errors of first graders were omissions. The children did not attempt to figure the words out by using any available cues. Second-grade children showed an increased tendency to try to "get" the word. This is shown by the somewhat higher percent of substitutions among the list errors of second-grade children. Third graders showed a pronounced increase in the percent of substitutions among their list errors. Children in successive grades used word attack skills with increased frequency though not necessarily with increased efficiency.

TABLE 4

One-Time Substitutions for Known Words in Stories

	Average Substitutions	Average Lines Read	Substitutions Per Line Read
Grade 1	3.7	50.2	.074
Grade 2	14.9	126.2	.118
Grade 3	16.9	118.7	.142

There was no instance of a child getting a word right on the list but missing it consistently in the story. But often children made an incorrect substitution in the reading of the story in individual occurrences of known words. As Table 4 indicates, second and third graders made more than twice as many one-time substitutions per line read as first graders. Third graders made more substitutions per line than second graders. Three possible causes of these one-time substitutions may be:

1. overuse of cues within words to the exclusion of other cues
2. miscuing by book language which differs from the language as the child knows it
3. ineffective use of language cues.

REGRESSIONS IN READING

This study also was concerned with regressions in reading, that is repeating one or more words. No statistics are needed to support one observation: virtually every regression which the children in this study made was for the purpose of correcting previous reading.

When a child missed a word on a list, unless he corrected it immediately he seldom ever went back. In reading the story, however, children frequently repeated words or groups of words, almost always to make a correction. Regressions themselves, then, were not errors but attempts (usually but not always successful) to correct prior errors.

TABLE 5

Regressions in Reading

	First Grade		Second Grade		Third Grade	
	Per Child	Per Line Read	Per Child	Per Line Read	Per Child	Per Line Read
Word Only						
To correct word	2.40	.048	10.11	.090	10.30	.087
To correct intonation on word	.09	.002	.49	.004	1.42	.012
Total	2.49	.050	10.60	.094	11.72	.099
Phrase*						
To correct word by repeating phrase	1.54	.031	5.77	.052	7.54	.061
To rephrase	.29	.006	1.97	.018	1.03	.009
To change intonation	.52	.011	2.83	.026	2.76	.023
Total	2.35	.048	10.57	.096	11.33	.093

*For these purposes a phrase is considered *any* two or more consecutive words.

If regressions are divided into two groups, word regressions—those which involve one word immediately repeated—and phrase regressions—those which include repeating two or more words—the two types each represent almost exactly half the regressions at each of the grade levels (see Table 5).

Regressions seem to function in children's reading about like this: if the child makes an error in reading which he realizes is inconsistent with prior cues, he reevaluates the cues and corrects his error before continuing. Otherwise, he reads on encountering more cues which are inconsistent with his errors. Eventually he becomes aware that the cues cannot be reconciled and retraces his footsteps to find the source of the inconsistency. Thus, regressions in reading are due to redundant cues in language. They are self-corrections which play a vital role in children's learning to read. In two cases errors go uncorrected:

1. if the error makes no difference to the meaning of the passage, and
2. if the reader is relying so heavily on analytical techniques using only cues within words that he has lost the meaning altogether.

A PRELIMINARY LINGUISTIC TAXONOMY

In a third phase of the study I categorized all errors of the subjects according to linguistic terminology. This analysis produced the *Preliminary Linguistic Taxonomy of Cues and Miscues in Reading.* The Taxonomy will be published in a separate article.

It should be noted that the 100 subjects of this study, though all attend the same school and have learned to read with a fairly consistent methodology, exhibited virtually every kind of reading difficulty and deviation which I could predict linguistically.

IMPLICATIONS OF THIS STUDY

There are several implications to be drawn from the description of the oral reading of these children. Some practices in the teaching of reading are made suspect.

1. Introducing new words out of context before new stories are introduced to children does not appear to be necessary or desirable.
2. Prompting children or correcting them when they read orally also appears to be unnecessary and undesirable in view of the self-correction which language cues in children.
3. Our fixation on eye fixations and our mania for devices which eliminate regressions in reading seem to be due to a lamentable failure to recognize what was obvious in this study: that regressions are the means by which the child corrects himself and learns.
4. Shotgun teaching of so-called phonic skills to whole classes or groups at the same time seems highly questionable in view of the extreme diversity of the difficulties children displayed in this study. No single difficulty seemed general enough to

warrant this approach. In fact, it is most likely that at least as many children are suffering from difficulties caused by overusing particular learning strategies in reading as are suffering from a lack of such strategies.

5. The children in this study found it harder to recognize words than to read them in stories. Eventually I believe we must abandon our concentration on words in teaching reading and develop a theory of reading and a methodology which puts the focus where it belongs: on language.

Use of standardized tests is a most common practice. What are the uses and misuses of such instruments? Brigham provides a challenging point of view.

STANDARDIZED TESTS: USE AND MISUSE

Bruce W. Brigham

Johnny has a 6.1 reading grade score on a group standardized test. That means that his reading is at the level at which most sixth-graders read, at the end of their first month in sixth grade . . . doesn't it? Or, does it mean he can effectively and independently read the beginning parts of all the books in the sixth grade? . . . or, that he needs teacher guidance with sixth grade materials?

Does it mean any of these things? It might, but then again . . .? The 6.1 score may be an average (let's see, mean or median?) of a 7.1 vocabulary score and a 5.1 comprehension score. In other words, if Johnny had one hand in a pan of boiling water and the other hand in the freezer, he'd have an (arithmetic) average temperature! But as long as he has done something we can put a number on, we know all about him . . . or do we?

WHAT IS "STANDARD" ABOUT STANDARDIZED TESTS?

There are several elements common to all standardized tests, including basic purpose, general approaches to construction and prepublication trials, administration requirements, plus limitations of application, meaning, and interpretation.

Purpose and Rationale

One frequently stated purpose for standardized measures is that of "objectivity," the removal of teacher bias from evaluating performance. A laudable aim, but in many, if not most, educational situations—particularly at the secondary levels and below—

From *Reading and Language Arts: Application and Research* (College Park: Reading Center, the University of Maryland, Autumn 1970), pp. 42-58. Reprinted with permission of Robert M. Wilson and the author.

misinformation and lack of information have been substituted for bias. Something has gone awry here somewhere; therefore, as Edgar Dale noted in the *Ohio State News Letter,* "We must get our ignorance organized."

The function of standardized tests is to reflect the range of performance of a defined characteristic possessed by a group of individuals. The degree to which an individual performs successfully on the items representing the characteristic to be measured, other things being equal, should indicate how much of the characteristic he possesses, in comparison to the others of the sample group. The latter is a hopeful *assumption* underlying the use of these measures. The involved techniques of test construction are directed toward increasing the likelihood that this assumption will be true.

Here, then, we have several "standard" (common) elements: the definition of the behavior to be measured, the underlying assumption that quantifiable differentiation is possible, plus the possession of the population of certain other characteristics in common.

Actually, what group paper-and-pencil standardized tests "measure" of an individual is simply his ability to obtain a particular score at a particular time in a particular activity, in comparison to those scores of the individuals in the standardization group. *That is all.*

At every stage—construction and development, standardization, administration, scoring, and interpretation—are explicit and implicit assumptions which are *subjective* in nature. It is more effective (and accurate) to consider standardized tests as organized attempts at controlled subjectivity, than as truly objective.

> EXAMPLE I: George, fourteen years old, sixth grade. *Stanford Achievement Test:* Total reading —*8.4* grade. However, George was a *complete nonreader.* He simply made patterns of the answer choices.

MAJOR ELEMENTS IN TEST CONSTRUCTION

Construction and Trials

Items that logically seem to represent aspects of the characteristic are developed by certain methods that are likely to result in their successfully discriminating between those individuals with much and those with little of the characteristic. Frequently items are borrowed or adapted from other measures where they have appeared to discriminate on the basis of the same or a similar characteristic.

The set of items is then tried out on one or more samples of the population for whom the test is designed. The set of items and the individual items are analyzed to determine if they do discriminate successfully, preferably on the basis of some different and more operational measure or criterion of the characteristic. The items that discriminate best are retained.

The *samples* on whom the items are standardized hopefully should represent a balanced cross-section of descriptive characteristics of the entire population for whom the test is designed. This may be accomplished by various methods, the best probably being stratified random samples. Taking into consideration each potentially influencing characteristic of the population, in relative proportion, while randomizing the possibility of any of its members being chosen, is quite time-consuming, but there are techniques for doing this to meet the basic statistical assumptions involved in standardization procedures. These criteria in practice are very rarely met, especially in the case of group paper-and-pencil tests, various shortcuts being employed instead. Result: particularly at junior high levels and below, truly "national" norms are largely of the stuff dreams are made of. Even if "national" norms are available, if they are twelve-fifteen-twenty years old, how comparable are they to today's population?

The measure is evaluated in terms of *reliability,* which can mean several things. Basically the concept concerns the extent to which individuals in a specified sample, over a period of time, with no indication of intervening differential influences, retain their relative rank in the group in terms of the test. In other words, do the items and the test *consistently* indicate the same rankings of the individuals, over a period of time, for the characteristic, or were the initial results largely from chance or uncontrolled factors? Consistency of rankings over time is the best approach to reliability; it is also the most expensive and difficult to utilize—and, unfortunately, the *least* used.

Most widely used measures of reliability are those of "internal" consistency, i.e., do half the set of items discriminate (with the same group at the same time) approximately as well as the other half? There are various techniques for determining this. Regardless of the details, these measures are the least expensive, easiest, and most widely used. The resultant coefficients of reliability tend to be much higher than those obtained by the first method noted. It is this kind of reliability that is most often reported by test publishers. However, there are serious questions as to the value and dependability of this kind of reliability which, in any case, is not the same thing as the original meaning noted above.

For a test to be *valid,* it should measure what it is supposed to measure. (To be valid, it has to be reliable, but it can be reliable without being valid.) This is the usual meaning of validity, although technically at least four variations have been developed. This is also a very difficult test factor to fulfill in actuality. Items and tests do *not* necessarily successfully measure a particular characteristic by logical definition, description, or labels. The most meaningful concept of validity requires an entirely independent measure, preferably discretely and empirically quantifiable. With this concept of validity, we face the greatest difficulty in practice—and it is least used.

EXAMPLE II: There are group standardized achievement measures where:

    a. If the paper is dated, a reading-grade score of 1.6 is obtained
    b. If all the first answer choices are marked, a reading score of 3.1 is received
    c. If all the final answer choices are marked, a reading score of 3.6 is found.

Administration and Application

Administration procedures are usually very specifically standardized, as they should be. This necessitates, however, that each and every administrative procedure be handled *exactly* as specified. Every time a change is made, the already limited interpretive value and meaning of the results is reduced drastically.

Use should be confined *strictly* to groups having the same descriptive characteristics (age, sex, etc.) of the population samples used to establish the norms of the test (*if* you can obtain complete descriptive data of the original samples.) Again, any significant variation in this factor and the scores are meaningless in relation to the original sample population.

However, local norms can be built over a period of time. Actually, considering the limitations noted previously, using local experience as the basis for comparison of current scores is probably the most worthwhile approach, providing the local population remains relatively stable.

Meaning and Interpretation

The branch of psychology most concerned with developing standardized tests is the field of Individual Differences. Oddly enough, the field has been concerned largely with the development of *group* measures, which are much more widely used than are individual standardized tests (the latter includes the Binet and the Wechsler Intelligence tests).

As a result, most of our commonly used standardized measures in the school situation are *most* effective as indicators of *group* characteristics. For these and other reasons, an individual grade or age "score" of a group standardized paper-and-pencil test has a very limited meaning. The comforting and pseudo-concreteness of the numbers and mathematics associated with standardized tests (which also make them appear impressively confusing) can be very misleading. The basic problem seems to center around the fact that the limited *meanings* of scores are neglected in favor of stressing an abstract number value. Let us consider this idea in relation to both individual and group measures.

Individual: A carefully standardized test such as the Wechsler intelligence test which involved thorough controls at each construction stage, and requires special training for administration and interpretation, results in a score, with a good examiner, that is considered to be within plus or minus 5 (five!) points of the hypothetical "true" score approximately 2/3 (two-thirds!) of the time. *One-third* of the time any individual score will probably be greater than plus or minus five points away from the "true" score. These are the statistical limits for the confidence we can put into such scores, based on the relatively stringent way they have been developed.

For example, Tom and Jane both recently obtained a Full Scale IQ score of 100 (average) on the *Wechsler Intelligence Scale for Children.* Is their "intelligence" (ability to learn) the same? What are some of the possibilities?

1. Tom's usual FS IQ score may be 96, while Jane's is 104.
2. Tom's 100 could be the result of depressed functioning; his potential capacity, with the removal of the interfering factors, could be in the superior range (120-129). Jane's 100, on the other hand, may represent the best she can possibly do.
3. Their Full Scale IQ scores may have resulted from partial scores somewhat like these:

   Tom: Verbal-90, Performance-110; FS = 100
   Jane: Verbal-110, Performance- 90; FS = 100

Even with the relatively rigorously developed, administered, and interpreted *individual* standardized tests, can we be confident that two or more similar scores represent exactly the same learning capacity? Is there actually any invariable reason to expect Tom and Jane to respond in exactly the same manner in various instructional situations . . . or even in a roughly similar way in a reading situation and a science experiment?

Group: With group standardized measures, much greater limitations of development procedures indicate that individual scores be considered much more cautiously.
Consider:

1. An individual score on a paper-and-pencil group standardized intelligence test, with many shortcuts, qualifications, and approximations involved in the ways in which they are interpreted, can usually be considered to be within plus or minus fifteen to thirty points of the hypothetical "true" score two-thirds of the time.
2. Group paper-and-pencil measures of intelligence and reading tend to cover basically similar factors of intelligence, general verbal abilities, and reading achievement. Students with reading problems frequently have depressed "intelligence" scores because of their reading difficulties.

   a. Approximately two-thirds of dozens of youngsters previously labeled "orthogenic backward" or mentally retarded on the basis of group tests, when thoroughly evaluated individually in an educational-psychological clinic, were found to have *average or better* overall intelligence, potentially.
   b. Surveys indicate that about eighty percent of retarded readers (retarded in terms of their capacity) have average or better intelligence.

3. An individual score in a group test of reading tends to be one to four levels *above* where the individual can usually profit from systematic instruction (at his frustration level, not his instructional level.)
   Reasons include:

   a. Test development limitations
   b. Limited sampling of skills
   c. Partial control of guessing
   d. Situation factors

4. Jack 16, 10th grade.

Iowa Advanced Reading: Total Score: 5.9 grade level. Therefore, he was assigned fifth and sixth level materials. But, on
comprehensive individual "informal" tests:

Word Recognition

	Flash Scores	Untimed Scores
Pre-primer	90%	96%
Primer	70%	90%
First Reader	24%	40%
Second Reader	4%	20%

Individual Informal Reading Inventory

Pedagogical Level	Reader Level
Independent	0
Immediate Instructional	Reading Readiness
Basic Instructional	Pre-primer
Frustration	Primer
Hearing Capacity	First Reader

5. Generally, there is no basis for comparing scores from different tests on the same individual: usually different standardization procedures involving different populations at different
times and places are involved—it is analogous to comparing
bowling balls and meteorites—what do you have?

Can we still believe Johnny's 6.1 reading level on that test tells
us all we need to know about his reading? No, but there are some
ways in which such scores may be useful.

Some Uses for Group Standardized Measures

1. As screening devices for separating probably very high, average, and very low potential achievers, for initial *tentative*
grouping. Provisionally beginning instruction should be
about two levels *below* the test scores obtained.

2. As a rough measure to compare relative achievement of individuals who may need careful individual study, for example:

   a. Those with very high test scores, but average or poor daily achievement

   b. Those with average or poor test scores, but very good to excellent overall general achievement

   c. Those with low to average scores whose oral verbal participation is superior, but whose reading and writing achievement is very low

3. To establish local norms on specific tests for a local population.

SUMMARY AND CONCLUSIONS

First, let us admit that with standardized group test scores we are talking about approximate abstractions umpteem times removed from the reality we think is being described.

Second, we should avoid "pigeonholing" individual youngsters by their scores on such tests.

Third, we should learn something about test construction and study the test manuals in order to better understand the uses and limitations of these measures.

Fourth, we need to demand adequate information of construction and standardization data until those supplying us with tests supply such information with them. In the long run, this will increase the likelihood of more dependable measures being built.

The most effective standard with standardized tests is a great deal of caution.

5

Clinical Diagnosis

Many diagnostic tests are on the market. What are their compara-tive values? The McCalls take a close look at five of them.

COMPARATIVE VALIDITY OF FIVE READING DIAGNOSTIC TESTS

Rozanne A. McCall
Robert B. McCall

ABSTRACT[1,2]

Five reading diagnostic tests were administered to twenty-seven fourth-grade children in an attempt to assess their interrelation-ships and comparative validity. Teacher ratings, standardized test

---

[1]This work was done while the senior author was employed by the Champaign Illinois School System and attending the University of Illinois. The authors wish to acknowledge the cooperation of Mrs. Margaret Greenman and Mrs. Dorothy Cox for making the children available and to Carl F. Brown and William R. Powell for their guidance and comments.

[2]Address reprint requests to second author, Yellow Springs, Ohio 45387.

From *Journal of Educational Research* vol. 62, no. 7 (March 1969): 329-33. Re-printed by permission of Joan Hartenberger, Editorial Supervisor for Wilson B. Thiede.

scores, and grades were used as criteria. All tests had acceptable validity coefficients, although they were somewhat lower than previous results. The Bond, McCullough, and Doren tests were quite similar and their validities were somewhat higher than the Roswell and McKee. Vowel related subtests contributed most heavily to the relationship between tests and criteria, and reading-arithmetic relationships were frequently higher than reading-reading relationships.

Diagnostic reading tests are drastically unresearched relative to their importance in school remedial programs. Particularly alarming is the lack of extensive and meaningful validity information. Although several studies of diagnostic instruments are available, data on the validity of different tests are almost non-existent.

Although previous research provides a beginning to the validation process, it hardly represents a corpus of data capable of justifying the various uses of these tests. First among the liabilities of available research is that there is not enough of it. Second, the validation samples are frequently not appropriate for the groups which will utilize the test. Data gathered on a sample heterogeneously composed of pupils in grades K-6 is hardly useful to a school system which desires to detect problems in Grades 2-4. Third, invariably the validity criterion used in these studies is some other standardized test (e.g., Metropolitan, Stanford Achievement Test). Although the relationship between these reading instruments and the more general standardized tests is of some interest, one runs the danger of obtaining high validity coefficients as a function of criterion contamination. For example, it is not surprising that the vocabulary score on the Bond, Clymer, Hoyt Diagnostic Reading Test correlates .93 with the vocabulary section of the Stanford Achievement Test (4). However, this figure hardly represents an index of validity. While selecting a criterion which is both satisfying and qualitatively different from the predicting instrument is a problem in any area of testing, at least a variety of criterion measures might be examined including some which are not standardized tests bootstrapped for the validation procedure. The results of selecting samples with a wide range of ability and using criteria which are remarkably similar to the reading test itself is a set of validity coefficients that are incredulously high (frequently in the .90s), so high in fact that they sometimes exceed the reliability of the test.

Lastly, there is no empirical basis for deciding which of the several diagnostic tests to use.

The purpose of the present study was: 1. to provide additional validity information on five reading diagnostic tests; 2. to restrict the sample to a single grade in order to avoid the spurious inflation of coefficients because of an unreasonable range of ability; 3. to employ a variety of criteria including teacher ratings and grades as well as standardized test scores; and 4. to use a relatively small sample, giving each subject five reading diagnostic tests, in order to obtain comparative validities.

METHOD

Subjects: Twenty-seven fourth-grade children from a class at Carrie Busey School in Champaign, Illinois, participated in the study.

Materials: The following reading diagnostic tests were administered: 1. Bond, Clymer, Hoyt Silent Diagnostic Reading Test, 2. Doren Diagnostic Reading Test, 3. McKee Inventory of Phonetic Skill, 4. McCullough Word Analysis Test (Experimental Edition), and 5. Roswell-Chall Diagnostic Reading Test of Word Analysis Skills.

The criteria included teacher rankings of pupil's reading comprehension, word recognition, and arithmetic ability; third-grade reading and arithmetic school grades; comprehension, reading and arithmetic grade placement scores on the Iowa Test of Basic Skills (ITBS); and the IQ score of the California Test of Mental Maturity (CTMM).

Procedure: Four diagnostic tests were group administered in the order listed above. The Roswell-Chall test was given individually at noon and after school. The group sessions were held over a two-week period (February 22–March 5, 1965) from 9-10 A.M.

Prior to the administration of the reading tests, the fourth-grade teacher rank ordered the twenty-seven pupils on the three scales listed above. The remaining criteria were obtained from the cumulative folders. The ITBS and CTMM scores were from tests given in the Fall, 1964, and the grades were from the second semester of Grade 3. Thus, while the criteria were independent of all predictors, the teacher rankings were not independent of the other criteria depending upon the degree to which the teacher was influenced by her knowledge of the performance of the children the previous year.

RESULTS

Table 1 presents the means and standard deviations of the test scores and criteria except teacher rankings. The means of the standardized tests suggested that the group was average or somewhat above average in ability. For example, the CTMM mean IQ score was 112.58. While this appears rather high, others have found mean IQ scores reliably above 100 (e.g., 1), and additional evidence suggests that CTMM yields too high a score (3, 5, 6, 7). Another index of the possible advanced standing of the group is provided by the grade placement scores on the ITBS. These tended to be approximately 4.5, when the test was given slightly prior to the 3.5 grade level.

In contrast, scores on the reading diagnostic tests were approximately average for fourth graders. For example, the mean total score on the Doren was 307 which compares favorably with (if not lower than) Doren's norms (2), and if the mean scores on the Bond, Clymer, Hoyt are placed on a grade-equivalent profile almost all means fall within the fourth-grade range. Thus, the sample, while perhaps slightly advanced, does not deviate markedly from the norms.

Table 2 presents the simple correlations between each subtest of the five reading tests and the criteria (r's of .38 are significant at the .05 level; r's of .49 are at the .01 level). First, it may be noticed that the tests correlate higher with the teacher rankings than with the other criteria. This may be a function of the artificially broad range of this variable and the fact that the rankings were more contemporary with the reading testing.

Second, with respect to teacher rankings, three of the four reading tests having a major subtest relating to "vowels" showed this content category to be most highly correlated with the rankings. Thus, in the McKee, Roswell, and McCullough tests, vowel-related subtests consistently showed the highest correlations, usually in the .60's. In the Doren, the prominence of vowels was shared with subtests concentrating on rhyming, blending, sight words, and beginning sounds. Some of these same concepts were involved in high correlations on the Bond test which did not have separate parts devoted to vowels. Words in isolation and in context, syllabication, word elements and synthesis, and rhyming provided the highest relationships with teacher rankings.

Although there was definitely a marked tendency for these same subtests to relate highly with third graders, the pattern was not as definite. Further, for the standardized tests, only the Word Synthesis subtest of the Bond appeared to have any consistent relationship with these criteria.

The bottom portion of Table 2 contains the intercorrelations among criteria. It is clear that the teacher ranked arithmetic, comprehension, and word-recognition ability very much the same. The rankings of reading related more strongly to the grades than to the

TABLE 1

Means and Standard Deviations

Predictors	x	s
McKee:		
Initial Consonants	45.18	8.76
Final Consonants	11.00	1.66
Structural Elements - C	12.93	1.71
Vowel Sounds	21.00	4.45
Initial Consonant Blends	5.41	.93
Structural Elements - F	7.44	.97
Common Elements	11.81	2.22
Roswell-Chall:		
Single Consonants	19.30	4.00
Consonant Combination	8.48	2.56
Short Vowels	34.56	4.31
Silent e Rule	9.30	1.17
Vowel Combination	10.67	2.29
Syllabication	5.67	1.57
McCullough:		
Initial Blends	29.70	.67
Vowel-Phonetic Discrimination	23.89	5.55
Matching Vowel Sounds and Letters	27.74	2.81
Syllabication	25.19	3.67
Bond, Clymer, Hoyt:		
Words in Isolation	50.81	3.15
Words in Context	23.63	3.55
Orientation	21.37	1.76
Locating Elements	33.48	4.26
Syllabication	14.33	4.39
Locating Root Words	22.67	5.14
Word Elements	24.33	3.04
Beginning Sounds	24.56	4.25
Rhyming Sounds	21.15	5.41
Letter Sounds	27.00	2.18
Word Synthesis	16.26	4.77
Doren:		
Letter Recognition	33.70	2.51
Beginning Sounds	24.41	1.12
Whole Word Recognition	43.67	1.07
Words within Words	27.96	2.07
Speech Consonants	19.15	1.75
Ending Sounds	19.41	.80
Blending	18.33	3.19
Rhyming	35.19	4.13
Vowels	67.59	1.11
Sight Words	17.89	5.65

Criteria	x	s
Grades:		
Reading	2.44	.65
Arithmetic	2.64	.81
ITBS:		
Reading	4.46	1.08
Comprehension	4.55	1.07
Arithmetic	4.36	.73
CTMM:		
IQ	112.58	12.13

TABLE 2

Subtest Correlations with Criteria

	Ability Rankings			Grades		ITBS			CTMM
	Arithmetic	Comprehension	Word Recognition	Reading	Arithmetic	Reading Grade Placement	Comprehension Grade Placement	Arithmetic Grade Placement	IQ
McKee									
Initial Consonants	.40	.32	.37	.35	.21	-.03	.11	.27	.28
Final Consonants	.31	.35	.43	.36	.15	.03	.01	.18	.67
Structural Elements C	.63	.53	.38	.58	.47	.32	.21	.59	.41
Vowel Sounds	.63	.64	.67	.64	.28	.52	.31	.48	.55
Initial Consonant Blends	.22	.24	.22	.27	.06	.16	.12	.19	.49
Structural Elements F	.41	.38	.28	.37	.31	.15	-.05	.33	.36
Common Elements	.48	.35	.03	.29	.38	.67	.39	.45	.15
Roswell-Chall									
Single Consonants	.35	.21	.33	.40	.30	-.07	.08	.30	.19
Consonant Combinations	.43	.42	.46	.37	.21	.13	.17	.33	.20
Short Vowels	.71	.68	.63	.67	.21	.38	.29	.54	.32
Silent e Rule	.57	.67	.68	.61	.22	.28	.01	.15	.33
Vowel Combinations	.61	.62	.69	.59	.19	.17	.01	.26	.33
Syllabication	.52	.59	.47	.56	.21	.61	.25	.38	.19
McCullough									
Initial Blends	.28	.28	.17	.18	.27	.31	.15	.37	-.04
Vowel-Phonetic Discrim.	.63	.56	.40	.42	.25	.41	.32	.63	.31
Matching Vowels—Letters	.67	.71	.41	.67	.56	.35	.19	.43	.38
Syllabication	.69	.54	.48	.47	.39	.50	.28	.58	.38
Bond, Clymer, Hoyt									
Words in Isolation	.68	.80	.65	.70	.46	.40	.15	.39	.35
Words in Context	.71	.76	.45	.72	.45	.57	.27	.41	.23

	C1	C2	C3	C4	C5	C6	C7	C8	C9
Orientation	.62	.61	.61	.55	.30	.59	.45	.49	.35
Locating Elements	.48	.44	.32	.37	.36	.23	.17	.35	.26
Syllabication	.79	.77	.68	.63	.45	.65	.19	.53	.25
Locating Root Words	.47	.53	.38	.52	.37	.15	-.04	.25	.50
Word Elements	.72	.72	.74	.48	.27	.47	.25	.47	.38
Beginning Sounds	.47	.59	.55	.28	.23	.03	-.01	.27	.43
Rhyming Sounds	.50	.71	.54	.54	.36	.61	.31	.55	.35
Letter Sounds	.70	.44	.59	.32	.11	.11	-.08	.14	.36
Word Synthesis	.70	.75	.53	.69	.67	.74	.72	.65	.19
Doren									
Letter Recognition	.24	.37	.42	.50	.12	-.03	-.15	.01	.35
Beginning Sounds	.65	.63	.46	.36	.26	.62	.39	.62	-.19
Whole Word Recognition	.13	.03	.07	-.04	-.09	.16	.24	.21	.02
Words Within Words	.42	.54	.37	.63	.48	.32	.19	.24	.39
Speech Consonants	.32	.44	.46	.33	.04	.23	.06	.23	.08
Ending Sounds	.21	.08	.05	-.01	-.12	-.05	-.16	.17	.08
Blending	.56	.66	.32	.60	.42	.48	.19	.39	.16
Rhyming	.70	.63	.29	.42	.47	.65	.48	.73	.18
Vowels	.61	.59	.58	.51	.23	.40	.27	.50	.23
Sight Words	.75	.71	.57	.68	.41	.49	.24	.54	.28
Rankings									
Comprehension	.90								
Word Recognition	.74	.80							
Grades									
Reading	.70	.81	.66	.71					
Arithmetic	.62	.68	.44						
ITBS									
Reading	.67	.66	.49	.52	.59	.66			
Comprehension	.46	.48	.37	.45	.66	.63	.62		
Arithmetic	.73	.67	.48	.55	.69				
CTMM									
IQ	.27	.36	.44	.49	.44	.06	.14	.12	

P < .05 for r > .38.   P < .01 for r > .49.   P < .001 for r > .60.

ITBS measures of the same concepts, which fact might suggest that previous grades influenced the teacher's rankings.

Since the CTMM IQ score is not as completely tied to reading as the other criteria and since the grades were formulated almost nine months prior to the diagnostic testing, the reading tests were not subsequently compared on these criteria. Since the sum of the child's scores on all subtests is sometimes suggested as a single index of reading ability, such a "total" score was computed for all subjects on each test and correlated with the remaining criteria. Further, the multiple correlations of the subtests were also obtained. This comparative data is presented in Tables 3 and 4.

Table 3 displays the correlations between "total" scores for the five diagnostic tests. Although moderately related to the other tests, it appears that the McKee is measuring something that the other four are not. Further, the Bond, McCullough, and Doren tests share considerable common variance (64 percent) and correlate somewhat higher with the Roswell than with the McKee.

TABLE 3

Intercorrelations of Total Scores on the Reading Tests

	1	*2*	*3*	*4*
1. McKee				
2. Roswell	.61‡			
3. Bond	.53†	.64‡		
4. McCullough	.54†	.70‡	.82‡	
5. Doren	.40*	.67‡	.80‡	.82‡

*p < .05.   †p < .01.   ‡p < .001.

Table 4 provides both the simple correlations between the total test scores and the rankings and ITBS and also the multiple correlations between the weighted subtests of each diagnostic instrument and these same criteria. The validity coefficients for the total scores, although running as high as .81, are somewhat more modest than those reported in the test manuals and previous research. Further, these relationships are somewhat higher for the criterion of teacher rankings than for the ITBS, which one would not expect if there was criterion contamination as a function of possible item similarity between reading test and standardized test. However, the ITBS was given almost a year before the reading tests were administered.

TABLE 4

Simple and Multiple Validity Coefficients

| | Rankings | | | | ITBS | |
	Arithmetic	Compre-hension	Word Recognition	Reading	Compre-hension	Arithmetic
McKee (130 Items)						
Total Score	.55†	.45*	.41*	.25	.17	.35
Multiple R	.80*	.71	.71	.87†	.64	.69
McCullough (210 Items)						
Total Score	.80‡	.73‡	.51†	.50†	.32	.68‡
Multiple R	.81*	.75*	.68	.55	.35	.72*
Bond (339 Items)						
Total Score	.76‡	.66‡	.52†	.67‡	.42*	.67‡
Multiple R	.94‡	.95‡	.94‡	.89†	.84*	.79
Roswell-Chall (78 Items)						
Total Score	.70‡	.66‡	.69‡	.27	.20	.46*
Multiple R	.75*	.79*	.78*	.64	.48	.65
Doren (315 Items)						
Total Score	.75‡	.71‡	.55†	.61‡	.41*	.70‡
Multiple R	.92‡	.90‡	.83*	.94‡	.91‡	.83*

*p < .05.   †p < .01.   ‡p < .001.

Comparatively, the McKee appeared to have somewhat lower relationships with both criterion sets. In addition, the Roswell did not predict the ITBS reading and comprehension scores as well as the other reading tests.

In terms of the multiple correlations, the Bond and the Doren tests were outstanding with multiple R's in the .90 s. However, both tests were longer and contained more subtests than the other instruments. Further, these R's should be cross-validated in order to assess shrinkage. It is interesting to note that the total score for the McCullough and to some extent for the Roswell-Chall predicted the criteria about as well as did the differential weighting of subtests. Although the relationships were not as high as for the Bond and Doren, the multiple R for the McKee was considerably higher than the simple r's for its total score.

Throughout these data one cannot ignore the consistently high relationships between the reading variables and the measures of arithmetic competence. For every reading test, the highest correlation for the total score was with a measure of arithmetic ability rather than reading (Table 4). The figures in Table 2 also indicate relationships between reading and arithmetic which are as high or higher than between two reading variables.

DISCUSSION

These data suggest that: 1. the validity coefficients for five reading diagnostic tests are somewhat lower than previously reported but nonetheless of acceptable magnitude; 2. vowel-related concepts might be the most salient single component in a teacher's evaluation of general reading performance; 3. the Bond, McCullough, and Doren tests yield very similar general assessments of reading performance and these three tests correlate somewhat higher with the Roswell than with the McKee; 4. the total score of the McKee correlates more modestly with teacher rankings and the McKee and Roswell are poorer predictors of ITBS scores than the other tests; 5. subject to cross-validation the Bond and Doren may provide excellent general assessment through a weighted combination of subtests rather than a simple total score; and 6. the reading variables appear to predict arithmetic ability as well or better than they predict other reading measures.

The interpretation of these comparative validity findings must be tempered with the use these instruments receive. The criteria used in the present study were teacher rankings and standardized tests of relatively general reading performance. Consequently, these results do not bear upon the potential ability of these tests to select which of many reading problems plagues a particular student. However, contrary to the insistence of one test publisher (personal communication), a "diagnostic" test does need validation for whatever purpose the test will serve. Nevertheless, one finds it difficult to accept the notion that a test can diagnose reading difficulties but not correlate with measures of general reading performance. Therefore, the present results may be interpreted to suggest that among the tests studied the McKee possesses less while the Bond and Doren have somewhat more potential in this area.

A theoretical consideration here is that the tests which had the highest validity coefficients had the most items and subtests. Since reliability places a ceiling on the extent of validity and since reliability may vary with test length, this factor could explain some of the differences in validity coefficients. From a practical standpoint, however, it is of little consequence to a school system whether or not the low validity of a test is a function of poor items or too few of them.

One cannot help speculating on the finding that the reading tests predict arithmetic as well or better than reading performance. Although it is not unusual to find high relationships between reading and arithmetic test scores (e.g., 5), no empirically validated explanation exists. Certainly, reading and arithmetic tests both require the pupil to read and comprehend the material and employ word and sentence analysis, but one wonders if these common factors explain why reading-arithmetic correlations are consistently (but slightly) higher than reading-reading indices.

REFERENCES

1. Burke, N. F., and Anderson, K. E. "A Comparative Study of 1939 and 1950 Achievement Test Results in the Hawthorne Elementary School in Ottawa, Kansas." *Journal of Educational Research* 47 (1953): 19-33.

2. Doren, Margaret. *Doren Diagnostic Reading Test of Word Recognition Skills.* Minneapolis: Educational Test Bureau, 1956.

3. Finley, Carmen J. "A Comparison of the California Achievement Test, Metropolitan Achievement Test, and Iowa Test of Basic Skills." *California Journal of Educational Research* 14 (1963): 79-88.

4. Karstens, H. "Procedures for Norming and Validating Bond Tests." *Field Bulletin #1-63.* Chicago: Lyons and Carnahan, 1963.

5. McCall, Rozanne A., and McCall, R. B. "A Comparison of First Grade Reading Tests." *Illinois School Research, II* (1965): 32-37.

6. Stake, R. E. "Overestimation of Achievement with the California Achievement Test." *Educational and Psychological Measurement* 21 (1961): 59-62.

7. Taylor, E. A. and Crandall, J. H. "A Study of the Norm Equivalence of Certain Tests Approved for the California Testing Program." *California Journal of Educational Research* 13 (1962): 186-92.

Most teachers know how to conduct diagnosis of one type or another. But how does one develop remedial prescriptions? No answer is easy, but Bannatyne has one for you.

DIAGNOSING LEARNING DISABILITIES AND WRITING REMEDIAL PRESCRIPTIONS

Alex Bannatyne

Diagnosis is a concept with many labels, and many people in different disciplines or having different viewpoints may choose a particular term to their liking. Some part-synonyms used for discovering "what is wrong" with fellow human beings are assessment, evaluation, task-analysis, investigation, check-up, finding out, observing behavior, problem-solving, etc. We will not be far away from a satisfactory definition of diagnosis if we accept Webster's three versions and slightly modify them. On this basis, a diagnosis is the act or process of deciding the nature of a disorder or disability by examination and through the examination making a careful investigation of the facts to determine the nature or basis of the problem. The final diagnosis is the decision from such an examination or investigation.

It is a little less easy to give a satisfactory definition of learning disabilities. The essential aspect of a learning disability is a discrepancy between the child's apparent potential and his performance in practice when he has to carry out some essential learning process. The learning disability itself is not primarily caused by inadequate mental ability, emotional disturbance, or sensori-motor organ defects. Of course, it is quite possible for a child with learning disabilities to *also* have defective sensory apparatus (for example, defective

From *Journal of Learning Disabilities* vol. 1, no. 4 (April 1968): 28-35. Reprinted by permission of the Professional Press, Inc.

vision) to be mentally retarded or to exhibit some form of emotional instability.

Almost always the remediation of learning disabilities will require specialized teaching techniques. Learning disabilities usually manifest themselves in disturbances of global end-result complex behavior, such as reading, and like the proverbial iceberg, they are nine-tenths hidden. Just as there are hundreds of reasons why a person may not be able to walk, so are there hundreds of possible discrete causal "states" which can result in the inability to learn to calculate, read, write or spell well. This is equally true for most other academic studies in which the child may engage. Not infrequently several separate specific deficits may combine in a multi-faceted disability to make the diagnosis and remediation quite complicated.

TEAM DIAGNOSIS

To ensure an unbiased accurate diagnostic examination, a team of specialists should work together with the child. The key members of the team, some of whom may be part-time, are an educator, psychologist, speech correctionist, pediatrician, and social worker. It will be obvious from the account of the diagnostic procedure below which team member investigates and supplies specific data and information. Either the educator or the psychologist should be the executive director of the team, both of whom should have been trained in the field of learning disabilities. Other experts such as an EEG specialist, psychiatrist, etc., may be consulted as the team thinks necessary. In fact, an EEG, electropolymyographs, a physical check-up, and an audiometry test should be obligatory in all cases.

THE PURPOSE OF DIAGNOSIS

The diagnostic objective must be the remediation of the deficit areas and the guiding rule should be, "remediate the deficit areas and reinforce through the intact areas." For example, if a boy had an auditory discrimination problem, one would thoroughly train him in phoneme discrimination, and if his writing ability was intact, he would be asked to write down for record purposes the mistaken (and corrected) words in which the difficult phonemes were presented auditorially, thus reinforcing the corrected discriminations through motor/kinesthetic activity. The word "reinforce" is used here in its original meaning and not as an operant reward.

From what has been said, it will be apparent that it is essential not to miss any area or facet of the child which might be contributing to the end-result learning disability either on the surface or manifest level, or on any of the other supporting levels which are less obvious. I shall describe each of the four major levels which require diagnostic analysis, indicate the tests and information used on each level, and describe cross-analyzing the data for the isolation of deficits.

THE ACADEMIC LEVEL

This is the area in which most teachers and many psychologists usually investigate the child's problems. Almost any of the major better-known achievement tests are valuable as an overall screening of the academic attainment of individual children or groups. It is very important to note, not only in which school subjects the child does well or poorly, but also his areas of success and failure with each subject. Even on achievement tests, indicators can be found as to which sensori-motor or cognitive skills are tending to lower the child's performance. Two useful reading tests are to be found in the Gates-McKillop Reading Tests and the Neale Analysis of Reading Ability (13). The Gates-McKillop is a very long test and the following sections may be left out if time is short: Words Flashed, Phrases Flashed, Recognition and Blending, Naming Capitals, Recognizing Nonsense Words, Recognizing Initial Letters, Recognizing Final Letters, and Vocabulary Syllabification. The Neale Reading Test has three scores: Accuracy, Comprehension, and Rate of Reading. The implications of each of these three scores in the final analysis of the data should be taken into account, although the comprehension score is (as are so many comprehension scores) mostly a test of verbal memory. The child should be examined for his knowledge of phoneme/grapheme matchings by using the flash cards in the *Writing Road to Reading* by Spalding and Spalding (1962) (16). Another academic test which may be found useful is the Ayres Spelling Test. However, there is a great need for a standardized comprehensive spelling test which not only examines the child both orally and in writing, but also examines him on words with a regular orthography and separately on words with an irregular orthography. The child's handwriting can be assessed from his written spelling, but he should also be given the opportunity to write as well as he is able.

It should be noted that if learning disability children make an intensive effort, many can produce quite good work, possibly near the class average, but it should always be remembered that this requires a very special effort which is not demanded of most normal children on an everyday basis. Within all these tests on the academic level, one can make quite a detailed diagnosis of the specific points with which the child needs help. However, it is quite possible that intensive instruction only on the academic level may not result in the rapid progress expected simply because more fundamental deficits underlie the child's problems with his school work.

COGNITIVE AND SENSORI-MOTOR ABILITY LEVEL

There are several major tests which should be given on this level and the Wechsler Intelligence Scale for Children is an essential one. The Stanford-Binet Intelligence Scale is far too verbal and unstructured in content and presentation for the assessment of learning disability cases. All of the subtests of the WISC except Mazes should be administered and the child's Full-Scale, Verbal, and Performance IQ's calculated. However, it is now well known from factor analytic studies that the verbal and performance breakdown scores do not have much psychological meaning. I have found it more useful to analyze the WISC in the following way (7).

A Spatial Score is obtained by adding together the scaled scores of three of the performance subtests which do not involve sequencing.

They are Picture Completion, plus Block Design, plus Object Assembly.

The Conceptualizing Score is compiled from scaled scores as follows:

Comprehension + Similarities + Vocabulary

A Sequencing Score is obtained by combining the scaled scores for:

Digit Span + Picture Arrangement + Coding

The composite mean standardized scaled scores expected for each of these groupings of three subtests is thirty. By comparing a child's Spatial score with his Conceptualizing and Sequencing score, one can obtain just that much more information as to where the child's deficit areas lie. Many genetic dyslexic children (1) will obtain a good spatial score and a poor sequencing score when these are compared with their overall ability, their deficit being more in auditory closure and sequencing.

The next major test in the cognitive and sensori-motor abilities level is the Illinois Test of Psycholinguistic Ability. A revised version, which is being published at the moment (11), contains twelve subtests which cover Auditory Reception, Visual Reception, Visual Sequencing Memory, Visual Association, Visual Closure, Verbal Expression, Grammar Closure, Manual Expression, Auditory Closure and Sound Blending. A profile drawn in accordance with the instructions in the handbook will indicate immediately many of the child's deficits and strengths. The third major test is the Frostig Development Test of Visual Perception (7). The Frostig Test has five subtests: Eye-Motor Coordination, Figure-Ground, Form Constancy, Position in Space, and Spatial Relations. This test is valuable for a quite detailed analysis of a child's visuo-spatial ability and visual perception in two dimensions. Other tests which should be given for a complete diagnosis are the Graham-Kendall Memory-for-Designs Test (8) which investigates just that—the child's memory for designs. However, as we are not investigating brain damage per se, but rather the child's ability to learn particular subjects, I have found that four or more errors of any kind on the M-F-D to indicate the likelihood of a visuo-spatial or visuo-motor disability of some kind. Most children nine years old and over who have no problems in this area will correctly remember and draw all the designs except perhaps for one or two exact reversals. A useful back-up copying test in this area is the Beery-Buktenica Developmental Form Sequence Test (3). Here, again, the older child should be able to copy all of these designs reasonably well, always allowing, of course, for one or two unintentional mistakes. A repeat test is always advisable.

A useful auditory discrimination test is the Wepman (17) or one issued by the Perceptual and Educational Research Center (18). Here, again, most normal children should attain an almost perfect score. Charles Drake suggests that more than five errors are indicative of an auditory discrimination problem which may need even more investigation. As auditory discrimination tests are very unreliable, one should always tape them using a clear woman's voice and administer twice with a week's interval between tests. As a consequence of the findings of two research projects separately carried out by Drake and Schnall (1966) and Wolf (18) (1967), we know that one excellent diagnostic indicator of auditory reading disabilities is the Melody Discrimination Test. I have made up my own version using a xylophone. Ten pairs of four-note melodies, some pairs being the same and some different, were recorded on tape allowing five-second intervals for answering. If the diagnostician can play the piano, an informal test of this sort could be recorded and administered to each child.

The Money Road Map Test of Direction Sense (12) and the Benton Right/Left Discrimination Test (12) will assess the child's understanding of the concepts "right" and "left" and indicate the extent of any confusion. His handedness can be investigated using the Harris Laterality Scale (19). The simultaneous writing subtest of this scale is a useful indicator of reversals by either hand but only if the child is asked to perform very quickly. Sometimes a nominally right-handed subject will reverse (mirror image) the right-hand letters but not the left ones, indicating he is basically left-handed. However, I never advise changing hands unless the change is quite spontaneous.

PERSONALITY, EMOTIONAL, MOTIVATIONAL LEVEL

One of the most useful sources of information on this level is the Family Information Form which the parents have to fill in at home. The questions on the form cover the following topics: the number and order of siblings; the walking, toilet training, and feeding "milestones"; speech acquisition; mother-child separation; symptoms of neurosis or other emotional disturbance; family language background and development; the child's physical development, mostly in terms of clumsiness; the incidence of learning disabilities in other members of the family; the occupation of the father and mother; and the number of schools and types of classes the child has been to. The mother is also asked for a full pregnancy, birth, and subsequent medical history of the child and, if possible, this should be cross-checked with medical informants.

A psychologist should be asked for a personality assessment of the child. (I have found the Bene-Anthony Family Relations (15) to be of value in assessing the child's attitudes to the members of his family. Some assessment of the amount of anxiety exhibited by the child is also useful.) The Sarason Test Anxiety Scale and General Anxiety Scale (15) can be used for this purpose. Other orthodox projective techniques can be administered by experienced clinical psychologists.

A careful winnowing out of the child's genuine interests in life will help in the remedial planning of high interest work programs and literature selection. A lengthy check-list combined with a conversational approach should prove effective here.

NEURO-PHYSIOLOGICAL LEVEL

On this level there is a need to investigate the electrical functioning of the brain, and, of course, a full EEG report is necessary. Even more important than an electroencephalographic record is an investigation of the child's motor functioning. It is now possible, as Prechtl (14) has done using a portable EEG machine, to obtain electropolymyographs which will help determine any muscle dysfunction which is attributable to neurological dysfunction. A useful test of finger agnosia is that suggested by Kinsbourne and Warrington (10) as it will pick up any tactile or haptic deficits in the hand and fingers.

The muscles of the eyes can be evaluated for normal functioning by using electrodes to obtain oculomotor tracings. By this means, any choreiform (twitching) or irregular eye movements will be detected. On the broader motor level there is always the Lincoln Oseretsky Motor Performance Scale. (I have found that if one gives a few impromptu tests of body balance and finger coordination one achieves the same diagnostic objective).

Along with the above tests, assessments of the child's vision and hearing should be made by competent professional people. Apart from the usual thorough audiometry examination, a speech and hearing expert should evaluate the child's articulation, recheck his auditory discrimination, and even administer a language assessment scale. Learning disability personnel can utilize the services of suitably trained speech and hearing people particularly in the diagnosis and remediation of articulation and listening-auditory deficits.

THE TECHNIQUE OF "FUNNELING-IN"

Although each child will probably require more than ten hours of testing and other examinations, there is no need to extend the procedure indefinitely. It is a useful practice to look at the information yielded by the Family Information Form, the WISC, the ITPA, the Frostig, and Auditory Discrimination Test with a view to discovering those areas in which the child functions well and those in which he appears to have broad deficits. For example, if he successfully completes the Frostig and spatial items on the WISC and ITPA, there will be no need to give him any further visuo-spatial tests such as the Beery or Memory-for-Designs. However, assuming his auditory functioning to be poor, there may be a need to investigate the problem in more detail using such tests as Melody Discrimination, Articulation Assessment, etc. Referral to the speech and hearing clinic might be advisable. When funneling-in on a deficit, it is better to give too many tests than too few.

CROSS-ANALYSIS AND CONSISTENT PATTERNING

Once all the test results and other information are at hand, all should be written up on a large chalk-board in separate chalk-drawn "cells" until the board looks like a vast mosaic. One then cross-analyzes all the figures and information searching for consistent patterns and profiles which will precisely delineate the areas of both dysfunction and sound performance on each of the four levels. Usually two or more people from the team, including the psychologist and educator, should carry through this cross-analysis.

THE DIAGNOSTIC REPORT FORM

The diagnostic coordinator next draws up a rather precise summary of these deficits, and he does so under each of the four headings: the Academic Level, the Cognitive/Sensori-Motor Level, the Personality/Emotional/Motivational Level, and the Neuro-Physiological Level. Underneath these is a space for further comment on etiology, inter-level complications, suspected compound deficits, and any other important special points in the child's background, such as parental or sibling suicide, *known* brain damage, multiple births, etc.

The sheet which is used for setting out the remedial prescriptions follows closely the one used for the diagnostic report. In other words, a prescription is written for *each of the several levels* in which defects have been identified and if there is no prescription for any particular level there should be entered in its place an explanation of why remediation is not necessary. As on the diagnostic sheet, there is space under the various remedial prescriptions for "Further Comment" in which detailed explanation of the choice of remedial topics, techniques, and other teaching ideas and devices can be entered.

MULTI-TRACK REMEDIATION

Normally several remedial or training tracks of learning on several levels will be in progress during the first half of the child's total time spent in tuition be it days, weeks, or months. Once their respective remedial objectives have been achieved, the individual tracks along which the child is progressing may be either slowly phased out or merged together as tuition progresses. For example, a child with a severe visuo-spatial problem may require on the academic level a considerable amount of a. writing and b. the reading of large-print stories. Once the child has mastered writing the two tracks would merge into a program of writing down summaries of stories he has read. The same child on the sensori-motor level may also have embarked initially on a Frostig Program of Developmental Perception, a task which might take up another ten minutes of his lesson time each day. If the child were poorly motivated some high interest technique might be used such as utilizing a boy's interest in racing cars as a theme for most of his academic work. On the neurophysiological level, the child might be given yet another learning track, for example, the training of eye-hand coordination on suitable (and one would hope enjoyable) apparatus.

As the child progressed along each of these tracks, they would in turn be phased out or merged until all were coalesced into one or two programs on the academic level. In most cases of reading disability these would obviously include reading, writing, and spelling. Similar multi-track programs can and should be devised for other learning disabilities, for example, in mathematics.

DIAGNOSTIC REMEDIATION

The diagnosis of learning disabilities does not stop with the onset of remediation. In fact, continuous diagnostic remediation should be practiced, the teacher being prepared to modify her procedures as need arises. I have invented the phrase "Track Advancement Effectors" to describe all those often unitary occasions, contingencies, situations, devices, actions, ideas, insights, steps, modifications, rearrangements, and inventions which cause the child to move nearer the academic, cognitive/sensori-motor, social, neurological, and physiological objectives which will have been suggested in the multi-track prescription for remediation. The teacher should watch for these track advancement effectors because they will help her structure future remediation for both the child in hand and other learning disability cases.

Task Analysis is a valuable technique in the process of diagnostic remediation. Each step of each lesson on each level should be examined before and after the remedial session for the purpose of isolating unit-deficits within the immediate tasks. This seems time-consuming but the overall result may be a considerable shortening of the entire program.

Since this is a paper primarily devoted to an overall description of diagnostic procedures and techniques, it is not the place to elaborate further on the valuable remedial technique of task analysis or the many other possible methods of remediation. Many of these I have described elsewhere (18).

GLOSSARY

Cognition, Cognitive: This is a general term covering all the various modes of knowing—perceiving, reasoning, conceiving, judging, and imagining. It is contrasted a. with affective functioning, that is an awareness of emotional, feeling sensations, and b. with conative functioning which is a striving or action-drive to fulfil some need.

Dyslexia: Dyslexia is the inability to learn to read, write or spell competently in persons who either have or are suspected of having average or above average intelligence (usually as measured on Full Scale IQ of the WISC). The discrepancy is not caused by primary emotional disturbance, mental retardation, aphasia, or severe communication disorders.

Electropolymyograms: The electrodes of an EEG machine can be placed on the skin over muscles in the limbs, neck, trunk, face, or eyes to detect choreiform (slight, jerky, irregular, arhythmical movements) discharges in either contracted or relaxed muscles. Choreiform discharges may be indicative of mild brain dysfunction.

Finger Agnosia: Agnosia refers to the inability to attach meaning to sensory impressions and as such is usually considered to be caused by brain dysfunction. Persons with finger agnosia are unable or less able to use the haptic sensitivity of their fingers to identify objects they are handling while blindfolded. It may interfere with writing ability.

Genetic Dyslexia: Genetic Dyslexia is the term used to describe those persons (almost always male) who exhibit a syndrome of specific linguistic skill disabilities which restrict their ability to learn to read, spell, and write as well as their full scale intelligence would indicate. There is a body of research evidence which indicates that the condition is inherited (See Bannatyne, 1966).

Grapheme: A grapheme is the written or printed (letter or letters) equivalent of the auditory/speech unit of sound, the phoneme. If the orthography of the language is irregular, the matching of phonemes to graphemes is not consistent. For example, the phoneme/eye/can be written as the graphemes, eye, *i, l, igh, ei, ie, uy, y.*

Haptic: Haptic refers to the cutaneous sense and it includes all the sensations derived from the receptors in the skin for contact, pressure, pain, warmth, and cold. They form one group or proprioreceptors.

Kinesthetic Sense: This sense is a general term covering *sensations* of muscle movement of any part of the body. It is a receptive feedback of information to the brain in the interests of sensori-motor coordination and planning for immediate action. Activities such as reading, writing, and speech depend tremendously on accurate *kinesthetic* information.

Oculomotor Recordings: Oculomotor means "eye-movement activity" and eye-movements can be recorded reasonably easily on an EEG machine during reading or visual field scanning by using two electrodes, one above and one below each eye. The resulting tracings can be examined for choreiform or other irregular eye movements, a not infrequent cause of reading difficulties.

Phoneme: A class or family of closely related speech sounds regarded as a single sound and represented in phonetic transcription by the same symbol, as the sounds of /r/ in b*r*ing, *r*ed and *r*ound. The discernible phonetic differences between such sounds are due to the modifying influence of the adjacent sounds.

Sensori-Motor: Sensori-motor is a generic term which includes all the senses (hearing, seeing, haptic, kinesthetic, etc.), and all motor or muscle activities (of fingers, eyes, articulation, etc.). When one reacts to a sensory stimulus of a complex nature, such as reading, considerable sensori-motor integration and coordination of a neurological nature is required.

Sequencing Ability: Sequencing ability is a time-oriented skill which may be active in almost all sensori-motor activities, singly or in combination, and memory is usually involved. When reading, one must visually recognize sequences of letters, sequences of graphemes and sequences of words; one must auditorially recognize the phoneme sequences the graphemes symbolize. In spelling, a reverse process of recalling phonemes and graphemes occurs. Writing involves motor sequencing habits.

Visuo-Spatial Ability: Visuo-spatial ability as an intellect-oriented term which can be defined as the ability to manipulate objects and their inter-relationships intelligently in multi-dimensional space. Architects, surgeons, dentists, builders, engineers, mechanics, pilots, drivers, sportsmen, many scientists, and the like operate in their daily work on a visuo-spatial intellectual basis which in essence is nonverbal.

REFERENCES

1. Bannatyne, A. D. *The Etiology of Dyslexia and the Color Phonics System.* Paper presented at the Third Annual Conference of the Association for Children with Learning Disabilities, Tulsa, Oklahoma, March 1966.

2. _____. *Matching Remedial Methods with Specific Deficits.* Paper presented at the 1967 International Convocation on Children and Young Adults with Learning Disabilities, Home for Crippled Children, Pittsburgh, February, 1967.

3. Beery, K. E., and Buktenica, N. *Beery-Buktenica Developmental Test of Visual-Motor Integration (VMI).* Chicago: Parkinson Division, Follett Publishing Co., 1967.

4. Bene, E., and Bene, Anthony. *Children's Version and Adult Version of the Family Relations Test.* The Mere, Upton Park, Slough, Bucks, England: National Foundation for Educational Research, 1966.

5. Benton, A. L. "Right-Left Discrimination and Finger Localization: Development and Pathology." In *Benton Protocol for Right-Left Discrimination.* New York: Hoerber-Harper, 1959.

6. Drake, Charles. *PERC Auditory Discrimination Test.* Wellesley, Massachusetts: Perceptual and Educational Research Center, 1966.

7. Frostig, Marianne. *Developmental Test of Visual Perception.* Palo Alto, California: Consulting Psychologists Press, 1964.

8. Graham, F. K., and Kendall, B. S. Memory-for-Designs Test. Missoula, Montana: Psychological Test Specialists, 1960.

9. Harris, Albert J. *Harris Test of Lateral Dominance.* New York: The Psychological Corporation, 1947.

10. Kinsbourne, M., and Warrington, E. K. "The Development of Finger Differentiation." *Quarterly Journal of Experiential Psychology* 15 (May 1963): Part 2.

11. Kirk, S. A. *The Illinois Test of Psycholinguistic Abilities,* rev. ed. Urbana: Illinois University Press, 1968.

12. Money, John. *Road Map Test of Direction Sense.* Baltimore, Maryland: Johns Hopkins Press, 1966.

13. Neale, Marie D. *Neale Analysis of Reading Ability.* London: Macmillan, 1964.

14. Prechtl, H. F. R. Reading Difficulties as a Neurological Problem in Childhood." In Reading Disability, edited by J. Money. Baltimore: The Johns Hopkins Press, 1962.

15. Sarason, S. B. et al. Test Anxiety for Children and General Anxiety Scale for Children." In Anxiety in Elementary School Children. New York: John Wiley, 1960.

16. Spalding, R. B., and Spalding, W. T. *The Writing Road to Reading.* New York: Whiteside/Morrow, 1962.

17. Wepman, J. Wepman Auditory Discrimination Test. Chicago: Language Research Associates, 1958.

18. Wolf, Clifton W. An Experimental Investigation of Specific Disability (Dyslexia). Bulletin of the Orton Society 17 (1967).

6

Remediation—A Place to Start

Remediation should start with success. What does success have to do with mental health? Waetjen presents a case which needs consideration by all educators.

ABOUT LEARNING AND MENTAL HEALTH: AN INTRODUCTION

Walter B. Waetjen

This yearbook is about learning and mental health. At first blush a person might think that there is no possible reason why such a volume should be produced. Behind such a thought would be the idea that for several centuries teachers have been concerned about the learning of their pupils. Some would aver that for at least a decade teachers have been concerned about the mental health of those whom they teach. The Yearbook Committee that has planned and

---

From *Learning and Mental Health in the School. 1966 Yearbook,* edited by Walter B. Waetjen and Robert W. Leeper (Washington, D.C.: Association for Supervision and Curriculum Development, 1966), p. 4. Reprinted with permission of the Association for Supervision and Curriculum Development and Walter B. Waetjen. Copyright © 1966 by the Association for Supervision and Curriculum Development.

written this volume could only agree with these points of view. Yet if members of the Committee had dismissed the issue without further thought, then there would have been no reason for proceeding with this yearbook.

Even a moment's reflection on the matter of learning brings to mind that the teacher is placed in a dilemma on this subject. For if a teacher is to help a pupil to learn, this means that the teacher must do something about his teaching. But what? Should he arrange his subject matter differently? Should he present it differently? Should he give the pupils more, or less, responsibility for planning the learning activities? Or should the teacher do all of these things?

To compound the dilemma, some of the learning theories to which most teachers subscribe require close scrutiny. The theories or laws of learning that many teachers believe in (if they believe in any) are based on data obtained using animals as subjects. If the subjects were human beings, then they, like the animals, were in highly controlled unclassroomlike situations. As a consequence, the findings are only remotely related to what the teacher experiences in the classroom. It seems strange that, in a society that does so much experimentation in psychological processes, we have a rather meager psychology of individual differences that may be utilized by the teacher. Yet these are observations that have relevance only to learning—what about mental health?

By virtue of the teacher-education process, mental health is not seen as a reality by either preservice or in-service teachers. This is not to say that they do not see some merit in fostering mental health in our schools, for indeed they do. Yet it seems that most teachers see mental health as something apart from teaching. Counseling, which is not part of the teaching act, would be perceived by teachers as a mental health function of the school. Likewise, they would view the activities of the school psychologist and the school social worker as the school's role in the development of better mental health. One cannot deny that these are mental health functions of the school, but it should be recognized that these functions are quite distinct from what occurs in the elementary school classroom, the algebra class, the chemistry class, or the civics class.

Some directors of curriculum would rise in hot protest against the previous statement and point with conviction to the fact that mental health is highly central to the teaching activity in their school system. Typically, in these cases the curriculum director is likely to produce a course of study or a curriculum unit that is taught at some given grade. Or perhaps the same type of unit with modification is taught at some given grade. Or perhaps the same type of unit with modification is taught at several different grade levels. Logic in such an approach seems to be that mental health is so important that we must make of it a highly cognitive activity. In this instance mental health is seen as a *thing* to be taught rather than as a *process* to be engaged in.

These two views of mental health have been disavowed by the Yearbook Committee. To our minds mental health is not something out of which one makes a curriculum unit but rather it is something that occurs in the context of the moment-to-moment discourse and interaction between pupils and teachers in classrooms. We have taken the position that there are potentialities for influencing mental health in teaching the skills and understandings necessary to cope with the environment, the skills of communication, the ways of identifying and solving problems rationally, and the basic requirements needed for pursuing a vocation. Viewed in this way, mental health is a process and processes usually have a product. In this case the product is the competent person, a term that will be used throughout the context of this yearbook.

To place blame on teachers for not doing more about mental health and learning of pupils would be unfair. It may be that there is a standardization of teaching practices, and attitudes in teachers. Yet, this may be caused by the fact that teachers are so surrounded by regulations and requirements and notions about teaching and learning that they stultify their teaching capacity and damage their trust in themselves. Teaching, to be good, must have large elements of creativity and spontaneity—neither of which elements can long survive in an atmosphere in which conformity to senseless regulations plays a dominant part. In such an atmosphere a teacher himself cannot learn and he in turn has difficulty teaching in such a way that his pupils can learn. The consequence is that pupils have difficulty in becoming competent persons.

In the pages to follow it will become readily apparent to the reader that the writers have subscribed to a certain kind of education. The education to which we have subscribed has one great and overarching purpose and that is the achievement of individual freedom. We do not use the words "individual freedom" in the way that they might be used by an aspirant to political office. In that context the words are often vague and rather meaningless. Nor does individual freedom mean just doing whatever one likes. Freedom is never free; there is always some price to pay. As will be pointed out in all of the chapters that ensue, the price that the mentally healthy, learning-oriented pupil pays for his freedom in the classroom is that he accepts the responsibility for his acts.

Pupils are only truly free when they are acting in accordance with reality. That is, with events, things, and people as they really are. They are bound and unfree to the extent to which they are incapable of seeing things as they really are. Thus, freedom has nothing to do with license, but it has a great deal to do with being sufficiently aware of ourselves and sufficiently aware of our feelings and thinking to be able to see and respond to things as they are. It takes only a moment's reflection, then, to see that education needs to concern itself with the liberation of the individual.

It is only the pupil who is free who can begin to see things as they really are and who can begin to live and act in harmony with the reality principle rather than principles of personal defensiveness. Of course, one could easily misinterpret the statement to the extent of believing that this yearbook holds curriculum content to be unimportant. This would be a most unfortunate interpretation, for actually we hold the view that curriculum content, if taught properly, can indeed be a liberating force for all pupils. This same curriculum content could enable a youngster not only to discover reality, but to test it; and the curriculum content would indeed give pupils a lever on the world, as it properly should.

Education is harmful to the extent to which it makes independent thinking difficult and to the degree to which it makes pupils distrust their own experience. If education is dominated by the belief that the accumulation of knowledge is valuable in itself, then we are only playing party to moving our society down the path of conformity and a spectacular lack of creativity and inventiveness. Significant learning and mental health start with questions that spring out of real life and that are forced upon us by pressure of events. This kind of learning is necessarily disciplined by objective fact. There is practically no value whatever in knowing things just for the sake of knowing them and nothing more.

The search for knowledge is either a search for that which has significance for human behavior or it is a relapse into unreality. The contents of Chapters 5 and 6 should make it crystal clear that what we are advocating can occur in a classroom in which there is a curriculum and in which the teacher accepts responsibility for "structuring" the classroom activities. So much of the so-called academic life, especially college academic life, has around it an aura of futility and barrenness because it has so little significance to and for the individual learner. If a learner has freedom, with its attendant responsibilities in the classroom, all other forms of learning necessary for living in our contemporary world come more easily to him —for learning comes easily to one who is unrestricted intellectually.

It is in school that a pupil can see his own small world of home from the outside and can begin to make his independent judgments of parents and their demands. School can provide a child with an opportunity for self-discovery. At school he is not imprisoned in the kind of personality that his parents have come to accept as his. At school he can experiment with new roles and thus find out who he really is and what he is capable of. But this kind of "role rehearsal" occurs best when the teacher makes provision for it. He does not rely upon chance occurrences. The school can encourage independence of thinking and create an atmosphere in which every belief is questioned. In short, school can become a place in which the doubt is prized. School can be a place where a pupil can be discontented with things as they are without fearing reprisal. Of course, the discontentment of the pupil must be expressed in ways that are socially acceptable and which lead to some constructive social action on his part. In this yearbook we have tried to point out that our schools can become places where a pupil learns the difference between experiencing and the explaining of experiences.

Every year new approaches to the problems of remedial readers are presented. What are the values of such approaches? Harris presents a classic analysis.

WHAT ABOUT SPECIAL THEORIES OF TEACHING REMEDIAL READING?

Albert J. Harris

Remedial Reading has become an exceedingly active area of reading instruction. As a result, new theories of diagnosis and treatment are continuously evolving. Among these new theories are the Delacato theory of neurological integration, Kephart's theory of motor and perceptual training, Frostig's theory of specific perceptual training, and the drug treatment theory applied in studies conducted by several investigators. Each of these theories will be described, and research concerning each one will be presented and evaluated in the scholarly papers that follow.

Majority opinion among remedial specialists has for many years favored the policy of beginning remedial reading by using perceptual and memory abilities which are normal or least impaired and, while the child is learning by a method with which he can achieve some success, working to strengthen those perceptual and associative abilities that are particularly weak. Major emphasis is on building up areas of weakness.

The contrast between the general remedial viewpoint and a newer point of view has been clearly stated by Silver and Hagin (39):

> Our initial concept had been that compensation was a basic principle; i.e., after assessing perceptual assets and deficits, we should train in the areas of greater perceptual strength, via the

From *Current Issues in Reading* (1969): 393-407. Reprinted with permission of the International Reading Association and Albert J. Harris.

most intact modalities. Results of the follow-up studies, however, suggest that this technique does not appear to enhance perception or to effect lasting improvement in reading. Efforts now are directed to the stimulation of the defective perceptual areas. This is almost a complete reversal of our earlier approach. Our purpose now is really to enhance cerebral maturation, to bring neurological functioning to the point where it is physiologically capable of learning to read.

This paper will attempt to explore several new approaches to remedial reading which share the viewpoint expressed by Silver and Hagin, to review the research currently available concerning them, and to arrive at tentative conclusions concerning their readiness for widespread adoption.

The writer had originally hoped to be able to include, under "special methods," those that attempt to simplify the reading task by using special alphabets, applications of programmed instruction and reinforcement psychology, and various forms of psychotherapy. However, limitations of time and space have made it necessary to limit the scope of coverage.

Most of the approaches to be discussed agree with the statement of Krippner (25): "Often a program of perceptual training, dominance establishment, and/or motor coordination improvement is needed before reading improvement will be helpful." The four major approaches to be discussed place emphasis on 1. developing neurological organization, 2. establishing a firm motor and perceptual base, 3. developing specific perceptual skills, and 4. using drugs to improve the learner's accessibility to instruction.

In attempting to appraise any new approach one must realize that the first efforts to study the value of an innovation are usually case reports or small-scale and poorly controled pilot studies which may indicate whether the procedure is worth more careful evaluation—but which cannot do much more. An ever-present danger is the placebo effect described by McDonald (29)—the power of positive suggestion which tends to enhance the effects of an innovation when used by its creator or by a devoted disciple. A second danger is the Hawthorne effect, the built-in advantage that almost any new experimental procedure has over the routine and comparatively unglamorous procedure assigned to a control group. A third problem is that of broad generalization from results obtained with small groups of doubtfully representative subjects over a short period of time. A fourth problem in evaluating the evidence is the researcher's temptation to use a statistical method which tends to maximize the possibility of finding a statistically significant difference, whether it is the most appropriate way to treat the data. In reviewing the evidence the writer has tried to keep these possible sources of error constantly in mind.

One must keep in mind, also, that as yet there is no good statistical evidence on the frequency of neurologically based reading disability or the percent of retarded readers whose problems fall into this category. Recently Morris (30), in a large-scale study, reported that

> ... The poorest readers were not in any reasonable interpretation of the term a neurological problem, and that the study as a whole lends little support to the idea that "specific developmental dyslexia" is an identifiable syndrome distinct from "reading backwardness." In other words, if "word blindness" exists as a condition which cannot be treated by good teaching within the state educational system it must be a rare condition indeed.

Nevertheless, there are many specialists in learning disabilities who believe in a special condition caused by heredity, severe environmental deprivation, or brain damage which makes it extremely difficult for some children with otherwise normal intelligence to learn to read. Among the characteristics stressed as frequently found in this group are poor visual and auditory perception, poor ability to make visual-auditory associations, and directional confusion; distractibility, motor restlessness, clumsiness, and short attention span are reported in many cases (20). Most of the special remedial methods have been advocated especially for this subgroup of disabled readers.

THE DELACATO APPROACH: NEUROLOGICAL INTEGRATION

Delacato has explained his theoretical basis and remedial procedures in three books (8, 9, 10). Obviously only a very sketchy summary can be given here. Very briefly, he believes that in some children a failure to achieve neurological integration below the cortical level of the brain is basic and must be corrected by such activities as sleeping in a particular position and learning to crawl and creep properly. When subcortical integration is present or has been developed, the major problem is lack of clear and consistent dominance of one cerebral hemisphere over the other. A variety of treatment procedures have the common purpose of strengthening the consistent use of the dominant hand and compelling the child to rely on the eye on the same side as the dominant hand. Among the precedures used are eliminating music, occluding one eye to force reliance on the other, creeping, crawling, and so on. Once neurological integration has been achieved, the child is said to learn to read by normal developmental teaching methods.

In his books Delacato has presented brief versions of fifteen studies, for several of which he did the statistical work on data supplied by others. A careful analytical review of these studies has recently been made by Glass and Robbins (18), who analyzed each of the studies in detail, considering research design and statistical treatment. Their conclusions are summarized in the following quotation:

> Twelve experiments are analyzed in light of the controls which were lacking in their execution and the shortcomings of the reported statistical analysis. Serious doubts about the validity of any of the twelve experiments are raised. An analysis of correlation studies reported by Delacato reveals a conclusion quite contrary to the implications drawn by him from the data. Without exception, the empirical studies cited by Delacato as a "scientific appraisal" of his theory of neurological organization are shown to be of dubious value.

The writer had read the fifteen studies before seeing the Glass and Robbins critique and reread them afterward. He finds himself in close agreement with their criticisms.

Recent research has cast doubt on the idea that crossed dominance—having the preferred eye on the opposite side from the preferred hand—has any relation to success in reading, although Delacato considers this condition sufficient evidence of neurological immaturity. In the writer's own research (21), crossed dominance was not significantly more frequent in severe reading disabilities than in an unselected school population, while mixed-handedness and directional confusion were found in a substantially higher proportion of reading disabilities. A study by Stephen, Cunningham, and Stigler (43) recently found no relationship between crossed dominance and reading readiness in kindergarten children.

Independent studies bearing on the Delacato approach have not produced supporting evidence. Yarborough (46) studied the value of the Leavell Language-Development Service, a procedure for strengthening the use of the eye on the same side as the preferred hand. Using a stereoscopic technique similar to one used by

Delacato, she found no evidence of significant benefit in reading. Robbins (35,36) tried out Delacato procedures with second graders. Not only did he find no benefit in reading but, after the training to establish consistent sidedness, there were two more children with crossed dominance than before the training.

Anderson (1) tried cross-pattern creeping and walking exercises with kindergarten children and found no significant improvement in readiness in the experimental as compared with a control group. He did a similar study with intermediate grade students and again found no significant differences for the total population, for lower IQ children, or for those with lower initial reading ability.

It may turn out eventually that the Delacato approach is useful for a small percentage of children with severe reading disabilities. However, the research efforts to date have failed to provide evidence of its value. In view of the widespread publicity given to these procedures and the considerable number of children who at present are spending a substantial part of their school time creeping and crawling, definitive impartial research on the Delacato system is urgently needed.

A rather extreme version of a point of view resembling that of Delacato is expounded by a private organization in Chicago called The Reading Research Foundation (33). In a brochure explaining its program the following statements are made:

> Development of the capacity to sustain concentration is influenced by continuous changes in the stimulus cues for the appropriate response-pattern and for signaling success and error of response. Furthermore, the intensity of the signals (loud hollers, for example) are used as one way of developing the stability of concentration. Cross-lateral patterns of movements are used extensively in order to promote neurological organization in each of the cerebral hemispheres as well as an integration in their functioning.

The writer has received from this organization two mimeographed papers reporting small-scale tryouts of their procedures with first-grade children. Although differences between the final reading scores of total experimental and control groups were not significant in both studies, the authors argue for significance in one case by restricting the comparison to low groups of twelve children each and in the other by disregarding a nonsignificant analysis of variance and stressing a comparison of gain scores, which is, in the writers opinion, a dubious statistical procedure (27, 28).

A very recent feature article in the *Chicago Daily News* describes this program and reports comments by two visitors. The following is a direct quotation from the article:

> Dr. E. R. Simmons, director of the Texas Reading Institute, San Antonio, visited the school and saw teachers shake, pinch, and pull the hair of students. He described his attitude as disbelief giving way to anger and distress. . . . James Weddell, director of Purdue University's Achievement Center for Children said some of his staff was "appalled" by the approach, fearing it may "tear some kids asunder emotionally."

It is not necessary for me to add to these comments.

KEPHART: MOTOR AND PERCEPTUAL TRAINING

Kephart (23) has advocated programs for slow or disabled learners in which much emphasis is placed on developing readiness. In a recent paper coauthored with Dunning occurs the following:

> Readiness for learning . . . consists of a hierarchical build-up of generalizations which allows the child to deal more effectively with his environment. Learning difficulties may be viewed in terms of difficulties in this developmental sequence. When such difficulties occur, then there are gaps in the sequence which will affect all future learning either by limiting or distorting it (11).

In the Kephart approach emphasis is placed on helping children changes from stereotyped, rigid movement patterns to variable, adaptive, and purposeful movement patterns. Specific graded sequences of exercises are suggested to develop balance and locomotion and to improve laterality, directionality, ocular pursuit, and temporal rhythm and succession. Essentially the same basic program seems to be recommended for mentally retarded, brain-injured, and reading-disability children.

There is as yet little published research on the effectiveness of the Kephart approach in improving reading. Rutherford (38) studied the effect of Kephart-type activities on the Metropolitan Readiness Test scores of kindergarten children. He found a significant gain for the boys in the experimental group but not for the girls. Whether this program would induce better reading later on is not known. Roach (34) used perceptual-motor training of the Kephart type with groups of reading-disability children averaging twelve years old and found no significant differences in oral reading. LaPray and Ross (26), selecting first graders who were low in both reading and visual perception, compared a group given training in large-muscle activities and visual training with one given extra time with simple reading materials; the former group improved more on perceptual tests and the latter, on reading tests. The writer has not yet found any controlled research that shows the Kephart approach to be useful in the treatment of reading disabilities.

Points of view quite similar to those of Kephart have been expressed by Barsch (3), Getman (17), and Bateman (4). The writer has not been able to find controled research relevant to their theoretical positions.

Since establishment of directionality is one of the objectives of Kephart, it may be appropriate at this point to mention a new method of preventing and correcting reversal tendencies. Daniels (7) has described a simple procedure which he says requires only one twenty-minute session and is effective two years later. He uses paired cutout forms which are mirror images, such as locomotives facing right and left. The child is shown a pair and then practices fitting each part into the correct form-board depression; this procedure is then practiced with many similar pairs. Daniels states that one lesson at about the age of four prevented reversals at the age of six. Certainly this procedure deserves to be tested by others; if it should be found to work, one of the big problems in reading could be eliminated for most children.

SPECIFIC PERCEPTUAL TRAINING

Emphasis on developing specific perceptual skills received major impetus with the publication of the Illinois Test of Psycholinguistic Abilities (24) and the Marianne Frostig Developmental Tests of Visual Perception (16). With analytical tests available, training programs were developed to improve the particular functional weaknesses disclosed by the tests. Although this approach seems reasonable and in accord with common sense, both the diagnostic validity of the tests and the value of spending time on perceptual training instead of remedial reading are at present questionable.

Olson (31, 32), studied the predictive value of the Frostig test and found that it had some predictive value when correlated with reading scores in Grades 2 and 3, but neither the total score nor the individual part scores were substantial predictors of specific difficulties in reading. Rosen (37) compared twelve experimental classes which received a half hour of Frostig training per day with thirteen classes receiving reading instruction only. The differences on reading tests consistently favored the control group but were not significant when adjustments were made to equate the groups for readiness.

According to Weener, Barritt, and Semmel (45), the Illinois Test of Psycholinguistic Abilities falls short of the statistical requirements for a satisfactory diagnostic test. They found that the reliabilities of ITPA subtests are too low, both split-half and test-retest, for adequate prediction and diagnosis from individual profiles.

Thus both of these tests, which have been widely adopted in reading clinics and by school psychologists, are imperfect instruments. A remedial program based on their high and low subtest scores may or may not fit the child's needs. It is to be hoped that revised versions or new perceptual tests will provide more accurate diagnostic analyses of perceptual and linguistic skills, information which will in turn permit research to determine whether remedial programs based on such tests will be valuable.

It should be noted that Frostig's descriptions (15) of her own remedial approach are broader and more flexible than study of her perceptual training materials might lead one to expect. She states that she includes physiotherapy, physical education, eye exercises, and help with fine motor coordination when indicated in an individual diagnosis (14) and employs varied teaching procedures for reading, including picture cues, phonics, and kinesthetic procedures when indicated (13).

Concentrated training in auditory perception as a preparation for remedial reading is advocated by Daniels (7), who reported that a group of retarded readers given one term of auditory training followed by two terms of phonics-oriented remedial reading improved more than a matched group given three terms of remedial reading. Since the control groups final average-age score was only 6.3, the quality of its remedial instruction would not seem to have been very high.

Silver, Hagin, and Hersh (40) have issued a progress report on what seems to be a quite important study. One group of disabled readers was given training in auditory and visual perception for half a year, followed by remedial reading during the second half year; the other group had remedial reading for the first half and perceptual training during the second half. However, the remedial teaching consisted of using a basal reader and following the teacher's manual —hardly an optimal remedial procedure. The authors concluded:

The results so far suggest that where perceptual defects are first trained out, reading instruction at intermodal and verbal levels will have a better chance of success. This is particularly true of the more severe language disabilities, those with defects in multiple modalities, and those in whom "soft" neurological signs may be found.

The final report of the study is not yet available.

A quite sophisticated study of the value of training in auditory perception was conducted by Feldmann and Deutsch (12) with third grade Negro and Puerto Rican children in New York City; all of the children were initially reading below middle second grade. The experimental children were instructed in small groups of two to four, three times a week for five months. In the first study there were three experimental groups: remedial reading only, auditory training only, and separate periods of reading and auditory training. None of the experimental groups did significantly better than the others or better than the control group that received only regular classroom reading instruction. On the assumption that the instruction program needed improvement, a second study was conducted with new but similar children. Changes were made in the auditory training program, and a new variable integrating auditory training with remedial reading was added. Again the results showed the control group doing as well as the experimental groups and no significant differences among the experimental groups.

The results of the Feldmann and Deutsch study demonstrate that one cannot assume that training in auditory perception will necessarily benefit retarded readers; transfer of what is learned during perceptual training to the act of reading is not automatic and sometimes does not take place.

DRUG TREATMENT FOR READING DISABILITY

The most ambitious effort to provide a theoretical and experimental basis for a drug treatment approach as an adjunct to a remedial teaching is that of Smith and Carrigan (41). Starting with the hypothesis that reading disability is based on a physiological difficulty in the transmission of nerve impulses in the brain, they developed theoretical models for five syndromes, based on various patterns of excess or deficiency in two chemicals, cholinesterase and acetylcholine. They then analyzed the results of a test battery given to forty cases of reading disability and reported that most of the cases fell into groups that corresponded to the models. Some of the children were given drugs chosen on the basis of the kind of change assumed to be needed in the child's brain chemistry. Statistically better response to remedial reading was reported for those taking medication as compared to other children not receiving medication. In 1961 the writer (19) prepared an evaluation of this study which may be briefly summarized as follows: the theoretical base is highly original, most interesting, and still possibly correct; the experimental evidence is unconvincing because of technical errors in design and execution. It is a pity that nobody has attempted to replicate the Smith-Carrigan study.

Staiger (42) studied the effects of a drug called Deanol on perception and reading improvement. He found a gain in perceptual speed for those taking the medication, but not in reading.

Baldwin and Kenny (2) tried twenty medications, singly and in combination, with 100 children having behavior disorders involving hyperactivity, impulsiveness, etc. The most effective treatment in reducing symptoms was a combination of Benadryl and Dilantin which produced some improvement in two-thirds of the cases to whom it was given, while only one child got worse. For children who are very hard to teach because of behavior disorders, the use of drugs to make them amenable to instruction seems quite plausible.

However, one should not confuse expectations with results. Valusek (44) did a carefully controled study on the use of drugs with retarded readers in a state mental hospital using Thorazine, Cytomel, and Dexedrine, tranquilizers that are quite popular in psychiatric practice. He found no significant differences between the medication and placebo groups in oral or silent reading or on psychological tests.

An interesting report of successful drug treatment for a specific subgroup of disabled readers comes from Calvert and Cromes (5). In the eye-movement photographs of children who were not responding to remedial tutoring they found evidence of fine tremors or spasms occurring at intervals of about eighteen seconds. Treatment of a few of these children with Primidone both stopped the tremors permanently and was followed by improved learning. The writer has not found any other study reporting either similar tremors or the use of Primidone, so this study certainly seems worth replicating.

These are the only studies the writer has found on the use of drugs with children having reading disabilities, studies which are certainly not definitive. It would seem logical that when children with reading disability are hyperactive or sluggish or depressed, appropriate drug therapy should be a useful adjunct to remedial teaching. New discoveries with animals open up possibilities of improving human mental functioning chemically, but as yet this area is something for the future. Certainly any use of medication should be prescribed and supervised by a physician, and we need much more research on the use of drugs with poor readers.

SUMMARY AND CONCLUSIONS

This paper has considered four main approaches to the treatment of reading disability by procedures other than teaching reading skills. All are interesting, but none has yet been firmly substantiated.

Most radically innovative is the Delacato's stress on neurological organization and laterality. Both Delacato's basic theories and the practical value of his procedures for treating reading disabilities are very much open to question. Publicity has far outstripped proof. Hopefully, careful objective studies will be done to discover if the method really helps any children with reading problems and, if so, how to identify the cases to which the method may be applicable. Adoption of cross-pattern creeping and attempts to alter patterns of lateral dominance are not justified for either schools or reading clinics on the basis of present evidence.

The Kephart approach, stressing the improvement of motor control and flexibility, the development of hand and eye coordination, and directionality, has not yet found verification as an improvement in remedial reading programs. However, it would seem to have some intrinsic value apart from reading. Better control of one's body can be a desirable goal in itself. Perhaps this kind of training will find a home in the physical education program rather than be judged in terms of whether it makes a direct contribution to academic learning.

Since there is ample evidence that visual and auditory perception are both significantly correlated with success in beginning reading, the main question would seem to be how to give perceptual training rather than whether to give it. Can it be most effective when it precedes or parallels reading instruction or when it is an integral part of reading instruction and emphasizes alphabetic shapes and the sounds of words and word parts? Here the evidence is somewhat conflicting. In the absence of proof to the contrary, the writer's preference is to combine perceptual training as closely as possible with reading instruction.

The fourth and final special approach considered here, the use of drug medication, is one in which future possibilities far outstrip the present inconclusive findings. If the particular drugs tried so far have not produced remedial reading miracles, perhaps some drug not yet discovered will do so. We must keep a close watch on the possible contributions of pharmacology to remedial education, and we should encourage continuing research in this area.

This paper began by pointing out the contrast between the classical emphasis on making use of the child's best avenues for learning and some newer approaches which concentrate on building up deficiency areas. As yet, the newer approaches have not provided convincing proof of their effectiveness. Those who have been obtaining satisfactory results with established methods of remedial teaching would do well to wait for more conclusive evidence before adopting any of the newer procedures that have been discussed here.

REFERENCES

1. Anderson, Russell W. *Effects of Neuro-Psychological Techniques on Reading Achievement.* Greeley: Colorado State College, 1965.

2. Baldwin, Ruth R., and Kenny, Thomas J. "Medical Treatment of Behavior Disorders." In *Learning Disorders,* Volume 2, edited by Jerome Hellmuth, pp. 313-25. Seattle: Special Child Publications, 1966.

3. Barsch, Ray H. "Six Factors in Learning," *Learning Disorders,* Volume 1, edited by Jerome Hellmuth, 323-43. Seattle: Special Child Publications, 1965.

4. Bateman, Barbara. "An Educator's View of a Diagnostic Approach to Learning Disorders." *Learning Disorders,* Volume 1, edited by Jerome Hellmuth, pp. 219-37. Seattle: Special Child Publications, 1965.

5. Calvert, James J., and Cromes, George F. "Oculomotor Spasms in Handicapped Readers." *Reading Teacher* 20 (December 1966): 231-36.

6. Cronbach, Lee J. *Educational Psychology,* 2nd ed. New York: Harcourt, Brace and World, 1963.

7. Daniels, J. C. "Children with Reading Difficulties." *Slow Learning Child* 13 (March 1967): 138-43.

8. Delacato, Carl H. *The Diagnosis and Treatment of Speech and Reading Problems.* Springfield, Illinois: Charles C. Thomas, 1963.

9. _____. *Neurological Organization and Reading.* Springfield, Illinois: Charles C. Thomas, 1966.

10. _____. *Treatment and Prevention of Reading Problems.* Springfield, Illinois: Charles C. Thomas, 1959.

11. Dunning, Jack D., and Kephart, Newell C. "Motor Generalization in Space and Time." In *Learning Disorders,* Volume 1, edited by Jerome Hellmuth, pp. 77-121. Seattle: Special Child Publications, 1965.

12. Feldmann, Shirley C., and Deutsch, Cynthia P. *A Study of the Effectiveness of Training for Retarded Readers in the Auditory Perceptual Skills Underlying Reading.* U.S. Office of Education Title VII Project No. 1127. New York: Institute of Developmental Studies, Department of Psychiatry, New York Medical College, 1965.

13. Frostig, Marianne. "Corrective Reading in the Classroom." *Reading Teacher* 18 (April 1965): 573-80.

14. Frostig, Marianne, and Horne, David "An Approach to the Treatment of Children with Learning Disorders." In *Learning Disorders,* Volume 1, edited by Jerome Hellmuth, pp. 293-305. Seattle: Special Child Publications, 1965.

15. _____. *The Frostig Program for the Development of Visual Perception.* Chicago: Follett, 1964.

16. Frostig, Marianne; Lefevre, D. W.; and Whittlesey, J. R. B. *The Marianne Frostig Developmental Test of Perception.* Palo Alto, California: Consulting Psychologists Press, 1964.

17. Getman, G. N. "The Visuomotor Complex in the Acquisition of Learning Skills." *In Learning Disorders,* Volume 1, edited by Jerome Hellmuth, pp. 49-76. Seattle: Special Child Publications, 1965, 49-76.

18. Glass, Gene V. and Robbins, Melvyn P. "A Critique of Experiments on the Role of Neurological Organization in Reading Performance." *Reading Research Quarterly* 3 (Fall 1967): 5-52.

19. Harris, Albert J. "A Critical Reaction to: The Nature of Reading Disability." *Journal of Developmental Reading* 3 (1960): 238-49.

20. _____. "Diagnosis and Remedial Instruction in Reading." In *Innovation and Change in Reading.* Sixty-seventh Yearbook, Part II, of the National Society for the Study of Education. Chicago: University of Chicago Press, 1968, 159-94.

21. _____. "Lateral Dominance, Directional Confusion, and Reading Disability." *Journal of Psychology* 44 (1957): 283-94.

22. Hasman, Karen. "What's All the Shouting About?" *Chicago Daily News,* 2 April 1968, p. 25.

23. Kephart, Newell C. *The Slow Learner in the Classroom,* 2d ed. Columbus, Ohio: Charles E. Merrill Publishing Co., 1971.

24. Kirk, Samuel A. and McCarthy, James J. "The Illinois Test of Psycholinguistic Abilities: An Approach to Differential Diagnosis." *American Journal of Mental Deficiency* 66 (November 1961): 399-412.

25. Krippner, Stanley. "Etiological Factors in Reading Disability of the Academically Talented in Comparison to Pupils of Average and Slow-Learning Ability." *Journal of Educational Research* 61 (February 1968): 275-79.

26. LaPray, Margaret and Ross, Ramon. "Auditory and Visual Perceptual Training." in *Vistas in Reading,* Proceedings of the International Reading Association, Volume 2, Part 1, 1966 (Copyright 1967), edited by Allen Figurel, pp. 530-32.

27. McCormick, Clarence C. et al. *Improvement in Reading Achievement through Perceptual-Motor Training.* Chicago: Reading Research Foundation, July 1967. Mimeographed.

28. McCormick, Clarence C.; Schnobrich, Janice N.; and Footlick, S. Willard. *The Effect of Perceptual-Motor Training on Reading Achievement.* Chicago: Reading Research Foundation, Inc., July 1967. Mimeographed.

29. McDonald, Arthur S. "The Placebo Response in Reading Research." *New Developments in Programs and Procedures for College-Adult Reading.* Twelfth Yearbook of the National Reading Conference 12 (1963): 220-29.

30. Morris, Joyce M. *Standards and Progress in Reading.* London: National Foundation for Educational Research in England and Wales, 1966.

31. Olson, Arthur V. "Relation of Achievement Test Scores and Specific Reading Abilities to the Frostig Developmental Tests of Visual Perception." *Perceptual and Motor Skills* 22 (1966): 179-84.

32. _____. "School Achievement, Reading Ability, and Specific Visual Perception Skills in the Third Grade." *Reading Teacher* 19 (April 1966): 490-92.

33. *Perceptual-Motor Training: A Program of Exercises Designed to Effect Remediation for Disorders Involving Underachievement, Learning Disabilities, Perceptual Handicaps, Minimal Brain Damage, Mental Retardation.* Chicago: Reading Research Foundation, 3849 West Devon, 1967.

34. Roach, Eugene G. "Evaluation of An Experimental Program of Perceptual Motor Training with Slow Readers." In *Vistas in Reading,* Proceedings of the International Reading Association, Vol. 11, Part 1, 1966 (Copyright 1967), edited by J. Allen Figurel, pp. 446-50.

35. Robbins, Melvyn P. "Creeping, Laterality, and Reading." *Academic Therapy Quarterly* 1 (1966): 200-06.

36. Robbins, Melvyn P. "The Delacato Interpretation of Neurological Organization." *Reading Research Quarterly* 1 (Spring 1966): 57-78.

37. Rosen, Carl L. "An Experimental Study of Visual Perceptual Training and Reading Achievement in First Grade." *Perceptual and Motor Skills* 22 (1966): 979-86.

38. Rutherford, William L. "Perceptual-Motor Training and Readiness." *Reading and Inquiry,* Proceedings of the International Reading Association, Vol. 10, 1965, edited by J. Allen Figurel, pp. 194-96.

39. Silver, Archie A. and Hagin, Rosa A. *Specific Reading Disability: An Approach to Diagnosis and Treatment.* New York: Department of Neurology and Psychiatry, New York University Bellevue Medical Center, 1966. Mimeographed.

40. Silver, Archie A.; Hagin, Rosa A; and Hersh, Marilyn F. *Specific Reading Disability: Teaching through Stimulation of Deficit Perceptual Areas.* New York: Department of Neurology and Psychiatry, New York University Bellevue Medical Center, 1965. Mimeographed.

41. Smith, Donald E. P., and Carrigan, Patricia M. *The Nature of Reading Disability.* New York: Harcourt, Brace and World, 1959.

42. Staiger, Ralph C. "Medicine for Reading Improvement." *Journal of Developmental Reading* 5 (Autumn 1961): 48-51.

43. Stephens, W. E., Cunningham, E.; and Stigler, B. J. "Reading Readiness and Eye-Hand Preference Patterns in First-Grade Children." *Exceptional Children* 30 (March 1967): 481-88.

44. Valusek, John E. *The Effect of Drugs on Retarded Readers in a State Mental Hospital.* Unpublished doctoral dissertation, University of Michigan, 1963.

45. Weener, Paul; Barritt, Loren S.; and Semmel, Melvyn I. "A Critical Evaluation of the Illinois Test of Psycholinguistic Abilities." *Exceptional Children* 30 (February 1967): 377-80.

46. Yarborough, Betty H. "A Study of the Effectiveness of the Leavell Language-Development Service in Improving the Silent Reading Ability and Other Language Skills of Persons with Mixed Dominance." Unpublished doctoral dissertation, University of Virginia, 1964.

7

Remedial Activities in Readiness Skills

Our concept of readiness for reading has changed over the past five decades. Is readiness a separate entity from reading or can reading opportunities be incorporated within a readiness program? Durkin presents an overview of these areas.

READING READINESS

Dolores Durkin

Dolores Durkin is a Professor of Education at the University of Illinois, College of Education, Urbana, Illinois

To understand how "reading readiness" got into professional vocabularies and then into the school curriculum, it is necessary to go back to the 1920s. That decade is relevant because it was characterized by the beginning of so-called "scientific" measurements of human behavior. Among the results of what became almost a craze to measure everything was the appearance of school surveys. Of special relevance to reading readiness is a finding common to many of the survey reports which indicated that large numbers of children

From *The Reading Teacher* vol. 23, no. 6 (March 1970): 528-34, 564. Reprinted with permission of the International Reading Association and Dolores Durkin.

were failing first grade, most often because of insufficient achievement in reading.

Within a short time—this was still the 1920s—concern about the finding became as widespread as the finding itself, for at least two reasons. Successful teaching of reading, then as now, was considered uniquely important among elementary school responsibilities. In addition, the failures that were occurring resulted in first-grade classrooms populated by many "over age" children. Behavior problems blossomed, and so did concern about why first graders were having difficulty learning to read.

Logically, it would seem, a study of reading problems—whether carried on in the 1920s or now—would look to such multiple and common sense causes as overly large classes, inappropriate materials, inadequate teacher preparation, lack of motivation on the part of the children, and so on. However, in the study of beginning reading problems that went on in the 1920s and 1930s, the factor given singular attention is to be found in a pronouncement appearing with great frequency in the professional literature of that period: First graders are having difficulty learning to read because they were not ready when the instruction started. Why beginning reading problems were attributed so exclusively to a lack of readiness and, secondly, why delaying instruction was soon proposed as *the* solution, can be understood only when the psychological setting of the 1920s and 1930s is brought into focus.

Described briefly, and therefore incompletely, the 1920s and 1930s was a period in which the ideas of Arnold Gesell dominated. As a physician, Gesell was especially interested in children's physical and motor development. Resulting from his work and his prolific writing about it came the notion that these aspects of development "unfold in stages." Or, to put it another way, a young child grows and develops as a result of maturation, not learning. Acceptance of this point of view would suggest that if a child is unable to perform some particular motor task—crawling, for example—it is because he has not yet reached that point or stage of development which allows him to crawl. Thus, he is unready. The solution? According to Gesell and his disciples it was to let time pass. That is, let additional maturity occur and then the child will be ready and he will be crawling.

INTELLECTUAL SKILLS MERGED WITH MOTOR SKILLS

Had Gesell and his followers confined their descriptions and explanations to motor skills, there would be little reason to quarrel with them because much about a child's physical development does depend upon maturation and, therefore, the passing of time. However, this is not what happened. Instead, prominent educators were soon using Gesell's explanation of motor skills to explain the development of intellectual skills. In fact, nowhere was this highly questionable merger more apparent than in the field of reading.

When, in the 1920s, school surveys revealed that children were failing first grade because of insufficient achievement in reading, the one "explanation" to get attention was that these first graders had problems because they were not ready when school instruction began. The solution? Still following the Gesell school of thought about motor development, some very influential educators were soon advocating that reading instruction be postponed so that the passing of additional time would insure a readiness for it. And so was born the doctrine of postponement. This doctrine fostered the notion that a. getting children ready to read and b. teaching them to read occur at distinctly different times in the school curriculum.

Such a notion is reflected, of course, in the long entrenched practice of having a readiness program followed by a reading program. In fact, and not many years ago, it was very common to find the first six or eight weeks of first grade given over to the goal of "readiness." This practice apparently assumed that a child could be "unready" for reading on, for example, Friday of the sixth week of school but quite "ready" on Monday of the seventh week. "What a week-end!" is one possible reaction to such an assumption. A less sarcastic and certainly more helpful response, however, is to think more carefully about what it means to help a child get ready to read and, secondly, what it means to teach him to read.

TRADITIONAL INTERPRETATION OF READING READINESS

Readiness—whether applied to reading or some other kind of learning—is an unquestionably valid psychological concept with permanent relevance. However, what is considerably less permanent and always open to question is how it is interpreted. Applied to reading, the concept of readiness was for a long time interpreted to mean that children become ready as a result of maturation. Or, to phrase this traditional interpretation somewhat differently, readiness for learning to read was thought to constitute a certain maturational stage in the child's development. Because this interpretation came into existence at a time when great efforts were being made to be objective and quantitatively precise about every description of behavior —these were the decades of the 1920s and 1930s—it was very natural for educators of that period to seek out a quantitative and precise description of the stage of development which they believed constituted readiness for reading. The end result was the proclamation that a mental age of about 6.5 years defines readiness.

How seriously this proclamation was taken by the man who had much to do with promoting it can be seen in a 1936 article. It was written by Carleton Washburne, then superintendent of the Winnetka, Illinois public schools and, more importantly, a leader of the Progressive Education Movement. In the article Washburne (1936, p. 127) noted:

> Nowadays each first grade teacher in Winnetka has a chart showing when each of her children will be mentally six-and-a-half, and is careful to avoid any effort to get a child to read before he has reached this stage of mental growth.

Washburne's comments are useful now because, in capsule form, they portray the once widely held belief that *getting* ready to read and *being* ready occur at completely separate points on some time line. It was just such a belief, of course, that led to the practice of having a readiness program at one point in the child's school life and a reading program at some later date.

ANOTHER INTERPRETATION

With the initial or traditional interpretation, readiness was viewed as a product; specifically, a product of maturation. Viewing readiness as a product is very defensible, but current knowledge indicates that it is the product of both maturation *and* learning. Within such a framework, readiness can be defined as various combinations of abilities which result from, or are the product of, nature and nurture interacting with each other.

A view of readiness which sees it as a product is defensible; yet, to view it only as a product is incomplete. What must be added is that dimension which brings into focus a relationship, a relationship between a child's particular abilities and the kind of learning opportunities made available to him. Within this framework readiness is still a product, but a product in relation to a given set of circumstances. Or, to use another's words, readiness is "the adequacy of existing capacity in relation to the demands of a given learning task" (Ausubel, 1959, p. 147).

This interpretation, if accepted, offers three important reminders to educators:

1. Readiness is not one thing. In fact, the variety of abilities, both in kind and amount, which add up to readiness suggests that a more accurately descriptive term would be "readinesses"—awkward, to be sure, but also accurate.
2. Although what makes one child ready for reading might be different from what makes another ready, *both* are ready because of the interplay of nature and nurture. This is a recognition that children are ready because of hereditary and maturational factors, but also because of the learning opportunities in their particular environment.
3. Because readiness depends not only upon a child's abilities but also upon the kind of learning opportunities made available to him, it is possible for a child to be ready when one type of reading program is offered, but unready when other kinds are available.

This dependence of readiness upon the type and quality of instruction that will be offered also has some implications for assessing a child's readiness. What it highlights right away, for example, is the inadequacy of any attempt to assess it apart from the kind of reading instruction that will be available. In positive terms the implication is: If readiness is "the adequacy of existing capacity in relation to the demands of a given learning task," then the best and even only way to assess a child's readiness for reading is to give him varied opportunities to begin to read.

PROVIDING READING OPPORTUNITIES

When should these learning opportunities be offered? In responding to such a query, it is of initial importance to remember that the practice of starting children to read in first grade and at the age of six is the result of convention, not of any evidence that there is something about six-year-old children which makes this a particularly productive time to start teaching reading. With such a reminder in the background, it seems appropriate to suggest—but with a little reservation—that since kindergarten is the first level of public school education now offered, kindergarten is the time to learn about children's readiness by giving them varied and interesting opportunities to begin to read.

The "little reservation" is rooted in the knowledge that some kindergartens are now bombarding children with whole-class, drill-oriented instruction. Knowing that this unfortunate practice is spreading, it seems wise to repeat the recommendation: Give kindergarten children *varied* and *interesting opportunities* to begin to read.

The wording for such a recommendation was carefully selected. For example, the emphasis on "opportunities" is there because it implies that with some children in some kindergartens the opportunities might not "take." Acceptance of this is of basic importance. It frees the kindergarten teacher from thinking that every child *must* learn to read and so, in turn, also frees her from feeling any need "to put the pressure on." Today, unfortunately, some kindergarten teachers *are* "putting the pressure on" with their whole-class use of drill and workbooks. Predictably, in the years to come, there will be a reaction against this—a reaction which is not likely to make a distinction between a timing that might be just right, and a methodology that is all wrong.

The need for *varied* opportunities is emphasized because the easiest way to become a reader is probably different for different children. Consequently the "varied" refers to opportunities to learn to print and spell and, too, opportunities to begin to learn about letters and the sounds they record. The end result of such varied efforts would be insight into the readiness of the children and, too, very specific information about the way into reading that seems easiest for each child. Of course, another result is that some of these kindergarten children would be reading.

Probably the best way to clarify "kindergarten opportunities to learn to read" is to describe some. Through these few examples it should become apparent that readiness instruction and reading instruction are not always two different things.

In the kindergarten, because five-year-olds love nobody quite as much as they love themselves, reading opportunities of a whole-word identification type might begin with attention to the children's names. Since attendance-taking is a daily routine, it could also become a source of daily "practice" as children tuck their names into a card holder when they arrive and, later, read all the name cards —at first with much assistance from the teacher—to find out who is present and who is absent. Other opportunities to learn to read other words of interest—days of the week, months of the year, and so on —could be provided too. How the children respond to such opportunities and what they learn from them will offer a teacher much information about their readiness to read *via,* in this case, a whole-word approach.

Art projects can often be a vehicle for assessments because, in this case, they provide occasions for children to learn to print labels or even short captions for their pictures. Such activities have direct relevance for readiness assessment because some young children who have no interest in reading *per se* are found to be very interested in printing (Durkin, 1966). With this in mind, the kindergarten teacher who offers opportunities to learn to print is providing herself with the opportunity to identify children whose way into beginning reading ought to be through writing and spelling. In addition, however, she is also becoming aware of other children for whom the motor skill of writing is a formidable task.

Because many young children seem to enjoy playing with the sounds of language, it also makes sense to provide kindergarten opportunities for learning about letters and the sounds they record. For example, it might happen that the word *magnet* takes on special interest. Perhaps it was first introduced in a story, and then simple experiments were done to show magnets, to demonstrate magnetism, and so on. The end result is that the word *magnet* is written many times for the children to see and thus—to learn to read. With *magnet* written on the chalkboard, a teacher might one day say to the children, "You know some other words that start with the same letter. Who knows the name of this letter? . . . Who remembers some other words that start with an *m?*" Quickly, children like Martha and Michael proudly offer their names as examples. And then another child recalls the word *Monday.*

The end result is a list of *m* words, but also the teacher's opportunity to introduce letter-sound associations. In this case, for instance, the teacher might read the list, point out again that all the words begin with *m,* then repeat the words—this time asking the children to try to hear how they all begin with the same sound. A natural follow-up question would be, "Can you think of some other words that begin with the sound that you hear at the beginning of these words? Listen. I'll say them again and then maybe you can think of other words that begin with the same sound."

As a result of this plus other instances of attention to letters and sounds, a teacher has the chance to learn which children are unable to name letters and, what will be more common, which are unable to hear initial sounds in words. At the same time, however, she is also learning that other children know the names of many letters and even are successful in hearing and distinguishing among beginning sounds.

These very few illustrations of "kindergarten opportunities to learn to read" hardly describe a total program. However, they ought to be sufficient to exemplify the main points suggested. They have illustrated, for example, that the assessment of readiness and the teaching of reading can result from the very same situation. Thus, the teacher's use of the children's names in attendance-taking was a chance for her to learn about their readiness to read whole words. In addition, though, for the children who were in fact "ready" it was the start of their learning to read—in this instance, children's names.

The few examples also ought to have shown that a single teaching procedure will be readiness instruction for some children, but reading instruction for others. For instance, the use that was made of the word *magnet* could result in beginning learning in phonics for some. Yet, for other less ready children, the teacher's questions about a particular group of words beginning with *m* would only be the first step in a series of steps which will finally result—perhaps during kindergarten—in the ability to hear and distinguish among initial sounds in words. For these latter children, the teacher was carrying on a type of readiness instruction. However, with the children who were very ready to grasp the connection between *m* and a certain sound, reading instruction was taking place.

In summary, then, three points seem particularly important:

1. Readiness for reading should not be viewed as comprising a single collection of abilities which will be the same for all children. Actually, what makes one child ready might be quite different from what makes another ready.
2. Whether or not a child *is* ready depends upon his particular abilities, but also upon the reading instruction that will be offered. This type of dependence means that readiness can be assessed only when a child is given varied opportunities to learn to read.
3. What a child is able to learn as a result of these opportunities offers very specific information about his readiness. With some children, a particular opportunity will result in reading ability and so, quite obviously, these children were ready. With others, however, the same opportunity will not "take," and so for them it is a type of readiness instruction. That the same teaching procedure can be reading instruction for some children and readiness instruction for others suggests serious flaws in school practices which seem to go out of their way to create an artificial separation between a readiness program and a reading program. A much more defensible way of working is to view readiness instruction as reading instruction in its early stages.

Acceptance of these views about readiness also entails acceptance of a variety of challenges for educators. Probably the major one has to do with the need for greater flexibility in the way schools handle beginning reading. Within the context of this view of readiness, for instance, there would be no room for thinking that there is one best age for starting reading; no room for thinking there is one best methodology and one best set of materials. Nor, certainly, is there a place for thinking that all children must accomplish the same learning at the same time.

Another and briefer way of stating these challenges is to insert the reminder that the important question for educators is not, "Are these children ready to learn to read?" but, rather, "Are we ready to teach them at a time, at a pace, and in a way that is just right for each child?"

REFERENCES

Ausubel, D. P. "Viewpoints from Related Disciplines: Human Growth and Development." *Teachers College Record* 60 (1959): 245-54.

Durkin, Dolores. *Children Who Read Early.* New York: Teachers College Press, Columbia University, 1966.

Washburne, C. "Ripeness." *Progressive Education* 13 (1936): 125-30.

Various authorities have suggested different approaches to remedial instruction. Should remediation have as its main thrust the rebuilding of basic schemata, or should the remedial program concentrate on intensive instruction beginning with presenting behaviors? Cohen provides one answer to this question.

CAUSE VS. TREATMENT IN READING ACHIEVEMENT

S. Alan Cohen

> *This is a paper written in response to critiques offered on Dr. Cohen's original article published in this journal in October, 1969. In this paper, Dr. Cohen further explains his position on visuo-motor development and reading achievement and includes responses to some of the rebuttals.*

Let us continue:

1. Learning disability patterns as measured on clinic tests of disadvantaged retarded readers do not differ markedly from the learning disability patterns of middle-class children who are retarded readers (Cohen, 1969, 1966). (Specifically for Dr. Solan.)
2. Perceptual dysfunctions as well as other psychophysical, psychosocial, psychodynamic and psycholinguistic factors are etiologically significant in reading retardation. Of course these factors are related to learning to read. This was not the issue I raised. I did not question the existence of the relationships between various visuo-perceptual factors and learning. I raised issues about the *quality* and about the practical implications of those relationships.
3. The etiology of a behavioral condition is usually irrelevant to its treatment except under two conditions:

From the *Journal of Learning Disabilities* vol. 3, no. 3 (March 1970): 43-46. Reprinted with permission of the Journal of Learning Disabilities and S. Alan Cohen.

a. When the etiology is physiological or medical, as in endocrine imbalance or in neurological impairments that generate neurological deterioration. This does not include NI without deterioration, in which case etiology is still irrelevant to treating the reading retardation.
b. When the researcher or practitioner is interested in *prevention*. Obviously, etiological factors are crucial to prevention of a condition that does not yet exist.

We call this the EBD or "Etiology-Be-Damned" point of view, explained in more detail in a forthcoming book by Dr. Barbara Bateman (Cohen, 1970a). Once the learning disability exists, and it is a nonmedical anomaly, etiology does not add an iota to the treatment. The presenting behaviors and related present conditions must determine the treatment. A *differential diagnosis* which differentiates the etiology is, in my view, useless. On the other hand, a differential diagnosis that "differentiates" the behaviors that must be learned and the present conditions that must be manipulated to modify behavior is most valuable.

4. "Schemata" that underlie cognitive processes are probably results of the genotype's interaction with its environment. Surely, Piaget has given us enough evidence to accept this. Especially at the early stages of development, perceptual and perceptual-motor experiences help develop "mind structures" underlying higher cortical processes such as reading (Hunt, 1961). But the school child is a developed psychophysical organism *not* devoid of underlying structures. Except for extreme cases who are obviously deficient in basic "schemata"—so deficient that we cannot even get them to sit at a desk—most learning disability cases do have enough "schemata" to learn to read.
5. Attempts to remediate *existing* problems in reading by restructuring these "schemata" will bear little payoff in reading (Jacobs, 1969; Arciszewski, 1967). Why? Simply because at this stage of development, for most children the further the independent or experimental variable (such as visuo-perceptual development) moves operationally from the dependent variable (reading), the less the measurable payoff in reading. An independent variable theoretically related to a dependent variable, but operationally far removed from that dependent variable, may have little observable influence upon the dependent variable; but it still may be related to it. We have fifty years of behavioral research to indicate this. Research-

ers know that given two experimental treatments, the one operationally closer to the dependent variable will yield the greater influence over that dependent variable. For example, Bannatyne intercorrelated various measurements of visuo-motor functioning and generated coefficients to the order of .50 to .70 (Bannatyne, 1969). These measurements are operationally close. But when he looks for a correlation between a visuo-motor variable and school-related task, the best he could find was an r of .39 with spelling. In this case, the operations are *not* close. Over thirty-five years ago one researcher found a .58 correlation between word pronunciation and spelling (Hartmann, 1931). Since then, researchers have found strong links between various aspects of visual and auditory memory and discrimination of letters, words, and sounds with spelling. If we want to guess at what kind of treatment would most likely give us a measurable increase in spelling, would we try visuo-motor training, or phonics instruction, or training in visual and auditory discrimination of letters and words? Obviously, the latter two are operationally closer to the dependent variable and are more likely to generate directly observable results in spelling. This does not deny Bannatyne's theory that the underlying schemata to the behaviors we call spelling may involve visuo-motor factors. The question is that for children who are *now* poor spellers, which treatment is most likely to pay off? The issue I raise is simply this: We have independent variables operationally close to the dependent variable (reading). These independent variables influence, in an observable and measurable manner, the dependent variable (reading). The independent variable happens to be intensive instruction. When dealing with children *currently* underachieving, why spend so much time and energy promoting the use of independent variables operationally far removed from the payoff?

6. Therefore, in modifying existing behaviors, manipulating behaviors that are operationally closer to the dependent variable will give us more pay-off? But in preventing certain conditions from developing, manipulating underlying schemata—such as visuo-motor learning—*may* be crucial. I emphasize *may,* for Dr. Solan appears to have misinterpreted the research on underlying schemata. Most of that research is what we call *ex post facto* design, not experimental design (Kurlinger, 1965). This is true of the studies Dr. Solan notes as well as others he might have cited (Hertzig, 1969; Birch, 1964; Pasamanick, 1960, 1946; Knobloch, 1953, 1956).

These studies show relationships, not cause and effect links. The independent variables in those studies have very obvious and important overlaps with intervening variables, and the authors of those studies are the first to understand, recognize, and communicate this. Those intervening variables may carry more weight in the causal chain.

7. Drs. Frostig and Solan may have confused teaching with learning. As I point out elsewhere (Cohen, 1970b), teaching is one thing—learning is another. Our analysis of underachievers indicates that they have not *learned* certain behaviors. For example, very retarded readers often have trouble discriminating letters. That a teacher may have exposed these children to letters is not the same thing as thorough, sequential instruction using carefully controlled contingencies and finely programmed stimuli. Too many professionals assume that "good" teachers have taught the retarded reader and the child still has not learned. They conclude, therefore, that the factor of pedagogy as an independent variable has been eliminated and that the child cannot read because something is wrong with him. Literally, this statement carries an element of truth, but pedagogically it is absurd. Our eight-dimension behavioral analysis of classroom learning in "good" teachers' classrooms indicates that very little learning may be occurring in most classrooms, and that what differentiates the successful from the unsuccessful readers is that the former learn to read in spite of this poor instruction (Cohen, 1970b). Under these conditions of poor instruction in general, the poor readers are unsuccessful because of the negative etiological conditions that I damned earlier in this paper. We may be able to assist these poor readers by painfully long-term rebuilding of basic schemata just as we may, theoretically, treat every case of neurosis by rebuilding the ego and superego. On the other hand, we can remediate them more quickly by intensive instruction beginning with their presenting behaviors. And the latter is my suggestion. For those who argue that my point of view leads to teaching splinter skills, I suggest that all we can ever hope to be is the fascinating interactions of our splinter skills.

CONCLUSIONS

I strongly disagree with Dr. Frostig's suggestion (Frostig, 1969) that "a more fruitful approach" is to explore underlying schemata's relationships to "task processes" (reading), if that relationship is gleaned from *ex post facto* research designs. If by "relationship" she suggests experimental research designs, then I would agree with her, pointing out again that previous experimental designs indicate that the closer the independent variable is to the dependent variable, the better the results.

Finally, may I point out to my colleagues working in the area of perception that I have not denied the validity of their "schemata"; my own personal and professional ego has had a vested interest in such theories (Cohen, 1965). But may I also remind them, as Skinner tried to remind us decades ago, that observable, specific operations can influence dependent variables, and that in the real world of underachieving children, we do not need to invent theories to engineer behaviors in children.

REFERENCES

Arciszewski, R. A. "The Frostig Approach: A Description of the Frostig Program." In *Perception and Reading,* p. 38. New Brunswick, New Jersey: Reading Center, Rutgers University, The State University, Extension Division, March, 1967.

Bannatyne, A. D. "A Comparison of Visuo-Spatial and Visuo-Motor Memory for Design and Their Relationship to Other Sensori-Motor Psycholinguistic Variables." *Journal of Learning Disabilities* vol. 2, no. 9 (September 1969): 451.

Birch, H., and Belmont, L. "Auditory-Visual Integration in Normal and Retarded Readers." *American Journal of Orthopsychiatry* 34 (1964): 852-61.

Cohen, S. Alan. "Dyspedagogia as a Cause of Reading Retardation: Definition and Treatment." In *Learning Disorders,* Volume 4, edited by Barbara Bateman. Seattle, Washington: Special Child Publications, 1970.

_____. "Some Learning Disabilities of Socially Disadvantaged Puerto Rican and Negro Children." *Academic Therapy Quarterly* vol. 2, no. 1 (Fall 1966): 37-41, 52.

_____. "A Study of Relationships among Measurements of Reading, Intelligence, and Vision in Socially Disadvantaged Junior High School Children." Unpublished doctoral dissertation, Boston University, 1965.

_____. "The Taxonomy of Instructional Treatments in Reading: Its Uses and Its Applications as a Classroom Analysis Scheme." New York: Reading and Language Arts Center, Graduate School, Yeshiva University, 1970. Available in mimeograph.

_____. *Teach Them All to Read: Theory, Methods, and Materials for Teaching the Disadvantaged.* New York: Random House, 1969, Chapter 4.

Frostig, M., and Maslow, P. "Reading, Developmental Abilities, and the Problem of Match." *Journal of Learning Disabilities* vol. 2, no. 11 (November 1969): 25.

Hartmann, G. W. "The Relative Influence of Visual and Auditory Factors in Spelling Ability." *Journal of Educational Psychology* 22 (December 1931): 371-81.

Hertzig, Bortner E., and Birch, H. "Neurological Findings in Children Educationally Designated as 'Brain Damaged.' " *American Journal of Orthopsychiatry* vol. 39, no. 3 (April 1969): 437.

Hunt, J. McV. *Intelligence and Experience.* New York: Ronald Press, 1961.

Jacobs, J.; Wirthlin, L. D.; and Miller, C. B. "A Follow-up Evaluation of the Frostig Visual Perceptual Training Program." *Educational Leadership* (November 1969): 169-75.

Kerlinger, F. N. *Foundation of Behavioral Research.* New York: Holt, Rinehart, and Winston, 1965, Chapter 20.

Knobloch, H.; Rider, R. V.; Pasamanick, B. A.; and Harper, P. A. "The Neuropsychiatric Sequelae of Prematurity: A Longitudinal Study." *Journal of the American Medical Association* (1956): 581-85.

Knobloch, H., and Pasamanick, B. A. "Further Observations on the Behavioral Development of Negro Infants." *Journal of Genetic Psychology* (1953): 137-57.

Pasamanick, B. "A Comparative Study of the Behavioral Development of Negro Infants." *Journal of Genetic Psychology* (1946): 3-44.

Pasamanick, B., and Knobloch, H. "Brain Damage and Reproductive Causality." American Journal of Orthopsychiatry (April 1960): 298-305.

8

Remedial Activities for Vocabulary Skills

Utilization of the language experience approach for the teaching of reading has increased. Upon what rationale can its implementation be defended? Hall supplies a linguistic rationale.

LINGUISTICALLY SPEAKING, WHY LANGUAGE EXPERIENCE?

MaryAnne Hall

MaryAnne Hall is an associate professor in the University of Maryland's Department of Early Childhood-Elementary Education and an officer in IRA's Language Experience interest group. Not content simply to list benefits, she presents seven "statements of linguistic rationale" for using this well-known approach with beginning readers.

The language experience approach has increasingly been employed for initial reading instruction in the last decade. In recent years, there has been growing interest in the implications of linguistic

From *The Reading Teacher* vol. 25, no. 4 (January 1972): 228-31. Reprinted by permission of MaryAnne Hall and the International Reading Association.

study for the teaching of reading. The term "linguistics" as related to reading instruction often signifies a beginning approach based on phoneme-grapheme correspondence through the presentation of a carefully controled vocabulary illustrating selected spelling patterns. However, linguistics is used here with a broader application. Since reading is communication through written language, all reading, therefore, is linguistic. Knowledge about language supplied by linguists should lead to reading instruction based on accurate information about the reading process.

The relationship of reading to spoken language is basic to a linguistic definition of reading. This relationship is also basic to teaching reading through the language experience approach. Seven statements of the linguistic rationale for the language experience approach are expressed below in terms of the beginning reader.

The beginning reader must be taught to view reading as a communication process: Language experience reading is communication-centered. Attention is on communication through the medium of print just as in speaking and listening the emphasis is on communication through the medium of speech. In beginning reading, children should feel a need to communicate naturally through print just as before learning to read they had felt the need to communicate through speech. A creative and competent teacher must provide the stimuli and opportunities for children to communicate in reading and writing.

The content of personally composed stories involves concepts within the scope of children's background knowledge and interests. Communication is present as children react while discussing their ideas, as they write or watch the teacher write those ideas, and as they then read their ideas. Comprehension is present since children do understand that which they first wrote.

The beginning reader is a user of language (Goodman, 1969): The spoken language which the child possesses is his greatest asset for learning written language. The normal child from an adequate home environment has mastered the patterns of his native language by the time of school entrance. This is not to overlook the fact that his linguistic facility is by no means complete. He has much to absorb in language flexibility and elaboration; still, he has more than sufficient linguistic ability to learn to read.

In discussions of reading readiness, great attention has been given to the experience background of children, and less to their language background. When attention has been given to language factors, usually that attention has been to the extent of vocabulary and general language facility in expressing and understanding spoken language instead of how this facility operates in learning to read. The child who learned spoken language in the preschool years displayed an amazing feat of linguistic performance. We should make it possible for him to learn to read with equal ease and to draw upon his existing linguistic background in doing so.

The beginning reader should understand the reading process as one of consciously relating print to oral language: As the beginning reader works with print he changes the unfamiliar graphic symbols to familiar oral language. Goodman (1968) defines reading as the processing of language information in order to reconstruct a message from print.

In the language experience approach the child finds translating print into speech greatly simplified since he is reading that which he first said. The message is easily reconstructed when the reader is also the author. In the beginning stages reading instruction must be geared to ensure success for the learner. The ease with which children can read their language should be capitalized on in language experience instruction.

Downing (1969) reports in studies of five and six year olds' views of reading that their conceptions of language are different from those of their teachers. Terminology such as "word," "sentence," "sound," and "letter" was unclear to the children in his research. He comments on the need to provide ". . . language experiences and activities which a. *orient* children correctly to the true purposes of reading and writing, and b. enable children's natural thinking processes to *generate understanding* of the technical concepts of language."

The beginning reader should incorporate the learning of writing with the learning of reading: Relating the written language code to the spoken code was discussed earlier as the task of the beginning reader. Learning the written code involves decoding—going from print to speech—and encoding—going from speech to print. In the language experience approach, writing is a natural corollary of reading as a child first watches the recording of thought he has dictated and as he progresses gradually to writing independently.

The integration of decoding and encoding should provide reinforcement in both processes. In studies of preschool readers, Durkin (1970) reported that interest in writing often preceded interest in reading. Dykstra (1968) reported in the National First Grade Studies that a writing component added to reading programs enhanced achievement in reading.

The beginning reader should learn to read with materials written in his language patterns: The language experience approach does use materials written with the language of the reader for whom they are intended. Reading materials should always convey meaning to a child in natural language phrasing which sounds right and familiar to him—not necessarily "right" to the ears of a Standard English speaker. For children who do not speak Standard English, the language of standard materials does not match their spoken language. While there are special materials written in nonstandard dialects, these materials are not available to all teachers of nonstandard-speaking children. Also, these materials may not fit all children in a group where they are being used. An often overlooked fact is that the limited preprimer language is also unlike the oral language of a child who does use Standard English.

The point to be remembered here is that the nonstandard speaker is a user of language. The absence of mastery of Standard English need not delay the beginning reading instruction when language experience materials are used. The teaching of oral Standard English will be another part of the total language program.

It is recommended that the teacher record the syntactical patterns of the children as spoken but using standard spelling. For example, if the child says "des" for "desk," the word will be written "desk," but if the child says, "My brother, he . . . ," this pattern will be written. The language communicates, and there is sufficient language to be used for teaching beginning reading.

The beginning reader should learn to read meaningful language units: In language experience reading, children are dealing with thought units from the flow of their speech. They are not dealing with a phoneme-grapheme unit or a word unit, but with a larger piece of language. From the total running flow of speech of others in their environment they learned to talk. The child gradually learned to pick words of very high meaning, "Mommy," "Daddy," "me," and others. From one-word utterances the child progressed to two-word patterns and built his linguistic knowledge from hearing natural speech around him.

In reading from language experience, children learn to read using the meaning-bearing patterns of language. They will be exposed to reading material which is not controled in vocabulary and which does not distort language in an effort to limit vocabulary or to emphasize phoneme-grapheme relationships. They gradually acquire a reading vocabulary by identifying words from stories which represent the natural flow of written language. Perhaps with the first experience story, children learn to read one story, perhaps two or three from the next one, and so on until their word banks represent a respectable stock of known words. These words were presented and learned, not in isolation, but in meaningful sentence and story units.

The beginning reader should learn to read orally with smooth, fluent, natural expression: The language experience approach provides oral reading situations in which children can truly "make it sound like someone talking." In the language experience approach, word-by-word emphasis in oral reading should not be permitted to occur. The teacher's model is important in illustrating fluent natural reading in the first pupil-dictated stories. In their concern that children learn vocabulary, some teachers may tend to distort the reading of experience stories with overemphasis on separate words.

Lefevre (1964) maintains that "single words, analyzed and spoken in isolation, assume the intonation contours of whole utterances. Single words thus lose the characteristic pitch and stress they normally carry in the larger constructions that comprise the flow of speech and bear meaning." He emphasizes that the sentence is the minimal unit of meaning, and that children should develop "sentence sense" in reading. In the language experience way of learning to read, the beginner does learn to supply the "melodies of speech" as he reads.

The relationship of oral and written language can also be shown as punctuation signals are pointed out incidentally, with emphasis on function and meaning. For example, after a number of experience stories have been written the teacher may casually say, "This is the end of your idea—so we put a period. The next word goes with the next idea so we start this part with a capital letter."

SUMMARY

The linguistic rationale for the language experience approach gives theoretical support to the teacher who is concerned with the implementation of this approach in teaching beginning reading. Language experience reading is truly a linguistically based method since the relationship of oral and written language is the key to teaching children to read through the recording and reading of their spoken language. The beginning reader is a user of language who must relate graphic symbols to the oral language code he already knows. Understanding the process of language communication through languge experience reading should enable the teacher to facilitate the task of learning to read for the beginner through use of relevant material which reflects *his* language. The most important consideration is how language communicates meaning—in language experience reading, *communication is the central focus.*

REFERENCES

Downing, John. "How Children Think about Reading." *The Reading Teacher* 23 (December 1969): 217-30.

Durkin, Dolores. "A Language Arts Program for Pre-First-Grade Children: Two Year Achievement Report." *Reading Research Quarterly* 5 (Summer 1970): 534-65.

Dykstra, Robert. "Summary of the Second-Grade Phase of the Cooperative Research Program in Primary Reading Instruction." *Reading Research Quarterly* 4 (Fall 1968): 49-70.

Goodman, Kenneth S. "Pro-Challenger Answer to 'Is the Linguistic Approach an Improvement in Reading Instruction?'" In *Current Issues in Reading,* conference proceedings of 13th Annual Convention, edited by Nila B. Smith, pp. 268-76. Newark, Delaware: International Reading Association, 1969.

Goodman, Kenneth S. *The Psycholinguistic Nature of the Reading Process.* Detroit: Wayne State University Press, 1968.

Lefevre, Carl A. *Linguistics and the Teaching of Reading.* New York: McGraw-Hall, 1964.

Several studies have been conducted concerning phonic generalizations. Of what value are such generalizations? How reliable are they? Burmeister conducts an interesting review.

USEFULNESS OF PHONIC GENERALIZATIONS

Lou E. Burmeister

Although most educators today favor the teaching of phonic generalizations, very few of them are able to enumerate with any degree of certainty the generalizations which are worthy of being taught. Evidence is beginning to accrue which would make any interested observer question the value of many phonic generalizations which have appeared for years in the literature and teaching materials in the field of reading.

PURPOSE

The purpose of this paper is to report and compare findings of seven recent studies which were designed to investigate scientifically the value of many commonly found phonic, structural analysis, and accent generalizations and in some cases to inductively formulate new generalizations which may prove useful.

STUDIES USED

The studies were reported by Oaks in 1952, Clymer in 1963, Fry in 1964, Bailey in 1965, Emans in 1966, Burmeister in 1966, and Winkley in 1966. All but Fry and Winkley utilized a "utility level" concept in determining the usefulness of generalizations. Fry used a "frequency approach," and Winkley selected useful generalizations "because of their applicability to multisyllabic words" (similar to the

From *The Reading Teacher* vol. 21, no. 4 (January 1968): 349-56. Reprinted with permission of Lou E. Burmeister and the International Reading Association.

utility level concept) "or because of their demonstrated usefulness to children in the identification of unknown multisyllabic words" (1965).

CONTENT OF THE STUDIES

Variations in findings among the studies might be expected because of the following factors:

1. Differences in the types of materials from which the sample words were taken.
2. Differences in the method of selecting the sample words from these materials when the materials are alike.
3. Differences in dictionaries, or phonemic systems, used as "authorities" for accepted pronunciation.
4. Differences in the author's definition of "short" and/or "long" vowel sounds (e.g., Is the unique sound of a vowel before an "r" considered in a separate category? Is a schwa sound considered to be a short vowel? etc.).
5. Differences caused by various ways of determining usefulness.

So that the reader may better understand basic similarities and differences among the studies, the following brief explanation of each study is offered.

Oaks looked at "vowel and vowel combinations which appear in certain basal readers designed for use in the primary grades" (1952, p. 604). She used Webster's *New International Dictionary* (1936).

Fry's frequency count is based on his 300 "Instant Words" (1960) and on comparisons made with findings by Moore (1951), Cordts (1925), Black (1961), and Kottmeyer (1954). He looked at phonic rules which were formulated from his own experiences in a reading clinic situation. The phonemic system which he used "was taken from Moore, which was based on work by Bloomfield. However, the rules make several departures from their system, most notable of which is the *Y* rule which states that *Y* on the end of a word containing another vowel makes a long *E* sound as opposed to the short *I* sound as is contended by most dictionaries" (1964, p. 759).

Clymer (1963) reported the utility levels of forty-five phonic generalizations found in grades one to three in four basal series. He used the combined vocabularies of these three levels from the four series plus the words from the Gates Reading Vocabulary for the

Primary Grades to determine the percent of utility of these generalizations. Webster's *New Collegiate Dictionary* was used.

Bailey's (1965) and Emans' (1966) studies were partial replications of Clymer's study. Both Bailey and Emans studied the same forty-five generalizations as Clymer. Bailey used as her source of words the entire vocabularies of all textbooks, Grades 1 through 6, of eight basal reading series: "Only words that appeared in two or more of the eight series were included, and place names, proper names, and foreign words were excluded. A composite list of 5773 words resulted."

Emans (1966) focused on words beyond the primary level (Grade 4). He took "a random sample of 10 per cent of the words (1944 words) beyond the primary level in *The Teacher's Word Book of 30,000 Words* by Thorndike and Lorge." Such a sample would include a heavy loading of words which occur infrequently since there are, for example, almost twice as many (5200) words that occur only once per million running words (according to the Thorndike and Lorge source) than there are words (2780) which occur from twenty to forty-nine times per million running words. (A frequency of forty-nine per million running words is the beginning point for Grade 4.0 according to Thorndike and Lorge [1944, pp. x-xi]). In addition, Emans inductively formulated eighteen generalizations which he found to be useful. Both Bailey and Emans used Webster's *New Collegiate Dictionary* (1959).

Burmeister (1966), in an attempt to obtain an even spread of easy and difficult words, chose her sample words from *The Teachers' Word Book of 30,000 Words* by Thorndike and Lorge at fourteen different "frequency of occurrence" levels. She took a 5 percent random sample at each of eleven levels for words which occur from six to over 100 times per million running words, and a somewhat smaller (percentage wise) sample at three levels for words which ranged in frequency from one to five occurrences per million running words. She looked at generalizations which are frequently found in materials at the fourth-grade level and above and also at generalizations which she had formulated through her own teaching experience. She tripled the number of sample words for her analysis of adjacent (double and triple) vowels and inductively arrived at generalizations which describe the sounds of such vowels. She used *The American College Dictionary* (1961).

Winkley (1965) reported on the applicability of eighteen accent generalizations suggested by Gray (1960) as they apply to multisyllabic words. The findings of her original study lent support to the teaching of seven generalizations; however her second study, the one being examined herein, suggests that twelve of these generalizations are worth teaching. By combining and rewording these generalizations she reduced the twelve generalizations to seven.

TABULATION OF FINDINGS

Each of the generalizations stated and examined by any one of the investigators was listed. For each, the results of each study which considered this generalization were tabulated. The percentage of utility was recorded from the data of the studies where such computations were made. From the others, the author's conclusion as to whether or not the generalization was useful was recorded. Two groups of generalizations were formed as a result of comparison of the findings: those generalizations which apparently are commonly included in instructional programs but, according to the studies, had limited utility value; and those which according to the results of the studies had reasonably broad application. Certain others, which seemed to be infrequently encountered in instructional programs and of little value in terms of application, were eliminated from consideration.

CONCLUSIONS AND IMPLICATIONS

Usefulness of Generalizations

Generalizations considered of limited usefulness: Certain generalizations appeared to be commonly taught but to have very limited usefulness according to the included studies. The following fell in this category:

> The vowel in an open syllable has a long sound.
>
> The letter *a* has the same sound (ô) when followed by *e, w,* and *u.*
>
> When there are two vowels, one of which is a final *e,* the vowel is long and the *e* is silent.
>
> In many two- and three-syllable words, the "final *e*" lengthens the vowel in the last syllable.
>
> When a word ends in "vowel-consonant-*e,*" the vowel is long and the *e* is silent.
>
> When two vowels are together, the first is long and the second is silent.

If the first vowel sound in a word is followed by a single consonant, that consonant usually begins the second syllable.

When two sounds are separated by one consonant, divide before
the consonant, but consider *ph, ch, sh,* and *th* to be single consonants.

It is recommended that teachers be particularly cautious when
instructing children in situations in which these generalizations
might apply in two or more specific ways until oral recognition is
achieved. For example, the following generalizations might be helpful:

Single vowels are usually short, but a single vowel may have a
long sound in an open syllable (approximately 30 percent of the
time), especially in a one syllable word.

If a word ends in "vowel-consonant-*e*" the vowel may be long or
short. Try the long sound first.

Generalizations of high utility value: Certain other generalizations appeared to be particularly useful. This in no way suggests that
other statements (or generalizations) are not important. The author,
for example, does not consider Fry's statement, "Single consonants
are quite consistent in making the same sound. They should be
taught in the following order: *t, n, r, m, d, s (sat), l, c (cat), p, s, f, v,
g (got), h, w, k, j, z, y,*" to be unimportant. She recognizes the need
for teaching single consonants but not necessarily in the order listed.
    The generalizations listed here are the most inclusive of the
group, or they are the ones with the highest utility level, or both.
Thus "*C* followed by *e, i,* or *y* sounds soft; otherwise *C* is hard (omit
ch)" was selected because it describes every situation in which a *C*
might be found; the other generalizations are more limited.

Especially useful generalizations: The following generalizations
are those from the studies which seemed most useful, except for the
"final *e*" generalization and the phonic syllabication number two
generalization. The latter two generalizations were formulated by
the current author as a result of the findings of the utility level
studies.

Consonant sounds

1. *C* followed by *e, i,* or *y* sounds soft; otherwise *c* is hard (omit
   ch) (certain, city, cycle; attic, cat, clip; success).

2. *G* followed by *e, i,* or *y* sounds soft; otherwise *g* is hard (omit *gh*) (gell, agile, gypsy; gone, flag, grope; suggest).
3. *Ch* is usually pronounced as it is in "kitchen," not like *sh* as in "machine."
4. When a word ends in *ck,* it has the same last sound as in "look."
5. When *ght* is seen in a word, *gh* is silent (thought, night, right).
6. When two of the same consonants are side-by-side, only one is heard (dollar, paddle).

Vowel sounds—single vowels

1. If the only vowel letter is at the end of a word, the letter usually stands for a long sound (one syllable words only) (be, he, she, go).
2. When "consonant + *y*" are the final letters in a one syllable word, the *y* has a "short *i*" (long *e*) sound (my, by, cry; baby, dignity).
3. A single vowel in a closed syllable has a short sound, except that it may be modified in words in which the vowel is followed by an *r* (club, dress, at, car, pumpkin, virgin).
4. The *r* gives the preceding vowel a sound that is neither long nor short (car, care, far, fair, fare) (single or double vowels).

Vowel sounds—adjacent vowels

1. *Digraphs:* When the following double vowel combinations are seen together, the first is usually long and the second is silent: *ai, ay, ae, ee, oa, ow* (ea may also have a "short *e*" sound, and ow may have an *ou* sound) (main, pay; eat, bread; see, oat, sparrow, how).
2. *Diphthongs (or blends):* The following double vowel combinations usually blend: *au, aw, ou, oi, oy, oo* (*oo* has two common sounds) (auto, awful, house, coin, boy, book, rooster).
3. *io and ia*: *io* and *ia* after *c, t,* or *s* help to make a consonant sound: vic*io*us, part*ia*l, music*ia*n, vis*io*n, attent*io*n (even o-c*ea*n).

Syllabication—determination of a syllable

Every single vowel or vowel combination means a syllable (except a "final *e*" in a "vowel-consonant-*e*" ending).

Syllabication—structural syllabication

These generalizations take precedence over phonic syllabication generalizations.

1. Divide between a prefix and a root.
2. Divide between two roots.
3. Usually divide between a root and a suffix.

Syllabication—phonic syllabication

1. When two vowel sounds are separated by two consonants, divide between the consonants but consider *ch, sh, ph,* and *th* to be single consonants (assist, convey, bunny, Houston, rustic).
2. When two vowel sounds are separated by one consonant, divide either before or after the consonant. Try dividing before the consonant first. (Consider *ch, sh, ph,* and *th* to be single consonants). [alone, select, ashame, Japan, sober; comet, honest, ever, idiot, modest, agile, general]
3. When a word ends in a "consonant-*l-e*" divide before the consonant. (battle, treble, tangible, kindle).

Accent

1. In most two-syllable words, the first syllable is accented.

   a. And, when there are two like consonant letters within a word the syllable before the double consonant is usually accented (beginner, letter).
   b. But, two vowel letters together in the last syllable of a word may be a clue to an accented final syllable (complain, conceal).

2. In inflected or derived forms of words, the primary accent usually falls on or within the root word (boxes, untie). [Therefore, if "a," "in," "re," "ex," "de," or "be" is the first syllable in a word, it is usually unaccented.]

Implications for Further Research

Vowel phoneme-grapheme relationships: It seems important when thinking of vowel sounds to differentiate between single vowels and double vowels. When two vowels are together, they ordinarily compose a phoneme. To lose sight of this causes a lack of clarity and a lessening of utility level of a possibly good generalization.

For generalizations to be especially useful and clear the grapheme must be clearly defined. For example, some generalizations listed under *vowel sounds*—"Single *or* double vowels" tend to be ambiguous. Vowels should always be looked at as *single vowels* or as *double vowels*. This can be clarified if we look at the following generalization: "When *y* is the final letter in a word, it usually has a vowel sound." Exceptions are, for example, words such as pl*ay*, tr*ay*, rep*ay*, k*ey*, th*ey*, words which end with two vowels which often form a digraph. Notice the 99 percent utility level, instead of the following more clearly stated generalization: "When 'consonant + *y*' are the final letters in a monosyllabic word, the *y* has a 'long *i*' sound; in a polysyllabic word the *y* has a 'short *i*' (long *e*) sound."

Another example might be cited. Generalization: "When the letter *i* is followed by the letters *gh* the *i* usually stands for its long sound and the *gh* is silent." Most of the common words which follow the generalization have a single vowel *i*: H*i*gh, n*i*ght, f*i*ght, fl*i*ght, bl*i*ght, etc. Words which do not follow the generalization are words with double vowels: n*ei*ghbor, str*ai*ght, w*ei*ght, etc. The generalization would have a higher utility level if it were stated thus: When the single vowel *i* is followed by the letters *gh* the *i* usually stands for its long sound and the *gh* is silent."

Sample Material: Apparently the variation in the sources from which sample words were selected usually makes very little difference in the findings. This becomes obvious when one compares the findings of Clymer, Bailey, and Emans in particular. When the size of the sample is large, the "utility levels" of almost all generalizations are fairly standard. An exception might be that of the *g* generalization. Clymer's primary materials yielded a lower utility level for this generalization than the other studies. This can be explained by noting that words of Anglo-Saxon origin supply the exceptions to this generalization and Anglo-Saxon words are our most common words—words likely to be found often at the primary level (give, get, girl, tiger, finger, etc.). Another exception involves the vowel digraph generalization. The primary materials used in Clymer's study yield a higher utility level for this generalization than do any of the other materials.

The observation that level of difficulty of words in general makes little difference in the utility level for a generalization can also be affirmed by examining the findings in Burmeister's study of the utility levels of each of the fourteen frequency of occurrence stratifications (Burmeister, 1966).

REFERENCES

Bailey, Mildred Hart. "An Analytical Study of the Utility of Selected Phonic Generalizations for Children in Grades One through Six." Unpublished doctoral dissertation, University of Mississippi, 1965.

Black, Sister Mary Carla, B.V.M. Phonics Rules Verification by a Thirteen-Hundred Word Count." Unpublished master's project, Loyola University of Los Angeles, 1961.

Bloomfield, L. *Language.* New York: Henry Holt, 1955.

Burmeister, Lou E. "An Analysis of the Inductive and Deductive Group Approaches to Teaching Selected Word Analysis Generalizations to Disabled Readers in Eighth and Ninth Grade." Unpublished doctoral dissertation, University of Wisconsin, 1966.

Clymer, T. L. "The Utility of Phonic Generalizations in the Primary Grades." *The Reading Teacher* 16 (1963): 252-58.

Cordts, Anna D. "Analysis and Classification of the Sounds of English Words in the Primary Reading Vocabulary." Unpublished doctoral dissertation, University of Iowa, 1925.

Dale, E., and Eichholz, G. *Children's Knowledge of Words.* Columbus, Ohio: Bureau of Educational Research and Service, 1960.

Emans, R. "The Usefulness of Phonic Generalizations above the Primary Grades." A paper given at the annual convention of the American Educational Research Association, Chicago, 1966.

Fry, E. "A Frequency Approach to Phonics." *Elementary English* 41 (1964): 759-65+.

————. "Teaching a Basic Reading Vocabulary." *Elementary English* 39 (1960): 37-42.

Gray, W. S. *On Their Own in Reading.* Chicago: Scott, Foresman, 1960.

Horn, E. "The Child's Early Experience with the Letter a." *The Journal of Educational Psychology* 20 (1929): 161-68.

Kottmeyer, W. A. "Phonetic and Structural Generalizations for the Teaching of a Primary Grade Spelling Vocabulary." Reported in Webster Publishing Company Reserve File No. 528-S and 529-S, St. Louis, Mo., 1954.

Moore, J. T. "Phonetic Elements Appearing in a 3,000-word Spelling Vocabulary." Unpublished doctoral dissertation, Stanford University, 1951.

Thorndike, E. L., and Lorge, I. *The Teacher's Word Book of 30,000 Words.* New York: Bureau of Publications, Teachers College, Columbia University, 1944.

Vogel, Mabel; Jaycox, Emma; and Washburne, C. W. "A Basic List of Phonics for Grades 1 and 2." *Elementary School Journal* 23 (1923): 436-43.

Winkley, Carol K. "Utilization of Accent Generalizations in Identifying Unknown Multisyllable Words." Unpublished doctoral dissertation, University of Chicago, 1965.

———. "Which Accent Generalizations are Worth Teaching?" *The Reading Teacher* 20 (1966): 219-24+.

Ways of helping students write and speak maturely, logically and interestingly have been pursued. What verbal behaviors are important enough to be taught in school, ones for which the school should take partial or full responsibility? Dale points the way and suggests directions for future research.

VOCABULARY MEASUREMENT: TECHNIQUES AND MAJOR FINDINGS

Edgar Dale

What are teachers of English? In what behaviors do they engage? Chiefly, they help children and young people develop an increasingly mature taste for excellence in literature, and they are responsible for guiding growth in language.

I say "responsible." This means that they have or should have certain insights into the growth of linguistic behavior which are useful in working with children, young people, their parents, editors, publishers. It may sound presumptuous and ambitious to say that teachers of English are the guardians of general growth in linguistic power, that they are the wise counselors of force and clarity in writing and speaking. But if they are not responsible for these goals, then who is?

The popular image of a teacher of English is much more restricted than the one I have just suggested. If you announce in a social gathering that you teach English, someone is likely to remark, "Oh, I must watch what I say." Or he may remain silent in the presence of this alleged authority, this super-tribunal on what is and what is not pure, undefiled English.

I need not say that the approach suggested by this image, the teacher as a guard in a correctional institution, is a fruitless one. Yet it does persist. Many see teacher aides as paid to *correct,* to excise dangling participles, to make specious and futile distinctions between *shall* and *will,* to correct repeated mistakes in spelling of words like *principal, their, to,* and so on. (By the way, the correction

From *Elementary English* vol. 4, no. 8 (December 1965): 895-901. Copyright © 1965 by the National Council of Teachers of English and Edgar Dale.

of most of such errors can be programmed and need require only a fraction of a teacher's time.)

I maintain that the goals we seek are bigger, more formidable. Immature writers need editing rather than correcting. It is the irrelevancies, the *non sequitur,* the cliches that we are after. True, there is much bad writing. I think of the teacher of English who received a theme that was so bad that she had to revise it before she threw it away.

But suppose that some divine magic suddenly turned all the incorrect writing into correct writing. I would then ask a simple question: Does it matter whether something *not worth reading* is written correctly? I would prefer a misspelled something to a correctly spelled nothing. Robert Frost once asked a group of students whether the papers they just handed in said anything important. When they replied "No," he dumped them all into the wastebasket.

I repeat: Let's go after bigger game. Let's search for ways of helping students write and speak more maturely, more logically, more interestingly. At this point the tired teacher of English says, "Go on, please tell me." My answer is: Let's get a much more accurate, more specific picture of language development seen as behavior. I believe that with better linguistic data, with patience and with lots of hope, we can build a strong curriculum in English for all students, a vigorous curriculum in English for all students, a vigorous curriculum that will enable us to "instruct with delight," as Horace put it. Vocabulary and its measurement are therefore of great importance as we develop a behavioral approach to language development.

Let's first put the topic of "Vocabulary Measurement" in its educational setting. Otherwise we may miss the central importance of verbal behavior in the life and education of the individual. Obviously, as teachers or students of the English language we have a concern with vocabulary and syntax—or words in patterned structures. I shall not emphasize the critical importance of language behavior. I remind you, however, that a test of vocabulary correlates highly with tests of mental development, and also with tests of reading ability. The vocabulary level is the best index of the readability level of materials.

Further, since language behaviors are so important, it seems wise to determine the specific language behaviors we are trying to develop in the school or college, the verbal behaviors. We are concerned with the language behaviors of speaking and listening, reading and writing, visualizing and observing. We need to describe these behaviors and then arrange them in some kind of graded programs of learning.

We should know which of these behaviors are achieved before children begin school, those they learn in school, those they learn after formal education is completed. Putting it, then, into typical curriculum language we ask: What verbal behaviors do we want the pupil to master at various stages of his development? What has he already mastered? How and when do we teach him to close this gap between desired performance and actual performance?

Let us look at the first question: What verbal behaviors are important enough to be taught in the school, ones for which the school should take partial or full responsibility? I note again that words are spoken and heard, written and read. Further, word experiences are also gained by "reading" photographs with captions, labeled graphs, charts, and the like.

What words are important in the varied subjects of the school, important for growth in language behavior? Spelling has important relationships to vocabulary development, and we have had many studies dealing with spelling, with the use of words in the writing of children and adults. The early spelling curriculum debates were concerned with whether we should depend chiefly on the studies of the writing of adults as our source of words, whether we should depend on the writing of children, or what combinations shall be made. Among key early studies of adult and child spelling vocabulary are: Ernest Horn, *A Basic Writing Vocabulary,* 1926; Henry D. Rinsland, *A Basic Vocabulary of Elementary School Children,* 1945; Frederick S. Breed, "What Words Should Children Be Taught to Spell? Vocabularies of Various Types," *Elementary School Journal* (November 1925). In general these studies have found that a small number of words constitutes the bulk of the words we write. Roughly it goes something like this: fifty words and their repetitions constitute about 50 percent of the words written by children or adults; 1000 words make up 90 percent; 2000 words, 95 percent; 3000 words, 97 percent; 4000 words, 98 percent; 10,000 words, 99.4 percent. We conclude that beyond a certain point it becomes impossible to predict the words that an individual will write. This then suggests the possibility of mastering principles relating to spelling.

Spelling is more closely related to reading than we may realize. Many errors in reading occur because the child or adult cannot spell. College students, for example, confuse *ingenious* and *ingenuous, interpellate* and *interpolate, appraise* and *apprise, filet* and *fillet, basilisk* and *basilica, forté* and *forte, fictitious, factitious,* and *factious, decry* and *descry.* Ability to recognize and spell prefixes, roots, and suffixes may also help in spelling and reading these words. We have some evidence that this is true. The more recent sophisticated studies, such as one now being conducted by Paul Hanna at Stanford

University, make use of computers to discover frequency of certain sound elements.

Let us look now at studies of verbal behavior made by analyzing reading materials. Thorndike, for example, published a series of studies culminating in *The Teacher's Word Book of 30,000 Words.* He sampled the *Bible,* children's literature, magazines, textbooks, etc.

What problems arise with such an approach to the measurement of vocabulary? First, one faces the extraordinarily complicated problem of sampling. Investigators miss simple words which may not appear in print but are well known. Common words are often omitted. Rinsland, for example, has *platypus* but not *pimple, mucus* but not *snot, bishop* but not *bitch, seminary* but not *scab, blacksmith* but not *blackhead.* Here are some of the supposedly difficult words found in Thorndike's list: *alumnae, appointive, avoidable, backache, barbed wire, bedbug, beefy, blurb, boodle, bootee, brassie, bucksaw, dragnet, bunghole, cashew, clubroom, cowbell, decode, éclair, featherweight, fluoride, iceman, milker, matador, orangeade, repetitious, shopworn, toreador, weatherproof, wristband, yak, zither.*

The weakness underlying many of the studies of children's speech and writing is the false assumption that Edward Dolch pointed out, "Children use all the words they know and they use them in proportion to their familiarity with them." The problem still remains but it is less acute as we move away from frequency studies which use *universal* samples. A remedy for this situation has been the study of terms in various subject matter fields. Here we have such studies as Luella Cole (Pressey), *The Teacher's Handbook of Technical Vocabulary;* George Klenzle's study of dental vocabulary; *The Language of Medicine, A Quantitative Study of Medical Vocabulary* by Edward M. Bridge, which includes words well known to doctors but unknown to most adults, e.g., *osteoblast, myasthenic, mitral, streptodornase, aureus.* Such technical words do not usually get into a general sampling such as Thorndike's.

In *Bibliography of Vocabulary Studies* we have listed 136 studies under the category, "Vocabulary and Use." It is clear, therefore, that attempts to measure vocabulary development or to measure outcomes of educational programs involve many different types of verbal behavior.

One of the major deficiencies of word lists which are supposedly concerned with meanings, not spelling, is that they have not usually studied frequency of *meanings.* The 30,000 Thorndike word list noted above did not differentiate meanings of words. This difficulty, however, was met by Thorndike and Lorge with their publication of

A Semantic Count of English Words in November 1938. In it they present 20,000 words with a statement of the frequency with which the varied meanings of words appear in print but not in the writing of children.

However, on words *spoken* and *heard,* we have very limited data. We have many studies of the words spoken before the age of six. These tend to be studies of middle-class and upper-class children and not deprived children. Today, however, more studies are under way which deal with the vocabulary and syntax of speech of children living under deprived conditions.

WHEN IS A WORD KNOWN?

To measure words known we must not only indicate what we mean by "knowing" but we must also define what we mean by a "word." How many meanings, for example, does the word *fast* have? The procedure in our nationwide study was to have two readers go over the words in the *Basic Dictionary of American English* and determine which of several meanings of a word were so unrelated that knowledge of one meaning would not automatically transfer to other meanings. Admittedly this is subjective, but this subjectivity is at present an inescapable necessity.

In testing vocabulary we also face the problem of inflectional forms. In general, we followed the rules on inflection stated by Thorndike on pages iv-v in *A Teacher's Word Book of 20,000 Words.* The assumptions made are that we have a new word when the inflection is likely to make it markedly more difficult. Thus you may know *like* but not *likely.* This problem is greater for the younger child who has not yet generalized the regular endings. I believe that these assumptions need more careful study to determine what inflections are satisfactorily generalized at what age levels with what children. This must be done both in writing and in spelling.

Another source of difference in size of vocabularies discovered as known is influenced by the nature of the test. Knowledge of a word can be placed on a continuum, starting with "I never saw the word before." For example, none of you knows the words *bittles, polentular,* or *fundular.* They do not exist as meaningful words. Second, we may say, "I know there is such a word but I don't know what it means." Such words might be *hugger-mugger, adnoun, adit, swingletree, detente, antidisestablishmentarianism, laser, serendipity.* A third stage is "a vague contextual placing of the word." You know you make the *welkin* ring and that *hustings* has to do with elections, but what do these words mean specifically? You *bask* in the sun. Can you bask in the shade? What are *kith* and *kin?* A *pied* piper? Was President Andrew Johnson *impeached?* These words are in what I call a "twilight zone."

Fourth, and finally we reach the stage where we have pinned the word down. We know it. We would recognize it again if we saw it, and we are likely to remember it.

But even beyond this stage we can make tests still more precise by requiring finer discriminations as between the *arresting* and *curing* of a disease; *irony, sarcasm,* and *satire; sympathy* and *empathy; bond* and *note; pride* and *arrogance; humility* and *humiliation.* This precision becomes especially important in distinguishing between general and specific terms. What in specific terms is "an educational breakthrough"? On our campus it is defined as "when you get $10,000 for your NDEA project."

How shall we test whether children know words? Here we turn again to word behavior. What are we called upon to do with words? Sometimes we *hear* them and must then carry out behavior that is appropriate. We may try to use a known word in our writing and discover that we can't readily retrieve it. Fluency in word retrieval then might be one aspect of vocabulary measurement. What is a person called who says he hates women? A *liar?* No, a *misogynist.* Recall is being tested here. The word association tests used by Buckingham and Dolch are examples of a word test which simply requires children to write as many words as they can without stimulus clues. This might be called word fluency and has many important correlations.

Or we may see the word in some kind of context from which we are required to infer the desired meaning. The word is given and recognition is required. But context can vary from no help to complete help in revealing the meaning of a word. So when someone says —"Test the word in context," we must ask: "What context?"

In school we commonly ask children to look up the meaning of words that they do not know. We assume apparently that this is a good way for them to check or measure this vocabulary. I tried this pupil judgment approach in three different studies. In the first study, pupils were asked to check words on a list—multiple meanings were put into clarifying context. It worked fairly well. Its deficiencies were that students were reacting to words whose spelling sometimes confused them. Thus *belie* was stated as known because some thought it meant stomach. *Eunuch* was confused with *unique.* The technique works fairly well on easy words and on hard words. We know that we know *house, mortgage, interest,* and that we don't know *syzygy* or *synovitis,* but there is a middle range where we are not certain whether we know the word or not (the twilight zone), and if we are poor spellers the difficulty is compounded.

I compiled data of this type on 800 of the most common words in the Thorndike list. The compilation was not published but proved very useful in compiling the 3,000 word list used in the Dale-Chall readability formula. Another by-product of this list was "A Topical List of Words" which is a classification of these 3,000 words into seven major categories and forty subcategories. These are variations of categories that Dolch developed but did not publish. Our list is not generally available but over 1,000 copies have been distributed in mimeographed form and it has been used chiefly in work with under-privileged children.

A second approach to the use of pupil judgment involved having children in the fourth grade read *Black Beauty* and underline the unknown words. I got some valuable data from it to use in the 3,000 word list, but the findings lacked needed accuracy. It does give, however, a rough indication of familiarity.

A third approach involved placing a paperback dictionary in the hands of college freshmen at Ohio State and Stephens College and asking them to read stated portions of the dictionary and check unknown words. This list proved valuable in discovering "hard" words but it did not give us data on easy- and middle-level words. But let's remember that the judgment of whether or not we know a word is a good test of "assumed familiarity," a worthy objective of re-search. It is not exact, but it is useful.

So we gave up the hope of developing an inexpensive, quick method for determining word knowledge and turned to a multiple-choice test. We have used a three-choice test and have now tested about a million children and young people throughout the United States. We shall finally have scores on about 40,000 word meanings in Grades 4, 6, 8, 10, 12, 13, and 16. Not less than 200 subjects were tested on each word in the elementary and high school testing and not less than 100 of the college freshmen and seniors. We turned to dictionaries of slang, lists of new words, mail order catalogs, patents data, and other sources to avoid missing new words.

Most of our tests were given during the middle months of the school year. We typically sent each test to at least five different school systems. We tested in all the states and tried to sample all kinds of schools. We asked our respondents to give the tests to typical pupils and pointed out that no data would be published which sin-gled out separate schools. We have every reason to believe that the testing was taken seriously by teachers and pupils.

Every test was expertly constructed according to a set of rules and was reviewed by two or three persons before testing was begun. These rules related to the nature of distractors, avoidance of spelling confusions, etc. The choices at lower levels were phrased in the idiom of children. As the study progressed, we could select distractors at known levels of familiarity.

Test findings were carefully inspected by experienced teachers, and when scores seemed inaccurate, samples were hand checked for scoring accuracy and the alternate choices carefully scrutinized. In cases of doubt, words were retested. Only rarely did these retests change results significantly. But we must never forget that a multiple-choice test is a subjective test objectively scored.

At least 200 children were tested on each word in each grade, 4 to 12. On the basis of twenty "control words" used on each twelfth grade test (thereby increasing the 200 word sample to over 2,800 students per test), we found that the scores were not altered by more than a -5 percent or a +2 percent. Therefore we assumed that a sample of 200 students per test was adequate to meet the desired accuracy and the practical demands of time and money.

How did we know what words to test at what levels? We had access, of course, to *Gates' Spelling Difficulties in 3,876 Words,* which gave us some clues. We also had access to the Diederich-Palmer unpublished list. But the sad fact was that we tested many of these words at three different levels before we found the level at which we could get a score of at least 67 percent and not more than 84 percent. Three-fourths of the words we retested moved to higher levels. We had underestimated their difficulty, as do many teachers.

A preliminary publication of this list was published under the title *Children's Knowledge of Words.* It included scores on about 15,000 words. The book is out of print.

Most of the testing has now been concluded on our study. A small number remain to be tested on the college level, and there will be some retesting at lower levels.

How can the list be used? It should help us know more about the "entry" behavior of students at the various grade levels. It will enable us to "control" vocabulary of written materials much better than we have done before. When we use hard unknown words in textbooks, we can explain them.

The list gives many clues as to the effect of inflections on the familiarity of words. The data show unmistakably that the literary vocabulary of college students is meager. They are not learning the harder words that are typically learned only by reading.

The list suggests approaches that can be used in vocabulary development. We can note the known words which have roots, prefixes, or suffixes such as *meter, tele, phon, gamy* (*as in polygamy*), *mono, bi, di, tri,* etc. We can put our study of vocabulary on a sounder, more developmental basis.

We shall also have information about the *number* of words known at the various levels. However, the study by Jeanne Chall and Irving Lorge titled, "Estimating the Size of Vocabularies of Children and Adults: An Analysis of Methodological Issues," *Journal of Experimental Education* (Winter 1963), has pretty well laid to rest the highly exaggerated data on words known by children at various grade levels. Word control is still needed in preparing materials of instruction.

How many words *do* children and young people know?

If we assume that children finish the first grade with an average vocabulary of 3,000 words, it is likely that they will add about 1,000 words a year from then on. The average high school senior will know about 14,000 to 15,000 words, the college senior 18,000 to 20,000.

WHAT RESEARCH DO I SEE FOR THE FUTURE?

1. *Less concern about data on "total" vocabularies and more study of special vocabularies in various fields.*
2. *An intensive study of technical terms with emphasis on various levels of growth in understanding specific terms.* Thus we would have a series of different scores for each word like *mortgage, bond, stock,* etc. We would note and distinguish between acceptable and inadequate definitions in discovering maturity of growth in understanding concepts. The use of teaching machines may speed this type of development, since small steps toward mastery are emphasized. The word *interest* as related to money may be tested on as many as four levels.
3. *The development of much more discriminating tests as we try to make more precise discriminations in words;* e.g., the differences between *investigation* and *inquisition; notorious* and *famous; suggestibility* and *suggestiveness.*
4. *More studies of spoken vocabulary with emphasis on expressive meaning as well as denotative meaning.* This is especially important with underprivileged children.

5. *Studies of ability of students to generalize new meanings from context, to develop new meanings through the use of known roots, prefixes, and suffixes.* There are very few studies in this field. Lee Deighton, Janice Harrison, and others have shown that we are overestimating the ability of children to infer meanings from context. How teachable is this skill?

6. *Studies of methods of developing vocabulary with special emphasis on programmed instruction.* Joseph O'Rourke and I have written three such books in cooperation with the Columbus (Ohio) Public Schools where they are now being widely used in Grades 6, 8, and 12.

7. *Studies of Vocabulary over a time span.* How do similar groups of children react to the same words after various spans of time? I tested a group of fifty business words at Winnetka in 1928, 1932, 1937 and 1960. A few words changed markedly in the first three testings. The means for a seventh grade shifted upward a few points. The means of the eighth-grade list shifted less than a percentage point over the three testing periods. However, the last test given in 1960 showed a sharp upward growth. Why? We don't know. We also need studies of individual vocabulary over a span of time. We need case studies of the life-history of slang terms—why do some of them survive?

   I see the vocabulary studies of the future more closely related to environing conditions, with better analysis for causative factors. What words, for example, show high differences between grades and which show much less difference? Apparently quantitative terms are in the latter group.

8. *We can discover the typical attitudes of students toward vocabulary study.* A report by Margaret Early indicated topics liked and disliked by the non-college-bound student. She found that studying vocabulary was listed among the most disliked topics. Interest in spelling was high. Dr. Early also reported that the typical teaching method was to have students look up a list of words in the dictionary and then write a sentence using each one, a process which kills interest in words.

9. *We need to discover how much we can increase and refine the vocabulary of children of varying backgrounds and competence.* I believe that even with what we now know we can increase nearly every student's vocabulary by about 10 percent. This growth would come, first, from helping him put

into sharp focus those words now in a "twilight zone." And second, sharp growth could come from helping him master the prefixes, roots, and suffixes which have the greatest possibilities for generalization.

10. *Perhaps the first major upthrust in future vocabulary study development will occur from work with the disadvantaged.* The studies of Riesman, Goldberg, Passow, Deutsch, Carroll, Whipple, and others should be helpful. I believe, also, that linguistic studies such as those of Strickland, Loban, Berko, Bernstein, Brown, and others will uncover important data concerning vocabulary development in its relation to syntax. Certainly we need a more comprehensive theory of vocabulary development which in turn can be coupled with sharply improved methods of measurement.

There are two basic problems in all vocabulary development. First, we must have experiences. Indeed, our vocabulary is determined in large measure by the richness, the depth of our experiences. Second, labeling and filing these experiences is a necessary factor in making them flexibly available under many and varied conditions. By thinking about the vocabulary outcomes of all experiences we can markedly increase the quality and range of the experiences. Thus, research on vocabulary development can make all language experiences more effective.

*What context clues are most beneficial as word recognition aids? Is
there a continuum for levels of difficulty for this skill? Emans and
Fisher present their findings.*

TEACHING THE USE OF CONTEXT CLUES

Robert Emans
Gladys Mary Fisher

THE PROBLEM

The purpose of this study was to develop a series of exercises for
teaching the use of context clues in word recognition. Used along
with phonetic and structural analysis, context clues provide one of
the best means for achieving the recognition of a word. Finding that
unlocking of a previously unknown word makes sense in context
provides a check as to the pronunciation of the word. Although
context clues can also be used for determining the meaning of a
word, the concern of this study was the use of context clues as a word
recognition device. As Miles A. Tinker states, "Context clues are
derived from the meanings of those words in the sentence already
known to the child. These meanings are used to obtain the pronunciation of the one or two new words in the sentence" (14).

Authorities such as Nila B. Smith (13), Arthur W. Heilman (6),
Emmet A. Betts (1), Homer Carter, and Dorothy McGinnis (3), and
many others agree to the importance of context clues in identifying
words. William S. Gray said, "Context clues are perhaps the most
important single aid to word perception" (5).

Not only is there wide acceptance of the importance of context
clues, but there is also wide acceptance of the value of teaching their
use. For example, Miles Tinker and Constance McCullough write,
"Few children will be able to make all the use they might of these
clues without such training" (15). Smith believes context clues require ". . . more than incidental attention if children learn to make
the most of the skill" (13). And Kathleen Hester agrees, "Systematic
guidance is necessary to help him (the child) to learn this important
technique for recognizing words" (7).

In spite of the importance of context clues in word recognition
and the need for explicitly guiding children in their use, little re-

search has been conducted in this area. Smith states, "Not many studies have been made in regard to children's use of context clues as a word identification technique" (13). McCullough makes this point dramatically when she states that the process of using context clues still remains "an area of considerable ignorance among us" (9). Nevertheless, a few studies have been conducted. McCullough has identified four types of clues which aid in the recognition of words as being experience, comparison or contrast, familiar expression, and definition (10). Paul McKee found that the average child in fourth grade can use context clues to identify the meaning of an unrecognized word in his textbooks about once in three times (11). H. Alan Robinson found that context clues alone were not sufficient for successful recognition by average fourth-grade children although he thought that children would probably profit from instruction in the use of context clues (12).

THE BACKGROUND

How can children learn to take advantage of context clues in word recognition? Because of the lack of research in this area, twenty-one teachers and administrators at Fort Atkinson, Wisconsin, decided they would try to develop a series of exercises for helping children develop this skill. Participants included special reading teachers, elementary teachers, teachers in special content fields, and administrators.

A survey of the literature indicates that many authorities believe context clues are best used when combined with other means of word recognition including word configuration and phonetic analysis. For example, Tinker and McCullough state ". . . context clues should be combined with such aids as word form, phonetics, and even use of the dictionary" (15). Bond and Wagner believe, "Context clues are practically always used in combination with other methods of word recognition . . ." (2). Robert Karlin goes so far as to say that, "Context clues should not be used separately to unlock unknown words, and the teacher does well to prepare exercises that utilize at least two word-recognition techniques simultaneously" (8).

Many exercises combine context clues with other word attack skills. However, no hierarchy of difficulty among the various forms was found. This is an important gap in our knowledge since it is almost always desirable to start with easy exercises and proceed with continually more difficult ones. It has been difficult, therefore, to develop a systematic, sequential program for teaching context clues.

THE TESTING SITUATION

Because of this need the participants devised six exercises to determine the relative difficulty of six different techniques found in the literature. To assure compatibility among the exercises, revisions of various forms of the already standardized test, *Gates Reading Survey* (4), were used. In Form I, the key word was omitted and a correct response was to be chosen from four choices supplied. In Form II, the beginning and ending letter of each word was given with the others omitted. In Form III, just the beginning letter was given. In Form IV, only the vowels were omitted from the key words. In Form V, the complete word was omitted and the line for each missing word was the same length. In Form VI, the entire word was omitted, but the length of the lines was determined by the length of the word.

Various exercises teach the use of context clues in word recognition somewhat indirectly. Instead of varying the context in helping to recognize a word, the exercises vary the amount of configuration and phonic clues provided. The exercises require the child to search his listening-speaking vocabularies to find the word that is suitable for the context and, also, consistent with other word attack clues including phonics and word form. The thinking is that meeting success in this fashion will prepare the reader to use a similar approach with an unknown word.

THE FINDINGS

These exercises were administered in eleven schools by the twenty-one participating teachers. The schools included a parochial school and a college campus training school, as well as nine public schools. The tests were given in all grades from three to ten. There was a range of from fifty to 150 pupils in each grade. A total of 781 subjects were given all six forms of the test. The order of administration for the tests was altered so that not all would take the tests in the same order in case any learning would occur from one or more of the tests. All of the tests were administered by participating teachers or under the supervision of a participating teacher.

The tests were partially scored at a meeting of the teachers to determine what answers were acceptable. Responses were considered correct if they made sense in light of the context, even though they might be misspelled or have an incorrectly inflected ending, or have an incorrect verb tense except where letters or words given limited the response. In the case of Form IV, an answer was considered correct if 50 percent or more of the vowels were correct. Individual participating teachers then scored each test, computed raw scores, and determined the rank of the six tests for each subject. After this, the frequency of each rank for the forms of the tests was computed for the entire group. The frequency of the ranks were compared using the Chi Square Test.

THE FINDINGS

The results showed, all significant at the .001 level, that:

1. Form IV, consonants given, was easier than Forms I, II, III, V, VI.
2. Form I, four word choices given, was easier than Forms II, III, V, VI.
3. Form II, beginning and ending letters given, was easier than Forms III, V. VI.
4. Form VI, length of word given, was easier than Forms III, V.
5. Form III, beginning letter given, was easier than Form V.
6. Form V, no clue given, was the most difficult.

It is interesting to note that Form III, with only the initial letter given, is the second most difficult type of exercise. This type is one of the most frequently mentioned exercises found in the literature. The importance of this study is verified since it shows a need for identifying easier exercises.

The results indicate that, in general, the more clues a reader has the easier it is to unlock an unknown word. In Form IV, where only the vowels were omitted, the subject was given phonetic and configuration clues, as well as context clues, to aid him in determining the correct response. This proved to be the easiest form of the test. On the other hand, Form V, which was the most difficult form of the test, provided the subject with no clues at all other than context. Furthermore, in Form V, a number of responses made sense in context and were correct which bears out the hypotheses that context clues must be used in conjunction with other word attack techniques if the appropriate response is to be made.

Analyzing the other forms of the test to determine the relationship between the number of clues given and the relative difficulty of the task showed a positive relationship in most cases. In Form I (in which the subject was given multiple choices to complete the items) phonetic and configuration clues, and possibly some structural anal-

ysis clues were available to help the subject make the correct responses. However, the limitations of the subject's own vocabulary
may have prevented him from making the correct response in some
cases. Even though he may have been able to sound out all of the
words, if he did not know the meaning of any of them, the clues
would not be helpful. Nevertheless, Forms I and IV did supply more
clues than any of the other forms and would certainly seem to indicate that the teaching of the use of context clues would be most
effective if additional word attack clues were included.

Form II included phonetic clues with the beginning and ending
letters given and with a rank of third easiest fits into the pattern
described—fewer clues make word attack more difficult. Then the
rank of Form III, with only the initial letter given, and Form V, with
no clues other than context, continue in the same pattern.

The rank of Form VI indicated that the length of the line would
give more of a clue than giving the initial letter, as in Form III.
However in scoring, no notice was taken as to whether the response
was short on a short line, or long on a long line as long as the
sentence made sense.

What difference does sex, intelligence, comprehension, vocabulary, and grade level make in the rank of difficulty of the tests? Did
IQ score make a difference as to which test was easier? To discover
the answer to these questions, the pupils' test scores were compared
in respect to various demographic variables. Table 1 shows the results obtained by this analysis.

TABLE 1

Summary Chart of Findings Pertaining to Demographic
Data and Difficulty in Context Clue Aids

Demographic Data	Spearman a	Kendall b	Probability
Sex	1.0		.01
Intelligence Quotient	1.0		.01
Comprehension Level		117.5	.05
Vocabulary Level		153.5	.01
Grade Level		149.5	.01

  a Spearman Rank Correlation Coefficient
  b Kendall Coefficient of concordance

These data showed that readers, regardless of sex, intelligence,
comprehension, vocabulary, and grade level, use the same clues in
unlocking words. The same sequence of difficulty in exercises could,

therefore, be used for all children in respect to the various variables studied.

This study demonstrated not one, but two, important conclusions. The first showed that a group of practitioners could plan and execute an experiment which had highly statistically significant and important findings. The second showed that it was possible to identify an heirarchy of easy to difficult exercises for orienting the child towards the use of context clues. These exercises can be put to practical use for teaching context clues in the classroom.

REFERENCES

1. Betts, Emmet A. *Foundations of Reading Instruction.* Chicago: American Book Company, 1946, p. 229.

2. Bond, Guy L. and Wagner, Eva Bond. *Teaching the Child to Read.* New York: The Macmillan Company, 1960, p. 172.

3. Carter, Homer L. J., and McGinnis, Dorothy. *Teaching Individuals to Read.* Boston: D. C. Heath and Company, 1962, p. 84.

4. Gates, Arthur I. *Gates Reading Survey.* New York: Bureau of Publications, Teachers' College.

5. Gray, William S. *On Their Own in Reading.* Chicago: Scott, Foresman and Company, 1960, p. 25.

6. Heilman, Arthur W. *Principles and Practices of Teaching Reading.* Columbus, Ohio: Charles E. Merrill Publishing Co., 1961, p. 182.

7. Hester, Kathleen B. *Teaching Every Child to Read.* New York: Harper and Row, 1964, p. 138.

8. Karlin, Robert. *Teaching Reading in High School.* New York: The Bobbs-Merrill Company, Inc., 1964, p. 91.

9. McCullough, Constance. "Context Aids in Reading." *The Reading Teacher* 11 (April 1943): 229.

10. _____. "Context Aids in Reading." *Elementary English Review* 20 (April 1943): 140-43.

11. McKee, Paul. *The Teaching of Reading.* Boston: Houghton Mifflin Co., 1948, p. 73.

12. Robinson, H. Alan. "A Study of the Technique of Word Identification." *The Reading Teacher* 16 (January 1963): 238-42.

13. Smith, Nila Banton. *Reading Instruction for Today's Children.* Englewood Cliffs, New Jersey: Prentice-Hall, Inc., 1963, p. 470.

14. Tinker, Miles A. *Teaching Elementary Reading.* New York: Appleton-Century-Crofts, Inc., 1952, p. 92.

15. Tinker, Miles A., and McCullough, Constance. *Teaching Elementary Reading.* New York: Appleton-Century-Crofts, Inc., 1962, p. 150.

9

Remedial Activities for Comprehension Skills

What relevancy do the Taxonomies of educational objectives have for your instructional program? What are the levels for classifying processes in the cognitive domain and the affective domain? Sylwester's article, another in his series dealing with leaders in modern educational theory, presents an overview and a challenge.

BENJAMIN BLOOM AND HIS TAXONOMY

Robert Sylwester

The longtime popularity of quiz programs, crossword puzzles, and other word games characterizes our society's infatuation with the power of random facts. Random facts abound in informal and standardized testing programs; and they come all too rapidly to mind when adults think back on their elementary school science and social studies instruction.

From *Instructor* vol. 80, no. 6 (February 1971): 67-68. Copyright © 1971 by The Instructor Publications, Inc. Reprinted with permission.

RANDOM FACTS

1. Who was the Egyptian sun god?
2. What is a scythe handle called?
3. What is the common two-letter name of the three-toed sloth?
4. What radio quiz program gave candy bars to contestants?
5. Who were the three regular panelists on INFORMATION PLEASE?
6. What TV quiz program was hosted by Johnny Carson?
7. Who was the original quizmaster on COLLEGE QUIZ BOWL?

1. Ra 2. snath 3. ai 4. Dr. I.Q. 5. Franklin P. Adams, John Kiernan, Oscar Levant 6. WHO DO YOU TRUST? 7. Allen Ludden

Consequently, thoughtful educators across the country applauded the 1956 publication of a handbook called *Taxonomy of Educational Objectives: Cognitive Domain* (Longmans)—a truly formidable title, but also a highly significant effort to put intellectual concerns into proper perspective. The title was quickly reduced in most educator's minds to *Bloom's Taxonomy* (after its senior editor), and the book and its 1964 companion, *The Affective Domain* (both are published in paperback by David McKay Company, Inc.) went on to help revolutionize contemporary educational thought.

BLOOM AND HIS FRIENDS

In 1948, Benjamin Bloom was University Examiner of the University of Chicago. He and his counterparts across the country belonged to an organization called the Association of College and University Examiners, and their 1948 conference dealt with problems faced by University Examiners when they try to write examinations that accurately evaluate the degree to which students meet objectives.

Most educational conferences die quickly and quietly after the last resolution of appreciation has been passed. This one didn't. The problem was too important. During succeeding years several dozen Association members continued to meet and work on the task they considered most pressing—that of developing a universal system for classifying educational objectives.

Their efforts led them to develop a taxonomy (a classification system) of educational objectives. The group felt that educational objectives stated in behavioral terms have a counterpart in the behavior of individuals, and that this behavior can be observed, described, and classified. They evolved a taxonomy that was sequential and cumulative—so arranged that each category in the system included some form of all categories that existed beneath it (just as in the biological taxonomy each living thing can be categorized by variety species, genus, family, order, class, and phylum).

They decided to organize their taxonomies around the three common educational objective domains: cognitive, affective, and psychomotor. They turned their attention to the cognitive domain first, because it was most significant to their work. David Krathwohl, Max Engelhart, Edward Furst, Walker Hill, and Bertram Masia, in addition to Bloom, played major roles in developing the two taxonomies that have resulted from the group's efforts to date.

Even though the books are addressed primarily to college teachers, elementary teachers will find that they give clear and concise background information on a critically important area of instruction.

The Cognitive Domain

1. Knowledge: *Bloom's Taxonomy* lists the acquisition of various kinds of knowledge as an important first-level educational objective, because knowledge is a necessary prerequisite to higher-level intellectual activity, even though not an end in itself.

The *Taxonomy* arranges knowledge into three major categories. During his school years a student should gain: 1. a knowledge of basic factual information and terminology; 2. a knowledge of conventional procedures for studying, organizing, and evaluating phenomena, trends, sequences, classifications, and categories; and 3. a knowledge of universals and abstractions such as major principles, generalizations, structures, and theories.

A student who has mastered knowledge objectives can recognize or recall facts, ideas, principles, procedures, and the like in the approximate form in which he has learned them.

2. Comprehension: Whereas knowledge is essentially information that has been stored for retrieval, comprehension is seen as the lowest level of understanding—the first step beyond merely repeating words. It implies an awareness of the significance of knowledge and insight into its meaning and intent.

The Taxonomy divides comprehension into three components: translation, interpretation, and extrapolation. Translation implies an ability to paraphrase a communication into another form or language without losing the original intent. Interpretation implies an ability to accurately explain or summarize a communication by viewing it from a different perspective. Extrapolation implies an ability to extend the interpretation of a communication beyond the limits of the available data—prediction based on somewhat limited information.

3. Application: The person who can apply and comprehend the knowledge he has is able to use it successfully under conditions that differ from those under which he originally encountered it. This suggests a more abstract and general knowledge, and an awareness of the existence of relationships and alternate possibilities.

4. Analysis: The person who can analyze something can dissect it into its logical elements, relationships, and organizing principles—clearly distinguishing among facts, principles, hypotheses, and the like.

5. Synthesis: Where analysis implies a taking apart, synthesis suggests a putting together into new forms that use unsuspected relationships—creative behavior. Synthesis might take the form of the production of a unique communication, the production of a plan or proposed set of operations, or the derivation of a set of abstract relations. Inquiry programs generally focus on the development of skills needed in synthesis.

6. Evaluation: Evaluation involves judging the adequacy of something on the basis of accepted internal evidence and external criteria. While judgments are necessary in working with all the foregoing categories, the notion of value is not introduced until this level. Thus, it ties in closely with the taxonomy of objectives in the affective domain.

Unfortunately, the elementary school program often expends so much effort in meeting the tremendous demands of the first two levels of cognitive objectives that it gives only lip service to the four succeeding levels in the hierarchy. Yet it is this latter kind of intellectual activity that gives meaning to knowledge and comprehension. It's a challenging concern for elementary teachers.

The Affective Domain

The *Taxonomy* committee encountered problems in trying to reduce the affective domain to a neat hierarchy of objectives. There is something intangible about attitudes, interests, emotions, and appreciations that doesn't lend itself easily to categorization and evaluation.

Nevertheless, the committee developed a hierarchy—and it's a good one.

1. Receiving (Attending): At the lowest affective level, a learner generally perceives the existence of a phenomenon in three ascending stages: 1. He becomes aware of the phenomenon although he does not pay special attention to it. 2. He indicates a willingness to come into contact with the phenomenon, to receive it. 3. He gives selected attention to aspects of the phenomenon.

2. Responding: The second level suggests responses that go beyond mere attention. The person becomes interested. He will comply with requests that arise out of the phenomenon. He will volunteer. And at the highest level in this category, he will achieve a sense of satisfaction in being involved with the phenomenon.

3. Valuing: At this level, a person is motivated not by a mere desire to comply, but rather because the phenomenon has worth. He accepts it. He prefers it. He has a commitment to it.

4. Organization: As a person accepts and adopts values, he encounters situations in which more than one value is relevant. Consequently, he reaches a point where he must conceptualize values and organize them into a value system he can accept and live with.

5. Characterization by a value or a value complex: At this highest level of internalization, a person has come to peace with his value system. He acts in a way that is consistent with his generalized set of values, and he has moved toward a philosophy of life—a world view—that, when completely formed, can characterize him completely.

YOUR CHALLENGE

These two taxonomies of educational objectives comprise only eleven major categories, and yet many of the activities in our society's formal and informal educational process can be subsumed within these categories. Thus they help define your role as a teacher in our society.

Read the handbooks and draw depth from the excellent explanations and illustrations they contain. In the last several years, other educators have sought to relate the *Taxonomy* to specific aspects of classroom life. Norris Sander's *Classroom Questions: What Kind?* (Harper and Row, 1966; $2.50 paperback) is a fine illustration of this kind of effort—well worth your while. Seek out others.

Of course, if your conception of teaching is still bogged down at the level of random facts, you might prefer to munch on a candy bar while you do a crossword puzzle . . .

Many instructional materials have been assigned levels of difficulty. How do publishers arrive at the grade-level designation of your instructional materials? Mills and Richardson present a provocative article.

WHAT DO PUBLISHERS MEAN BY "GRADE LEVEL"?

Robert E. Mills
Jean R. Richardson

Teachers and remedial clinicians frequently express despair about securing from publishers materials that are accurately graded for level of difficulty. Nevertheless, most parents, and too often teachers, assume that what the publisher states is a "third-grade" book is written at third-grade level. Recent studies of readability variances between the publisher's grade listing of a book and the grade level as determined by a readability formula suggest the need of a common formula in the grading of books by a single publishing company and among various companies. It is true that factors such as concept load and individual differences within any school grade level add to the difficulty of evaluating texts. Too often, however, it would seem that publishers and educators excuse themselves from concern over level of difficulty because they are unable to control *all* variables. It is our contention that every effort should be made to control at least the more mechanical, objective variables to get the selection of reading books and materials out of the realm of pure guesswork.

Two hundred basic readers and other texts recommended for use in grades one through three were graded by remedial clinicians using the Spache formula. This formula takes into account both vocabulary and sentence complexity and, with a little practice, can produce very consistent reliable gradings. These texts came from seventeen publishers and included most of the primary texts used in the United States today. While many of them agreed closely with the publishers' stated grade level, there were some wide disparities.

From *The Reading Teacher* vol. 16, no. 5 (March 1963): 359-62. Reprinted with permission of the International Reading Association and Robert E. Mills.

There was, for example, a "primer" that turned out to be written at second grade-third month level. This seemed such a wide disparity that it was independently regraded by two other clinicians, with comparable results. There was also the series of three first-grade readers which scored at second grade-fourth month, second grade-sixth month, and second grade-ninth month.

Attention was then turned toward books on higher levels. The books selected were from a group of children's books, grades four through eight, published by well-known companies. These books were then graded by the Dale-Chall formula for books above fourth-grade level, which like the Spache takes into account both vocabulary and sentence complexity. The results were comparable to those found in the study of elementary texts.

The findings indicated a need for examining the methods by which the publishers determine the grade level of their books. Twelve companies were then chosen from well-established publishers of children's books, grades one through eight. These publishers were sent a letter and a questionnaire designed to secure only data pertinent to this study. The list of publishers included: Bobbs-Merrill, Grosset and Dunlap, E. M. Hale, Houghton-Mifflin, J. D. Lippincott, Charles E. Merrill, Macmillan, Row-Peterson, Scott-Foresman, Webster, and World Book Company.

The main part of the letter consisted of the following paragraph:

> We are requesting information regarding your formula for grading children's books, grades one through eight. A research study is being conducted on the need for a more consistent formula in grading books within a single publishing company, and between various companies. When your company lists a book as "for grades 1 - 3," it is difficult to understand such labeling because of the extreme difference in sentence complexity, vocabulary load, and interest level for a first grader as contrasted with a third grader.

The questionnaire posed six questions in three groups. 1 and 2. Do you use specific formulae for grading books? If Yes, what method is used and by whom is it done? 3 and 4. Is this formula used for all books, grades one through eight? What other procedures are used, i.e., experts in field grading books? 5 and 6. Do you employ specifically trained people to grade books? How is the level of interest established?

From the publishers to whom we addressed our requests, seven replies were received. From these seven only four completed the questionnaire. Second and third letters were sent to the five publishers who did not respond the first time, but to no avail.

We might speculate as to why five of the publishers gave no response whatsoever. Do they feel there is no need for a readability formula? Were they purposely avoiding the subject for some reason? Or is there an indifference on the part of publishers toward the readability of their books? Or did they "not have the time" to be bothered with research projects such as ours?

The replies we received were astonishing and somewhat discouraging. Two large publishing firms were unabashedly annoyed at our inference that a readability formula should be used. One publisher stated

> ... it is impossible to grade children's books exactly, for reading standards vary widely in different parts of the country and even in different parts of the same state, but those of us working in this field have found it necessary to use very elastic gradings— Preschool to 3rd Grade, 4th to 6th, 7th to 9th, 10th to 12th. . . . We strive to make the reader stretch his mind, imagination and interest."

A child reading on a primer level cannot be expected to read and comprehend a book written on a third-grade level because of the tremendous development of vocabulary between these grades. To give a child who is reading on a first-grade level a third-grade book is unwarrented, unfair, unrealistic, and damaging. A young reader's mind can be "stretched" only so far before he loses interest. Besides frustrating the child, these "elastic gradings" rob the teachers of a criterion for judging a child's reading. How many parents would accept a report card which read, "Your child is reading somewhere between a primer and third-grade level"?

Another publisher wrote:

> The most important thing in determining actual readability is probably none of the mechanical factors which include the word list, sentence length, complexity of sentences, etc., but rather the motivational factors. These are quite hard to assess, but include such things as writing in conversational style, personalizing the material, giving dramatic openings and dramatic handling of material, and a considerable additional range of factors that make material interesting and easy to read and of particular appeal to particular grade levels.

It does not seem possible that motivational factors could determine to this extent the readability of a book. An adult who is a sailing enthusiast cannot read a book on sailing written in Arabic if he does not know Arabic; nor can a child who is reading on a first-grade level read a third-grade book with much profit. To present such books to the adult or child highly motivated in a particular field would only prove that much more frustrating. The problem is obviously a matter of vocabulary development.

About one-half the publishers reported that no standardized formulae were used; they relied on the judgment of their authors or educational consultants to determine the grade level of their texts. Authors and educational consultants are, however, too often out of touch with the school system and have too little opportunity to observe the child as he reads. They do not realize the obvious need for a consistent systematic progression of graded texts.

Furthermore, there is the problem of variations in texts at the same grade level. The assumption that books labeled by their publishers as third grade are actually written at third-grade reading level has already been shown to be fallacious. This variance works a tremendous hardship not only on the student, but also on the teacher, for the teacher is thus required to work with virtually no universal criteria. Consistency in graded texts cannot be accomplished without the use of standardized, comparable formulae.

Books of all varieties from the publishers queried in this survey were graded by at least two evaluators. The results were then compared with the grade level listed on the individual publisher's catalogue. It is true that approximately 50 percent of the two hundred books graded were appropriately labeled. A selection of twenty of the books which showed disparity is presented in the table to indicate some of the differences which exist. These books varied from the publisher's listing from one to four school years. One in every five books (20 percent) was below the grade level listing; and four out of every five books (80 percent) were above the grade level listing. Therefore, we would conclude that the tendency is to upgrade books and that there are enough discrepancies in these gradings to warrant some positive action being taken to remedy this very real problem.

In these days when we are asking young readers to read more texts than ever before, it is our contention that providing them with a systematic progression of graded texts is an important step in developing confidence and minimizing frustration. Our findings certainly indicate the need for publishers to use some more consistent means of grading their texts. We believe that the use of comparable readability formulae is the best solution. It would be well if teachers, librarians, and others charged with the responsibility of selecting books for young readers started questioning publishers more closely as to what means they employ for grading their books and perhaps make purchases accordingly.

It would appear from the lethargy shown in the responses of publishers to this type of study that if anything constructive is to be done, it will have to be initiated by educators and parents.

TABLE 1

Grade Levels of Publishers and Researchers Compared

Book	Publisher's Grade	Researcher's Grade	Difference
Buckie's Friends	Pre	2.5	2½+
Making Friends	1	3.2	2+
Skipping Along	2	3.4	1½+
The New Round About	1	2.2	1+
The New Wishing Well	Pre	2.3	1+
The New Anything Can Happen	1	2.4	1½+
Runaway Home	6	5.2	1-
Parades	7	5.9	1-
New Days and Deeds	5.1	6.1	1+
Jack and Janet	1	2.0	1+
Bright Peaks	6	7.1	1+
Young Audubon	4.0	5.4	1½+
Molly Pitcher	4.0	2.5	1½-
Dan Webster	4.0	2.6	1½-
Boy Sailor	4.0	5.9	1½+
Little Fat Gretchen	1	3.3	2+
Stagecoach Sam	2	5.3	3+
Cowboy Tommy	3	5.6	2½+
Cowboy Tommy Roundup	3	5.9	3+
The Little Cowboy	1	5.3	4+

The importance of comprehension in the process of reading has been documented. Can a hierarchy for comprehension skills be identified? Huus gives an overview of comprehension skills and suggests strategies for assisting students achieve high levels of analysis and reasoning.

CRITICAL ASPECTS OF COMPREHENSION

Helen Huus

It is not enough that students learn to pronounce words and read aloud with ease and fluency. The purpose of reading is communication with the author, interpreting and reacting to his ideas, then assimilating what one will to become a permanent part of him. Too long have students been able to survive and progress in school with low-level reading skills, even in word recognition. If there is any doubt about this, just ask a high school student to read aloud his basic text for a course or have an elementary school student read at sight unfamiliar material at his ability level. Even very good readers —those who have mastered the skills of being able to pronounce nearly all words they meet and to understand what they read—can profit from work on skills that require high levels of analysis and reasoning. Critical reading is one of these skills.

LEVELS OF COMPREHENSION

There are at least three levels on which a reader can understand an author's ideas, each requiring skill and practice.

The first is at the literal level, where the reader grasps the work as a whole and knows "what the book says." As he reads, he notices the movement throughout the work, until upon completion, he can view the total as a unit. He can then outline, paraphrase, or summarize the ideas expressed by the author. This rather parrotlike repeti-

From *Elementary English* vol. 48, no. 5 (May 1971): 489-94. Copyright © 1971 by the National Council of Teachers of English and Helen Huus.

tion indicates that the reader at least has the word recognition skills that allow him to identify the printed words and the vocabulary and language skills that allow him to comprehend sentences in sequence and to put groups of sentences together.

Much of what goes on in school is, unfortunately, at this level. Teachers assign readings and expect students to be responsible for summarizing and repeating what they find in this material. Those who do this very well are often, mistakenly, given credit for being superior students when all they are doing is merely repeating what they have absorbed. However, this is not completely to their disadvantage, for this level is prerequisite to higher levels of reading and thinking.

At the second level of comprehension lies interpretation— "what the author really means" regardless of what he says. Marc Antony's funeral oration for Julius Caesar is a case in point . . . "For Brutus is an honourable man," you remember, or the many proverbs found in the language of various peoples. Among these are the well-known "When the cat's away, the mice will play," which in Scotland becomes, "Well kens the mouse when the cat's oot o' the house," and in Haiti, "When the cat's away, the mice dance the calinda." Then, too, there is the Russian one that states, "When the Tsar has a cold, all must cough," the Chinese one, "He who rides on a tiger can never dismount," and one recently quoted by a student from Nairobi, Kenya, "When two elephants fight, the grass suffers." Obviously, these do not mean what they literally state, and to take them thus misses the meaning completely. Yet among our pupils are a few literally minded ones who need help in delving for themselves the deeper meanings involved.

Many facets of meaning can be deduced through interpretation —content, sequence, time, place, theme, character development, mood and tone, style, and relationships of various types, such as cause-effect, fact-fancy, agents-events, part-whole, conclusions, and predictions. Each of these is worthy of separate treatment and of special attention by teachers, but they are mentioned here only to show their place in the total complex that is comprehension.

At the third and highest level is assimilation or psychological integration, where the reader asks himself, "What does all this mean to me?" or "What have I to do with this?" It is this recognition of a personal connection, of accepting into one's apperceptive mass or background the ideas freshly gained from reading and then making these ideas a part of one's total knowledge that characterizes the individual who obtains the fullest meaning from his reading. In this way, "Reading maketh," as Francis Bacon said, "the full man," and affects the nature of his personality and his actions. Truly, each individual is a part of all that he has seen and heard and read.

This phenomenon operates in a circular fashion, for as the reader enriches his background, then can he find more connections with what he subsequently reads than was possible before; as he continues reading, he can fit more and more pieces into his mental mosaic and, like the overtones in music, these enhance his comprehension by more than sheer addition.

While these three levels of reading increase in complexity and require progressively higher levels of creative thought, they do not progress sequentially in that the higher levels are reserved for older and more mature readers than those found in primary grades. Quite the contrary. Young children can, at their level of mental maturity, apply these aspects of comprehension to their reading. The skills required are interdependent and build one upon the other and continue to be applied with increasing maturity and skill in reading.

CRITICAL READING DEFINED

Critical reading as an aspect of comprehension needs to be viewed against this total background. It belongs, I think, between levels two and three and might be considered as an extension of interpretation, for inference is certainly involved in the process of critical reading.

During the last decade, much attention has been given to critical reading, but it is only recently that there has come to be some consensus of opinion regarding what is involved. Critical reading is not, I would maintain, problem solving *per se,* though such an approach might be used; it is not drawing conclusions and making generalizations from the content, though conclusions must be drawn in the process of reading critically; it is not interpreting figurative language or noting cause-effect relationships, which are in the province of interpretation, though inferences are made regarding those aspects which are within the province of critical reading.

One dictionary definition of a critic is "a person who makes judgments of the merits and faults of books, music, pictures, plays, acting, etc."[1] From this definition, critical reading would require the making of judgments of the merits and faults of the material read —notice it is both positive and negative. It requires the reader to judge and evaluate the worth, validity, and quality of what is read. The key words are "judge" and "evaluate"—to compare the material with established criteria that set forth the standard or norm against

[1]E. L. Thorndike and Clarence L. Barnhart, *Thorndike-Barnhart High School Dictionary* (Chicago: Scott, Foresman and Co., 1957), p. 234.

which the material is measured in order to decide just how good it is. This presumes that a reader has the necessary background to provide him with an adequate norm or standard for judging. It also presumes that this base is of high quality, obtained from exposure to the best of its type, whatever the dimension may be.

Worth

The worth or value of a selection is related to the purpose—the purpose of the author in writing the work and the purpose of the individual who reads it. Unless the author has explicitly stated his purpose, it can only be inferred from what is known about him, his way of working, and his ideas and philosophy. The work could have sprung from inspiration or from studied design, and the value to the author may have been in the expression of his idea directly, or indirectly through some symbolism that is meaningful to him. With living authors, it is often possible to find out what their thoughts and motives were in connection with a piece of writing, but with those long dead, the critics can only infer most of the time.

To the reader, however, the worth of the material may depend upon its content, directly, or indirectly when its symbolic implications are those which serve the reader's purpose. In order to be able to judge the worth, the reader must be able to understand the literal meaning, to see the symbolism involved, and to note the relevancy of either or both to his immediate needs. The value of different works for a student will vary from time to time as he judges each selection for relevancy to his central purpose. He learns to be selective, ruthlessly eleminating that which does not fit in favor of that which does.

Validity

Validity as a criterion for evaluating printed works denotes that which is not false, which agrees with fact, and which is accurate and correct, real and genuine. Some sordid facts, some negative approaches, and some unethical practices may be uncovered as fact and must be judged for what they are. The difficulty here is knowing when all the information has been assembled, or at least enough so that additional data do not change the total. A related problem is knowing whether or not the facts are accurate and in proper perspective. Still another problem stems from the shifting nature of what is valid as the result of changes in our society and of scientific studies that have unearthed (sometimes literally) new information and exploded old theories. The acceptance of these findings precipitates a constant revising of facts to coincide with the most recent data. A case in point is the discovery by Helge Ingstad of the Viking settlement in Newfoundland, indicating they were here before Columbus![2] And you know that the President and Congress have recognized this by designating October 9, as Leif Ericson Day.[3]

Validity is relative in another sense, also, in that facts can be accepted intellectually, but rejected emotionally. The study by Crossen[4] on the effect of the reader's prejudices pointed out the need for guiding students in the selection, interpretation, and evaluation of materials when dealing with topics on which unfavorable attitudes are held. There is also evidence to suggest that information contrary to that of the reader leads to confusion and irritation rather than to change in attitude.

Quality

In judging quality, the ultimate criteria remain goodness, truth, and beauty. "Goodness" is the characteristic identifying that which is admirable, noble, uplifting, ethical, just, right, proper, genuine, honorable, worthy, and so on, and it embodies positive attributes as opposed to negative ones. The determination by an individual of which is right or proper depends upon his knowledge, his experiences, and his bias.

"Truth" as a criterion for criticism is closely related to "validity," yet it connotes a greater good than mere accuracy. While it is essential to quality, it is also the sine qua non of the total act of critical reading, for sometimes exaggerated claims are made, in advertising for example, or willful distortion of facts appear in propaganda, or perhaps a typographical error slipped through the copy reader.

"Beauty" refers to the delight of the mind and senses caused by the presentation of something that is pleasing to see or hear because of its excellence and harmony. Beauty may be found in content, form, or treatment, and like other criteria of quality, depends upon the individual's knowledge, experiences, and bias.

The application of these criteria form the essence and taste, and to the degree that the individual has been exposed to a wide range of material is he able to judge what is at hand. Unless he has seen the very best, he may have no notion of how good it can be or how

---

[2]Helge Ingstad, "Vinland Ruins Prove Vikings Found the New World," *National Geographic,* 126. (November 1964): 708-34.

[3]"News in Brief," *News of Norway* (October 16, 1967): p. 131.

[4]Helen J. Crossen, "Effects of the Attitude of the Reader upon Critical Reading Ability," *Journal of Educational Research* 42 (December 1948): 289-98.

far removed the material he is reading actually is from the superior model.

In this connection, Frye states that:

> Good taste follows and is developed by the study of litera-
> ture; its precision results from knowledge, but does not produce
> knowledge. Hence the accuracy of any critic's good taste is no
> guarantee that his inductive basis in literary experience is ade-
> quate. This may still be true even after the critic has learned to
> base his judgments on his experience of literature and not on his
> social, moral, religious, or personal anxieties.[5]

To repeat, then, critical reading is judging and evaluating the worth, validity, and quality of the material read.

CRITICAL READING APPLIED

If teachers are to develop critical readers, what are the factors to be considered, and what are the aspects, the materials, and the methods to be used?

Factors

First of all, teachers must recognize that the student's personal characteristics and background, his intelligence, maturity, social level, experiences, attitudes, and values will affect his ability to read critically. This is not meant to imply that young children cannot learn to read critically, only that they will operate at their own level, using materials they can read. However, their skills will also be limited by their obviously limited background of information.

Readers may not always *see* the other side of an argument, even when these are understood, for their preconceived notions, biases, and prejudices stand in the way. It takes time and repetition, plus irrefutable facts, to change attitudes. The development of objectivity in dealing with emotionally loaded content is an important goal in all teaching.

The critical approach to material varies with the purpose of the reader. To be able to discern relevancy and applicability requires an acute understanding of the problem and the ability to see connections between it and the material being considered. While obvious connections are not difficult to note, it is the ability to see the subtle ramifications and relationships that distinguishes the scholar from the pedant.

---

[5]Northrop Frye, *Anatomy of Criticism* (Princeton, New Jersey: Princeton University Press, 1957), p. 27.

Aspects of critical reading

The aspects of critical reading which need evaluation include the author, the content, and the style.

A critical reader wants to know: "Who says this? Who *is* he? What does he know about the topic? Has he practical experience to back up his statements? Why did he write this? What is he trying to do—to me? Why should I believe him, especially if I don't agree with him?" Such are questions in the mind of someone who is thinking about his reading.

Checking the background and competency of the author is not always easy, particularly if he is not well known. If he is not included in the various *Who's Who* or *Who Was Who,* information can sometimes be found in journals where he has appeared, in advertisements of his works, on the dust jacket of his books, in newspaper publicity, or as a last resort, from his publisher. Even elementary school children know their favorite authors, have read their complete works (on their level, of course), and are familiar with homey details about them. Inviting authors to talk with pupils is a pleasant way to help students see that authors are human beings who happen to write and get their works in print.

A publisher shares the reputation of his authors, and vice versa, for reputable publishers with astute editors are responsible for locating unknown writers and presenting them to the public. As the reputation of an author grows, so too, does that of the publisher. Learning which publishers produce which types of material and noting the level of quality generally maintained may also aid the student in selecting and judging the work done by an author new to him. The checks on content which will be mentioned subsequently also aid in evaluating the competency of the author, as does his particular style of writing.

Teachers can ask children to find what they can of the author's background, especially as it relates to the content under consideration. Does the author have firsthand information about it? Is it in a field in which he should be expected to know something? Is his experience recent? Has he the educational background that assures a firm grounding in the subject? Has he written on the topic before? Has he a vested interest or an "axe to grind"?

But when information about the author is unavailable, the student can still evaluate, merely by analyzing the content itself. Is the material accurate, or if fantasy, is it plausible fantasy? Are complete facts given, or at least adequate enough to give an accurate perspective of the total? How do you know? Is the material documented so that you can check it for yourself? Is the material recent? Is it logical and internally consistent?

Teachers can help students by assignments such as these:

1. Choose five important facts given in this selection. Check each fact with at least two other sources.
2. What is the date of this work? Look up the chronological development of the topic and determine the status as of this date.
3. What personal experiences can you cite that bear out or refute the central idea expressed?
4. State the conclusion in your own words, then list the items that lead to this conclusion. What other arguments can you think of that might support this conclusion? What arguments that refute this? What arguments, if any, in the work refute each other?
5. Does this argument always hold? In other words, is this a generalization? How do you know?
6. Is this a true story or is it an imaginary one? Why do you say so? Is it based on facts or on what someone thinks or believes?

Those interested in pursuing the idea might read the report by Wolf on their experiment in teaching critical thinking at Ohio State,[6] or the early study by Glaser.[7]

The third aspect for critical reading is the manner in which the material is written—the aesthetic, literary, and ethical qualities inherent in its presentation. "Aesthetic" refers to the artistic aspects which in part are inherent in the conception and approach and in part dependent upon the style of writing. Lofty and grand ideas, like those in the myths and epics of a civilization, demand dignified and formal language that is elevated above the ordinary, whereas the homey folk tales that originated among the people of the countryside can be couched in the national vernacular, in the colloquialisms of everyday discourse. When style and idea are incongruous, humor results, as Mark Twain illustrated so well.

"Literary" qualities in the style of writing enhance the spirit of the work, and figures of speech add a lustre and freshness that cause

---

[6]Willavene Wolf, "The Logical Dimension of Critical Reading," *Reading and Inquiry Proceedings of the Annual Convention, X* (Newark, Delaware: International Reading Association, 1965), pp. 121-24.

[7]Edward M. Glaser, *An Experiment in the Development of Critical Thinking,* Teachers Contributions to Education, Number 843 (New York: Teachers College Columbia University, 1941), p. 212.

the reader to view the topic in a new light. The use of original similes and metaphor strike the reader, such as Vachel Lindsay's "The moon's the North Wind's cooky," Rowena Bennett's "The train is a dragon that roars through the Dark," and R. L. Stevenson's wind, "Like ladies' skirts across the grass," which may take some tall explaining today!

The basic "ethic" in stories for the young requires that Good will triumph over Evil, and that the villian will get his just due. However, this must be evaluated from the child's point of view, not from that of the adult, for otherwise how would Puss in Boots escape the electric chair or the First Chinese Brother go scot-free? It is soon enough to introduce the "debunking" school of biography when students are mature enough to cope with it. This admits to a kind of censorship of books for children until they attain the maturity enabling them to make judgments. On the other hand, children do have a kind of indigenous good taste that results in their recognizing the shoddy and accepting the best—assuming, of course, that they have access to it.

In this category, too, is the recognition of the various propaganda devices: bandwagon, testimonial, transfer, card-stacking, and so on. An interesting assignment in this connection is to ask children to categorize advertisements in magazines or on television according to the propaganda device used for appeal. Then have them choose a product they wish to advertise and let them write their own ads. Another variation could be tried by asking them to write several ads for the same product, using a different technique each time. Even kindergarten children could set up criteria for choosing toys, clothes, or food, then compare what the different advertisements tell them as the teacher reads them the contents.

10

Evaluation in Remedial Reading

In the curriculum field a controversy exists concerning the involvement of students in activities for which there have been no preset objectives established. Can such objectives be justified, or is the primary purpose of schools the changing of behavior through specific, predetermined objectives? Raths' article presents a challenge and provides some answers.

TEACHING WITHOUT SPECIFIC OBJECTIVES

James D. Raths

A central issue in the curriculum field is the dilemma, perhaps oversimplified, between *discipline* and *freedom.* Lawrence S. Kubie stated it most clearly:

> To put the question even more specifically, the educator must ask, "How can I equip the child with the facts and the tools which he will need in life, without interfering with the freedom with which he will be able to use them after he has acquired

From *Educational Leadership* vol. 28, no. 7 (April 1971): 714-20. Reprinted by permission of the Association for Supervision and Curriculum Development and James Raths. Copyright © 1971 by the Association for Supervision and Curriculum Development.

them?" We have learned that both input-overload through the excessive use of grill and drill, and input-underload through excessive permissiveness, may tumble the learner into the same abyss of paralysis and ignorance. (1)

The aim of this paper is to argue that by accepting the basic assumption that the *primary* purpose of schooling is to change the behavior of students in specific predetermined ways, schools are only making the problem defined by Kubie more acute. In addition, this paper asserts that activities may be justified for inclusion in the curriculum on grounds other than those based on the efficacy of the activity for specifically changing the behaviors of students. It is also proposed that schools, while accepting a minimum number of training responsibilities, would take as their *major* purpose one of involving students in activities which have no preset objectives, but which meet other specified criteria.

TEACHING FOR BEHAVIORAL OBJECTIVES

Regardless of the underlying bases on which curricula are selected for inclusion in a program, a major problem is that of justifying the activities children are asked to experience. Clearly, the selection process always involves subjective and value-related judgments.

Consider the junior high school teacher of science in his efforts to defend the behavioral objectives of his program. He may argue that a particular objective is justified on the grounds that it is related to student success in senior high school; that the objective has traditionally been taught as a part of the curriculum; that it reflects the behavior of scientists and as such is important to his students; or more simply, that the objective is "in the book." None of these justifications, either singly or collectively, seems especially convincing.

The problem is seen most clearly in the affective domain. Lay persons and professionals alike have long asked, "What values should be taught?" Krathwohl, Bloom, and Masia (2) have argued that one reason which partially accounts for the erosion of affective objectives in our schools is that teachers hesitate to impose values on their students through the lever of giving grades. On the other hand, teachers seem to feel that manipulating students in the cognitive domain is ethical. For instance, a science teacher may want his students to acquire behaviors associated with the scientific method. Manifestly, there is no one scientific method, just as there is no one view of justice, yet teachers seem to feel no compunction about "forcing" students to learn the scientific method they have in mind while shying away from teaching one view of justice.

It is important in terms of the central thesis of this paper to consider the long range implications a teacher and his students must accept once it has been decided that all students are to acquire a specific instructional objective. The teacher's task becomes at once difficult and tedious. He must inform his students of the objective to which they are expected to aspire; he must convince them of the relevance of this objective to their lives; he must give students the opportunity to practice the behavior being taught; he must diagnose individual difficulties encountered by members of his group; he must make prescriptions of assignments based on his diagnoses and repeat the cycle again and again. Needless to say, this "method" of instruction has proved itself effective, if not provocative. It is the training paradigm perfected during both World Wars and utilized extensively in the armed forces and in industry to prepare persons for specific responsibilities.

It is the rare teacher who implements this procedure with the precision implied by the foregoing description. Few teachers have the energy, the knowledge important for making diagnoses, the memory needed to recall prescriptions, or the feedback capabilities of a computer. The ultimate training program is the research-based IPI model used experimentally in a few schools throughout the country. This observation is not meant to fault teachers as a group but merely to observe that in terms of the ways schools are organized, for example, teacher-student ratios, availability of special technical assistance, etc., only the most gifted and dedicated teachers can offer an effective training procedure to students. So instead of a rigorous training paradigm, most students are presented with "grill and drill" techniques, as cited by Kubie, repetitious to some and meaningless to others. Yet even if all programs could be set up on the basis of behavioral objectives, who could argue that such a program would be other than tedious and ultimately stultifying? This last comment applies both to the students and to the teacher. Usually, teaching for objectives is dull work. Most of the student responses are familiar ones and are anticipated by a teacher who is fully aware of the range of possible problems students might meet in acquiring the behavior. Hopefully, both teachers and students aspire to something other than this.

TEACHING WITHOUT SPECIFIC OBJECTIVES

To suggest that teachers plan programs without specific instructional objectives seems to fly in the face of many sacred beliefs—

those dealing with progress, efficiency, success, and even rationality. On the other hand, such a proposal evidently does not fly in the face of current practices. Much to the distress of empiricists (3, 4), teachers do from time to time invite children to participate in activities for which specific behavioral objectives are rarely preset. Examples of some of these activities include taking field trips, acting in dramatic presentation, having free periods in school, participating in school governments, putting out a class newspaper, and many others. While teachers evidently hope that students, as individuals, will acquire learnings from these activities, the learnings are generally not preset nor are they imposed on all the children in the class.

Instead, teachers may intend that these activities will provide students with some of the skills they will need in life, either through the direct experience they undergo in the classroom in carrying out the activity or through subsequent follow-up activities. In addition, teachers learn to expect that some children will become bored with any single activity—whatever it is. This response can be found in most classrooms at any one time and teachers simply make plans to involve those students suffering from momentary ennui in other provocative activities later in the day or week.

While carrying out a program composed of such activities, a teacher must perform many important and difficult tasks, but the functions seem less perfunctory and more challenging than those carried out under the training regimen described previously. A teacher must listen to the comments and questions of his students with the intent of clarifying their views and perceptions; he must encourage students to reflect upon their experiences through writings, poetry, drawings, and discussions; he must react to their responses in ways that suggest individual activities students may consider in following up on their experiences. In these ways, teachers provide an environment that is sufficiently evocative to encourage children to become informed and capable, but in individual ways that would be difficult to anticipate either in the central offices of a board of education or in the test construction laboratories located at Palo Alto or Iowa City.

CRITERIA FOR WORTHWHILE ACTIVITIES

If we accept the argument that the major focus of our schools should be away from activities designed to bring about specific behavioral changes in students, then on what basis can activities be justified for inclusion in the curricula of our schools? This section advances some criteria for identifying activities that seem to have some inherent worth. The criteria set down here for identifying worthwhile activities are not advanced to convince anyone of their wisdom as a set or individually, but merely to suggest value statements that might be used to justify the selection of particular activities in a curriculum.

The value statements are couched in terms that can best be used in the following manner. As a teacher contemplates an activity for his classroom, each of the value statements may suggest ways the activity might be altered. For instance, if a teacher were to consider an assignment which requires students to write a report on Brazil, he might revise his assignment to include one or more of the value dimensions suggested by the criteria. With all other things being equal, the revised assignment would be considered, according to these criteria, more worthwhile than the original one.

A relevant question to raise at this point is, "Worthwhile for whom?" The answer necessarily is for the child and for society. While there can be no empirical support for this response, neither can any other activity or behavioral objective be justified through data.

1. *All other things being equal, one activity is more worthwhile than another if it permits children to make informed choices in carrying out the activity and to reflect on the consequences of their choices:* An activity that requires children to select topics for study, resources for use, or media for the display of ideas, after some exploration of alternatives, is more worthwhile than one that provides children with no opportunities or another that gives choices at rather mundane levels, for example, a choice of now or this afternoon, or using a pen or pencil.

2. *All other things being equal, one activity is more worthwhile than another if it assigns to students active roles in the learning situation rather than passive ones:* An activity that channels students' energies into such roles as panel members, researchers, orators, observers, reporters, interviewers, actors, surveyors, performers, role players, or participants in simulation exercises such as games is more worthwhile than one which assigns students to tasks such as listening in class to the teacher, filling out a ditto sheet, responding to a drill session, or participating in a routine teacher-led discussion.

3. *All other things being equal, one activity is more worthwhile than another if it asks students to engage in inquiry into ideas, applications of intellectual processes, or current problems, either personal or social:* An activity that directs children to become ac-

quainted with ideas that transcend traditional curricular areas, ideas such as truth, beauty, worth, justice, or self-worth; one that focuses children on intellectual processes such as testing hypotheses, identifying assumptions, or creating original pieces of work which communicate personal ideas or emotions; or one that raises questions about current social problems such as pollution, war and peace, or of personal human relations is more worthwhile than one that is directed toward places (Mexico or Africa), objects (birds or simple machines), or persons (Columbus or Shakespeare).

4. *All other things being equal, one activity is more worthwhile than another if it involves children with realia.* An activity that encourages children to touch, handle, apply, manipulate, examine, and collect real objects, materials, and artifacts either in the classroom or on field trips is more worthwhile than one that involves children in the use of pictures, models, or narrative accounts.

5. *All other things being equal, one activity is more worthwhile than another if completion of the activity may be accomplished successfully by children at several different levels of ability:* An activity that can be completed successfully by children of diverse interests and intellectual backgrounds is more worthwhile than one which specifies in rigid terms only one successful outcome of the activity. Examples of the former are thinking, comparing, classifying, or summarizing, all of which allow youngsters to operate on their own levels without imposing a single standard on the outcomes.

6. *All other things being equal, one activity is more worthwhile than another if it asks students to examine in a new setting an idea, an application of an intellectual process, or a current problem which has been previously studied:* An activity that builds on previous student work by directing a focus into *novel* locations, *new* subject matter areas, or *different* contexts is more worthwhile than one that is completely unrelated to the previous work of the students. (This position is an example of one that is impossible to build into every activity presented to students. Obviously a balance is needed between new areas of study and those which are related to previous work. Value dimension number six asserts the need for some continuity in a program.)

7. *All other things being equal, one activity is more worthwhile than another if it requires students to examine topics or issues that citizens in our society do not normally examine—and that are typically ignored by the major communication media in the nation:* An

activity that deals with matters of sex, religion, war and peace, the profit motive, treatment of minorities, the workings of the courts, the responsiveness of local governments to the needs of the people, the social responsibilities of public corporations, foreign influences in American media, social class, and similar issues is more worthwhile than an activity which deals with mundane "school topics" such as quadratic equations or short stories—topics usually considered safe and traditional.

8. *All other things being equal, one activity is more worthwhile than another if it involves students and faculty members in "risk"-taking—not a risk of life or limb, but a risk of success or failure:* Activities that may receive criticism from supervisors and parents on the basis of "what's usually done," that may fail because of unforeseen events or conditions are more worthwhile than activities that are relatively risk-free—using approaches which are condoned openly by the community and the school administration and which have served teachers well in the past.

9. *All other things being equal, one activity is more worthwhile than another if it requires students to rewrite, rehearse, and polish their initial efforts:* Rather than having students perceive assignments as "tasks to complete," activities should provide time and opportunity for students to revise their themes in the light of criticism, rehearse a play in front of an audience, or practice an interviewing technique to be used in a project so that they will begin to see the value of doing a task well. Activities that communicate to students that their efforts are approximations of perfect work—and that efforts can be made to improve their work—are more worthwhile than ones that merely suggest that once an assignment is completed the first time, it is finished.

10. *All other things being equal, one activity is more worthwhile than another if it involves students in the application and mastery of meaningful rules, standards, or disciplines:* Using standards derived from students as well as authorities, panel discussions can be disciplined by procedures; reporting of data can be disciplined by considerations of control; essays can be regulated by considerations of style and syntax. Activities which foster a sense of meaningful discipline, either imposed or chosen by the children themselves, are more worthwhile than ones that ignore the need for the application of meaningful rules or standards.

11. *All other things being equal, one activity is more worthwhile than another if it gives students a chance to share the planning, the*

carrying out of a plan, or the results of an activity with others: One facet of the current trends in individualizing instruction found in some programs is that of minimizing the chance for children to work in groups and to learn the problems inherent in any situation that calls for individual desires to yield at times to group requirements. An activity that asks children to play a role in sharing responsibilities with others is more worthwhile than one which limits such opportunity.

12. *All other things being equal, one activity is more worthwhile than another if it is relevant to the expressed purposes of the students:* While a prizing of children's purposes might well be protected by the value dimension previously expressed, of providing choices for children, it is important enough to stress in a value dimension of its own. As students are invited to express their own interests and to define problems in which they feel a personal involvement, and as the activities of the curriculum reflect those interests, the ensuing activity will be more worthwhile than one that is based on attributions of interests and concerns made by teachers.

Obviously, not all of the value components identified in this section can be built into a single activity. Also, not all the values listed deserve the same amount of emphasis in terms of time within a given program. For example, some assignments involving "risk" may be titillating for students and teachers, but a program which has more than a few activities reflecting the "risk" value would probably be out of balance. Finally, the list above is not exhaustive. It is meant to illustrate values that might be used in defining a program of worthwhile activities. The value-criteria are merely working hypotheses at this time, subject to analysis if not empirical testing. Others are encouraged to develop their own set of criteria.

CAVEAT

It must be emphasized that all teachers, whether working at the first-grade level or in graduate school, generally need to do some teaching for objectives as well as some teaching without specific objectives. Whitehead has suggested that in terms of the rhythm of education, many more of the tasks assigned to younger children should be justified on noninstrumental values, while those assigned at the upper levels might reasonable contain more performance-related activities (5).

EVALUATION

All of the foregoing is not to suggest that school programs need not be evaluated. As in the past, those activities which are justified in terms of the objectives they are designed to meet can be evaluated through criterion-referenced achievement tests. Other procedures need to be developed to describe school programs in terms of the characteristics of the activities which comprise the programs. The following procedure might serve as a way of communicating information about a given course or program which would be meaningful to administrators and parents.

Assume that a teacher accepted as the major values of his program those previously identified in this paper. (Presumably, this procedure could be used for any set of values.) He could periodically describe his program using a chart similar to the one presented in Table 1. The chart could be completed according to the following ground rules:

Column 1: This column would simple number the activity for purposes of identification.

Column 2: This notation would place the activity in the sequence of activities carried out during the reporting period.

Column 3: This entry would be another way of labeling the topics under study for purposes of identification.

Column 4: The number of students who successfully completed the activity would be entered here to communicate the extent to which all students in the class were involved in the activity.

Column 5: To give emphasis to the centrality of the activity to the scope of the course, the estimation of the average number of hours spent on the activity would be entered in this column.

Column 6: In this column, teachers would check those components of the activity which in their eyes serve to justify it in their program. In the example entered in the table, the teacher has justified an activity, not in terms of what students can do on finishing it that they could not do before, but on the grounds that it gave students a chance to make a choice (#1); involved them in active roles (#2); included experiences with realia (#4); provided various levels of achievement which could be judged as successful (#5); and required students to apply meaningful standards to their work (#10).

If each line of every teacher's log were punched on a computer card, a program could easily be written which would yield output describing the percentage of time spent on each activity and the number of children who were involved with programs under each value dimension. At present, no generalizations are available which could be used to rate definitively a given course description as adequate or inadequate, based on these data. Nevertheless, if a science program profile indicated that almost no time was spent with students in active roles, if students were almost never involved with realia, and if students had few opportunities to apply meaningful rules or standards to their work, then a person sharing the values espoused in this paper would have serious reservations about the quality of that particular science program.

TABLE 1

Teacher's Log

Subject: _____ Teacher's Name: _____   Unit: ___ Dates: From ___ To ___

(1)	(2)	(3)	(4)	(5)	(6)		
Activity Number	Dates	Title of Activity	Number of Students Completing Activity	Estimated Number of Hours of Participation per Student	Justified by Criteria (Check Those Relevant) 1 2 3 4 5 6 7 8 9 10 11 12		
1	Jan. 8	Experiment with electricity	15	2 hours	x x x x x		

In summary, the argument has been presented that an activity can be justified in terms other than those associated with its instrumental value for changing the behavior of students. In addition, this paper has presented a set of criteria for identifying worthwhile activities, proposed a modest procedure for describing programs in terms of those criteria, and issued an invitation for others to present alternative criteria. Most of all, it has asked that some concern be directed toward the quality of opportunities for experiences offered through our schools.

REFERENCES

1. Kubie, Lawrence S. "Research on Protecting Preconscious Functions in Education." No date, p. 4. Mimeographed. Also in *Nurturing Individual*

Potential edited by A. Harry Passow, pp. 28-42. Washington, D.C.: Association for Supervision and Curriculum Development. 1964.

2. Krathwohl, D. R.; Bloom, B. S.; and Masia, B. B. *Taxonomy of Educational Objectives Handbook II: Affective Domain.* New York: David McKay Co., 1964, p. 16.

3. Popham, W. James. *The Teacher-Empiricist.* Los Angeles: Aegeus Press, 1965.

4. Walbesser, Henry H. *Constructing Behavioral Objectives.* College Park: Bureau of Educational Research and Field Services, University of Maryland, 1970.

5. Whitehead, A. N. *The Aims of Education.* New York: Mentor Books, 1929, pp. 27ff.

Matching students with instructional level materials is a problem for educators. Can the cloze procedure offer a valid method of predicting academic success? This article reports an investigation relevant to the predictiveness of the cloze procedure in a specific content area.

CLOZE PROCEDURE AS A PREDICTOR OF COMPREHENSION IN SECONDARY SOCIAL STUDIES MATERIAL

James Geyer

INTRODUCTION

The investigation upon which this presentation is based involved the following problems:

1. The major problem investigated how predictive of a student's ability to comprehend social studies materials are cloze procedure scores when compared with IQ scores, previous social studies grades, and standardized reading test scores.
2. The secondary investigation dealt with the problem, does rewritten social studies materials on an easier readability level improve the comprehension of that material?

DEVELOPMENT OF READABILITY MEASURES

Interest in assessing printed materials has existed for some time. Lorge (1944, p. 544) indicates that the Talmudists in AD 900 counted words in a usual or unusual sense. One of the first scientifically

From *Proceedings of the College Reading Association*, vol. 7 (1970). Reprinted by permission of the College Reading Association.

oriented attempts to quantify a readability factor occurred in 1889 when F. W. Kaeding attempted to ascertain the frequency of occurrence of 11,000,000 words. The importance of the above study along with Thorndike's investigation (1921) of word frequency is suggested by the initial inclusion of vocabulary factors alone in the Lively and Pressey readability formula (1923, pp. 92-95). This formula is credited by Chall (1958, p. 17) as being the first quantitative study of readability.

By 1928 the emphasis on vocabulary factors as the basis of predicting readability was recognized as being inadequate. During the second period of readability exploration, extending through 1939, investigators of readability searched for factors other than vocabulary which would provide more accuracy in prediction. Representative of this period is the work of Gray and Leary (1935). In studying previous findings in readability and securing the opinions of about 100 experts and 170 library patrons, Gray and Leary found 389 factors which were assigned to the categories of content, style of expression and presentation, format, and general features of organization.

Difficulties in evaluating qualitative factors and the interrelatedness of many of the variables investigated by Gray and Leary were instrumental in ushering in the next period of readability investigation. During this period, which began about 1939 with the appearance of the Lorge Readability formula (1944, pp. 404-19), the basis for development of readability formulas rested on the premise that a small number of factors could validly predict readability. The two-factor Flesch and Dale-Chall formulas were credited by Chall (1958, p. 156) with giving a readability prediction comparable to the five-factor Gray and Leary formula.

Limitations of Readability Formulas

In the process of objectifying and simplifying the application of readability formulas, a measure of vocabulary and sentence factors was usually included. A source of criticism of these formulas lies in their avoidance of measuring other factors of readability.

Lorge (1949, pp. 90-91) indicates that readability formulas measure four elements. They are vocabulary load, sentence structure, idea density, and human interest. He adds that no other internal elements of comprehensibility have been useful in predicting passage difficulty although the lack of a measurement of conceptual difficulties and organization of the printed material is a fundamental weakness of formulas.

Chall (1958, pp. 31-32) adds reinforcement to the above statement. She suggests that readability formulas do not measure abstractness, vagueness, illogical organization, difficulty of words, conceptual difficulty, content, and physical features.

Smith and Dechant (1954, p. 251) support the above statements while attending to certain variables not previously mentioned. They state that readability formulas pay little attention to six factors which are determinants of readability. These factors are density and unusualness of facts, number of pictoral illustrations, interest and purpose, concept load and abstractness of words, organization of material and format, and interrelationship of ideas.

Dale and Chall (1949, p. 23) suggest that three variables affect readability. Included are the printed material and its stylistic elements, the criterion measure and the method used to make the readability estimate, and the reader along with all the qualities he brings to the printed page.

In summary, a limitation of the readability formulas appears to be evident with consideration of the variables mentioned above by Dale and Chall as only two of these factors are quantified. Since individual capabilities and characteristics are not considered in application of readability formulas for evaluation of written materials, difficulties may be encountered when one attempts to equate the reader and instructional material on the basis of such quantification. The discussion below expands and supports this statement.

Readability Formula Application and Effect on Comprehension

The statements above note certain limitations which are associated with quantitative evaluations of printed materials. Results of empirical assessments of readability formula procedures are presented below.

Since one of the elements common to the most widely used readability formulas is some measurement of vocabulary, this variable would logically be included in investigations of readability assessment. Nolte (1937, pp. 119-24; 46) investigated the effects of comprehension on mechanically simplifying vocabulary terms. Pictoral tests and personal interviews were employed to measure comprehension. Nolte reported, "Many vocabulary difficulties and numerous erroneous concepts were disclosed. . . ."

Wilson's study (1948, pp. 5-8) included a 300-word passage which was amplified into 600- and 1200-word versions. Since students comprehended the longest and structurally most difficult version significantly better, the efficacy of simplifying sentence factors as a means of improving comprehension may be open to question.

McCracken (1959, pp. 277-78) investigated the effectiveness of applying readability formula criteria in producing more readable materials. He rated the difficulty of two passages by the Yoakam and Dale-Chall formulas. By adjusting the vocabulary load, the readability levels were interchanged. Multiple-choice results based on factual comprehension led McCracken to conclude that

> Selections written to confirm with a set of vocabulary standards in order to increase or decrease their readability actually may not increase or decrease their readability as much as indicated. A selection thus written would seem to have a contrived or artificial readability level.

As a secondary purpose, the present study investigated the effectiveness of rewritten social studies materials as a means of improving comprehension. Two social studies texts were included in the study. These texts contained identical topics and visual aids such as pictures and maps; however, the readability levels were different as determined by application of the Dale-Chall Readability formula. The easier text was rated at a fifth-sixth grade level in readability while the more difficulty text was placed at the seventh-eighth grade level. A single, multiple-choice test was constructed to measure knowledge acquired after reading a randomly selected chapter. Analysis of covariance was applied to factor out the effects of reading achievement levels, IQ, and previous social studies grades. The null hypothesis of no significant differences between adjusted means was not rejected.

It is not the intent of this paper to suggest that readability formulas have no validity in adjusting readability levels. However, the above findings indicate that attempting to provide more readable materials by reducing sentence and vocabulary factors may not benefit the students for whom it is intended.

THE CLOZE PROCEDURE

In 1953 Wilson Taylor (1953, pp. 415-33) initiated a completion system which he termed the cloze procedure. This system is defined as being a method of intercepting a message (written or spoken), mutilating it by deleting parts, and then administering it to receivers (readers or listeners). The degree of success in restoring the missing elements is indicative of the individual's capacity and/or ability to deal with that message. This interaction between the reader and the printed material appears to circumvent certain limitations of readability formulas. Taylor (1953) suggests that the cloze procedure seems to measure the effects of many elements of reading by involving the reader with the material to be read.

Validity and Reliability of the Cloze Procedure

Many studies have confirmed the validity of the cloze procedure as a measure of readability. In his initial experiment, Taylor (1953, p. 431) finds that several reading passages were ranked in the same order by the Dale-Chall Readability formula, the Flesch Readability formula, and the cloze procedure. Rankin (1958, p. 138) reports correlations between standardized reading test scores and cloze test scores ranging from .65 to .81.

A number of studies relate reliability findings for the cloze procedure in pre- and post-test scores. Taylor (1957, p. 23) states that such correlations for three cloze forms employed in his investigation ranged from .80 to .88. Coleman and Miller (1968, pp. 369-86) find a correlation of .93 between pre- and post-test scores. Hence, the above findings appear to confirm reliability and validity of the cloze procedure as a measure of readability.

Cloze as a Predictor of Comprehension

As a rationale for this study which investigated the effectiveness of the cloze procedure as a predictor of ability to comprehend social studies materials, two studies appeared to be pertinent. Bormuth (1967, p. 295) established a frame of reference between cloze test scores and equivalent comprehension scores. Hafner (1964, pp. 135-45) investigated the effectiveness of the cloze procedure as a predictor of course grades in a college methods class with a resultant correlation of .65 being reported. These data suggest that the degree of comprehensibility an individual finds in instructional material may be predicted by prereading cloze scores.

Procedure and Findings

Data were obtained for this study by the following procedure. Students first completed a prereading cloze test from one of the two texts utilized in the study. An every fifth-word deletion system was employed. After completion of the cloze test, the student read the chapter from which the cloze test had been constructed and completed a fifty-item multiple-choice test.

To test the hypothesis concerning the predictive effectiveness of the cloze procedure as compared to the predictive effectiveness of standardized reading test scores, IQ scores, and previous social studies grades as predictors of how well students comprehend social studies materials, significant differences between two correlation coefficients involving a common variable were investigated with application of a procedure described by Tate (1965, pp. 282-83). At the .01 level the cloze procedure was not found to be significantly better than other variables in predicting comprehension levels. In reference to the standardized reading test scores, the findings were in the opposite direction of the prediction. At the .05 level, however, cloze scores were found to be significantly better predictors of comprehension of the social studies material as measured in this study than I.Q. scores and previous social studies grades.

DISCUSSION

A difference in the opposite direction of the prediction was found in comparing the effectiveness of prediction of cloze and standardized reading test scores. This result might be attributable to the similarity of the kinds of questions, i.e., multiple-choice items in the criterion measure and the standardized reading test. Completion of the cloze test may have required a different, more subjective type of comprehension ability than did the standardized reading test.

The efficacy of rewritten social studies materials on a lower readability level as a means of improving comprehensibility of such material was investigated. Reinforcement was given to certain previous studies in that objectively reducing vocabulary difficulty and sentence complexity may not significantly improve comprehension scores.

Continued investigation of the cloze procedure as a predictor of comprehension appears to be warranted. Numerous studies indicate that the cloze procedure is a valid and reliable measure of readability. The significant differences at the .05 level in comparing the predictive effectiveness of cloze scores to IQ scores and previous social studies grades also support the above suggestion.

Bormuth's frame of reference was mentioned previously. The findings of this study suggest that a universal frame of reference may not be feasible.

REFERENCES

Bormuth, John R. "Comparable Cloze and Multiple-Choice Test Scores." *Journal of Reading* 10 (February 1967): 295.

Chall, Jeanne S. *Readability, An Appraisal of Research and Application.* Columbus: Bureau of Educational Research, Ohio State University, 1958.

Coleman, E. B., and Miller, G. R. "A Measure of Information Gained during Prose Learning." *Reading Research Quarterly* 3 (Spring 1968): 384.

Dale, Edgar and Chall, Jeanne S. "The Concept of Readability." *Elementary English* 26 (January 1949): 23.

Gallant, Ruth. "Use of Cloze Tests as a Measure of Readability in the Primary Grades." In *Reading and Inquiry* edited by J. A. Figurel. Newark, Delaware: International Reading Conference Proceedings. The International Reading Association, 1965.

Gray, W. S., and Leary, B. E. *What Makes a Book Readable . . .: An Initial Study.* Chicago: The University of Chicago Press, 1935.

Hafner, Lawrence E. "Relationships of Various Measures to the 'Cloze' " in *New Concepts in College-Adult Reading* edited by Eric L. Thurston and Lawrence E. Hafner. Thirteenth Yearbook of the National Reading Conference. Milwaukee, Wisconsin: The National Reading Conference, Inc., 1964.

Lively, Bertha, and Pressey, Samuel L. "A Method for Measuring the Vocabulary Burden of Textbooks." *Educational Administration and Supervision* 9 (October 1923): 389-98.

Lorge, Irving. "Predicting Readability." *Teacher's College Record* 45 (March 1944), 404-19.

––––––. "Readability Formulae—An Evaluation." *Elementary English* 36 (February 1949): 90-91.

––––––. "Word Lists as Background for Communication." *Teacher's College Record* 45 (May 1944), 544-45; 49.

McCracken, Robert A. "An Experiment with Contrived Readability in Fifth and Sixth Grade." *Journal of Educational Research* 52 (March 1959), 277-78.

Nolte, Karl F. "Simplification of Vocabulary on Comprehension in Reading." *Elementary English Review* 24 (April 1937): 119-24; 46.

Rankin, Earl F. "The Cloze Procedure—Its Validity and Utility." In *Starting and Improving College Reading Programs* edited by Oscar and Eller Causey. Eighth Yearbook of the National Reading Conference. Fort Worth: Texas Christian Associated Press, 1958.

Smith, Henry P. and Dechant, Emerald V. *Psychology in Teaching Reading.* Englewood Cliffs, New Jersey: Prentice Hall, Inc., 1961.

Tate, Merle W. *Statistics in Education and Psychology.* New York: The Macmillan Company, 1965.

Taylor, Wilson. "Cloze Procedure: A New Tool for Measuring Readability." *Journalism Quarterly* 30 (Fall 1953): 415-33.

_____. "Cloze Readability Scores as Indices of Individual Differences in Comprehension and Aptitude." *Journal of Applied Psychology* 41 (February 1957): 26.

Thorndike, E. L. *The Teacher's Word Book.* New York: Bureau of Publications, Teacher's College, Columbia University, 1921.

Wilson, Mary C. "The Effect of Amplifying Materials and Reading Comprehension." *Journal of Experimental Education* 13 (September 1948): 5-8.

11

Parental Roles in Diagnosis, Remediation, and Prevention

Volunteer programs have been on the educational scene for over a decade. What should be the major thrust of volunteer activity? King and Coley take a stand and suggest directions for appropriate utilization of volunteers.

VOLUNTEERS IN THE INSTRUCTIONAL PROGRAM (VIPS)

Marti King
Joan Coley

INTRODUCTION

The first organized school volunteer program began in New York City in 1956, under the sponsorship of the Public Education Association and with the help of a Ford Foundation grant. Volunteers were used in a variety of ways, including the teaching of reading. In 1962, this volunteer program became an official activity of the New York City Board of Education. The New York City program continues to

From *Implementing Theory and Research in Reading: Position Papers in Reading.* College Park: Reading Center, College of Education, University of Maryland, 1972. Reprinted with permission of the authors.

be a model for the formation of volunteer programs throughout the country.

As a result of the success of the New York City School Volunteer Program, the National School Volunteer Program was organized in 1964 and funded by a Ford Foundation grant. The purpose of this organization was to help local citizens and boards of education in the next twenty largest cities to establish their own school volunteer programs. When the National School Volunteer Program came into being there were seventeen organized and established school volunteer programs in the country. By June of 1969, the number of school systems having volunteer programs had grown to 163.

The basic aims of most of these programs are to relieve teachers of nonprofessional chores, to provide individual attention and assistance which the classroom teacher is not able to supply to children who are not performing well in a group situation, to tap the human resources of the community for the enrichment of the school program, and to develop greater citizen understanding of the problems facing the school in order to enlist their support in securing better budgets, thus involving them in the total effort to improve public education.

One such program began in the public schools in Prince George's County, Maryland, in 1966. Volunteers have provided a wide variety of instructional assistance, with the major focus of the program being in the area of reading-language arts.

Based on our experience with the Prince George's County program, and our observation of other volunteer programs across the country we take the positions which follow:

> *Position:* The major thrust of volunteer activity in the schools should be directly with pupils in the instructional program.

Traditionally, mothers have volunteered to count milk money, to be roommothers, to go on trips, and to perform other noninstructional duties in the school. It is a great waste of human resources if this is the major contribution which volunteers are allowed to make. The need for staff utilization which is more effective than the old way of one teacher who must be all things to all children must be recognized as essential to the effective operation of a school. Involved in this is the use of volunteers.

> If we believe in effective staff utilization in our schools, we must also believe in providing paraprofessional and auxiliary person-

nel. It is not a good argument to say that we cannot afford to have clerks, aides, technicians, and volunteers in the schools. The plain fact of the matter is that we cannot afford not to have these positions staffed by competent people. After all, the human beings who work in the schools are our most precious and most expensive resources. It is wasteful not to have effective staff utilization (Becker, Foreword).

From the beginning in Prince George's County we were committed to providing a program in which volunteers would work directly with children for the purpose of enhancing self-concept and academic skills. For this reason volunteers were trained to work in the areas of oral language development, related speech and reading activities, tutoring in content areas, and the development of positive self-concept. A very careful distinction was made as to whom the volunteer owed primary responsibility. This distinction involved the concept of the volunteer being an aide to children and young people rather than being an aide to the teacher. In those schools where volunteers have been used as aides to teachers their duties have usually been of a clerical nature; thus their contribution to children has been lessened; they have begun to feel they are not making a contribution; and they have often dropped out. In those schools where teacher and volunteer are partners in helping children, in which the distinction is understood, the volunteer can see the contribution he is making directly to children and he then often increases the amount of time he is giving and recruits additional volunteers.

Although the program was not designed for research purposes our experience has been that volunteers whose first responsibility is to pupils are able to make significant contributions to the enhancement of self-concept and academic skills. In addition to informal evaluation of the program two studies have been done to measure the academic progress of pupils being assisted by volunteers.

In the elementary program two hundred primary children were pre- and post-tested with the *Dailey Language Facility Test*. Post-test results showed gains in oral language development of three to five years after one semester with a volunteer.

In the secondary program a comparison of report card grades before and after the help of a tutor was made. Ninety-five percent of the 500 young people in the program in 1968-69 showed an improvement of one or more letter grades in the area in which they were being tutored. In many cases attendance records for those students being helped dramatically improved as a result of the individual attention of a tutor.

Perhaps the area in which a volunteer can make the greatest contribution to a child or young person is in improved self-concept. When the volunteer's only function is to type experience stories or make book folders this vital contribution is lost. A school volunteer who has the time and the enthusiasm to encourage a child, to offer instant help for his mistakes, and instant recognition of his successes can do much toward enabling him to develop a positive self-concept. The volunteer, perhaps because he does not have the same kind of responsibility for the child as the parent or teacher, can more readily recognize and accept that

> every child has his own limitations. The really essential thing is this: that having given the child all the help one can, he is accepted for what he is, with his limitations and assets; that he should be helped to the extent of his ability to face his limitations and develop his assets to the fullest; and that at all times he should feel loved and wanted (Illingsworth, p. 68).

Position: Teacher-training institutions should provide training for teachers in the effective utilization of all paraprofessionals in the schools.

In a study conducted by the Bank Street College of Education on the new role of teachers, Bowman and Klopf provide evidence that the "... involvement of persons with a wide range of skills, training, experience, background, and potential may provide a better learning environment than the assignment of all educational tasks in a classroom to one person who, alone, must attempt to meet the individual needs of many pupils" (Bowman and Klopf, p. 215).

The experience of volunteer programs in every state has been that most teachers, however well trained and dedicated, are almost totally unprepared to effectively use or relate to auxiliary personnel. The overriding recommendation of the Bank Street College Team which studied the demonstration project of auxiliary utilization in Berkeley, California was: "The restructuring of the process of preservice education for teachers to include this facet of classroom functioning seems essential" (Bowman and Klopf, p. 105).

There are large numbers of people at all socioeconomic levels who have a desire to serve as volunteers in the schools. The potential of the contribution of this vast untapped supply of capable, resourceful, and talented citizens is just beginning to be recognized in many communities and school systems. Teachers need to be trained to effectively use this resource. Part of the preservice training for teachers should include a unit on the use of paraprofessionals in the classroom. A good working relationship will not come through administration proclamation. It will come only from the careful perception of and appreciation for the contribution each member of the team can make. Mutual respect and open lines of communication are essential for an effective working relationship. If teachers are trained to use volunteers of all racial, language, and educational backgrounds the climate for learning will be greatly enhanced.

Position: It is necessary that volunteers be trained for the job they are asked to do.

Just as it is necessary for teachers to be trained to effectively use volunteers, it is also necessary to train volunteers in their role in the school. A survey of volunteer programs across the country found that the range of training given to volunteers varies from no preservice training to fifteen sessions in which volunteers are trained in child development and in specific methods and materials they will be using. Those programs which provide little or no training have a high rate of teacher dissatisfaction with the use of volunteers and a high rate of volunteer drop out.

The training program for volunteers in Prince George's County consists of four phases. There are three formal preservice training sessions including lectures, discussions, seminars, demonstrations, and practice sessions. The content of these sessions deals with child development, language development, reading, speech, the role of the volunteer in relationship to the school, the community, and the pupil, and the use of specific methods and materials. The second phase of the training involves observation by the new volunteer of an experienced volunteer working in a situation similar to what the new volunteer's assignment will be and observation in at least one classroom in the school where he will be working. The third phase of the training involves a discussion session with the volunteer, the teacher (s), the principal and/or counselor, and a member of the Volunteer Program staff. The specific needs of the pupils to be involved are discussed as well as how the program will operate in that school. These discussions are held periodically throughout the time the volunteer works in the school. The fourth phase of the training involves monthly in-service meetings. Both preservice training and in-service training are geared for the service the volunteer is expected to perform with separate sessions on techniques and materials for elementary and secondary volunteers. In addition, members of the Volunteer Program Staff, all of whom are trained teachers, observe the volunteers periodically as they work with pupils.

CONCLUSION

That volunteers can "make the connection" and provide important instructional and personal services to children and youth has been clearly demonstrated (Cloward, PACE, Janowitz). Educators must not close their minds to the infinite and creative possibilities for utilizing this human resource which it could not possibly buy. From the instant help center in which a volunteer is available every period of every day for the student who just needs help one time to the tape recording of a science text book for the secondary nonreader by a mother who can't leave home to volunteer, we must open ourselves up to a partnership which will allow us to help each child and young person reach his potential. In doing so, we must remember that if volunteers are not given challenging work, if they are not used at their level of competence, they will be short-changed in the rewarding experience volunteering can be, schools will lose a valuable resource, and children will be denied an opportunity which might make the difference between success and failure.

REFERENCES

Bowman, Garda W., and Klopf, Gordon J. *New Careers and Roles in the American School.* Washington, D.C.: Office of Economic Opportunity, 1969.

Cloward, Robert D. "Studies in Tutoring." New York: Research Center, Columbia University School of Social Work, 1966.

Early Reading Assistance—A Reading Tutorial Program. Cleveland, Ohio: The PACE Association. 1968.

Janowitz, Gayle. *Helping Hands, Volunteer Work in Education.* Chicago: University of Chicago Press. 1965.

King, Martha. "I Alone—The School Volunteer Program in Prince George's County, Maryland." Board of Education, 1969.

————. "The Volunteer Program in Language Development." Prince George's County, Maryland: Board of Education, 1967.

National School Volunteer Program, Inc. *Basic Kit.*

_____. "A Survey of School Volunteer Programs." 1970.

Volunteers in Education—Materials for Volunteer Programs and the Volunteer. Washington, D.C.: U.S. Department of Health, Education, and Welfare, 1970.

Parental involvement in educational efforts—a concern of under-
graduate teacher-education training? Rentel provides a rationale.

PARENTS: THE MISSING
INGREDIENT IN TEACHER
EDUCATION

Victor M. Rentel

In the play, *Lady Windermere's Fans,* one of Oscar Wilde's charac-
ters remarks, "Experience is the name everyone gives to his mistakes."[1] Before I begin, then, I think it only fair to warn you that
I intend to share the benefit of my experience with you.

In teacher education one of our serious mistakes has been to pay
only peripheral attention to the tremendous educational potential of
the home. While there are numerous parent education programs,
there are few teacher-training programs which give adequate emphasis to providing teachers with the skill and knowledge to utilize
parents effectively as educative catalysts.[2] By and large, our efforts
to prepare teachers for work with parents have been hampered by
a characteristic campfire girl boldness and sophistication. In many
cases, our attitudes toward parents have been ritualistic and condescending. We tend to know but not understand that children learn
largely from the home their language, their attitudes, their values,
their conceptions of reality and possibility, their likes and dislikes,
and, in essence, what and who they are. By default and neglect, we
inspire teachers to ignore parents. There are several reasons why
teachers must be trained to utilize the educational potential of the
home. First, with the advent of television, both children and parents
have ready access to information in a format that the school simply
cannot compete with. Schools must look beyond information-proc-
essing to provide parents and children with guidelines for self-
directed learning and independent evaluation. Both the tremendous

From *Proceedings of the College Reading Association* 10 (1969): 188-90. Reprinted with permission of the College Reading Association and the author.
[1]Oscar Wilde, *Lady Windermere's Fans* Act 3, Scene 1 (New York).

[2]Gabrial Della-Piana, "Parents and Reading Achievement," *Elementary English*
45 (February 1968): 190-200.

increase of knowledge and the rate at which knowledge grows obsolete have rendered the schools helpless and unresponsive when judged by the standards children and parents have come to expect of television.

Schools are being outdistanced in their ability to provide relevant learning experiences not only by the impact of mass media, but also by the lack of time, space, teachers, techniques, and facilities. Teachers must be prepared to offer parents and children those things which mass media by its very nature cannot provide. Teachers can help parents to take advantage of home learning by counseling, guiding, evaluating, and providing methods of independent study. But, if they are to help later, preservice teachers must first be trained to work with parents.

If independent learning has indeed become a signal feature in modern life, then teachers and the school must be prepared to serve as a resource for diagnosing learning difficulties and prescribing highly individualized curricula. Today's and tomorrow's teachers will have to learn to do far more listening and far less talking. They will need to be expert at solving problems and more adept at communicating solutions. Teachers must accept the fact that everything that is worth learning cannot be and should not be taught in school.[3]

Wynn suggests that parents of disadvantaged children will need more than just information. Instead they will need to be encouraged to create an atmosphere in the home which stimulates learning. Disadvantaged parents, moreover, will need to be engaged in activities which involve no additional expenditures and which are easily accessible to them. Specifically, parents of disadvantaged children should be shown how to take advantage of free learning situations in the near community; they should be helped to make extensive use of the public library and selective use of mass media. Teachers in these situations will need to know how to motivate and how to plan wisely.[4]

THE TEACHER OF READING

Studies of the home unquestionably show that it is a major factor in school success, especially where reading and language development are concerned. Artifacts in the home, parental interest and encouragement in the child's conversation, and, finally, opportunities to

---

[3]N. R. Dixon, "Home as Educative Agent," *Educational Leadership* (April 1968): 632-36.

[4]S. J. Wynn, "Beginning Reading Program for the Deprived Child," *Reading Teacher* 21 (October 1967): 40-47.

model and practice speaking have all been shown to be significant influences on language development.[5] Mothers' attitudes affect articulation, their modes of discipline influence cognitive functioning and language development, their supportive behavior correlates with reading achievement.[6]

Where school systems have taken it upon themselves to establish training programs for parents, these programs have met with considerable success.[7] Evidence that schools and teachers can make a difference in a child's reading development by working with parents is not hard to come by. Guidelines as well as the "experience" of those who have already tried are becoming increasingly frequent in the professional literature.

This past fall a group of parents broke with the New York City school system to form an experimental alternative to neighborhood public schools. In Boston a nonprofit group known as the Committee for Community Educational Development was awarded $390,000 by the Ford Foundation to develop plans for a small experimental school system. The system will probably receive all of its operating funds from the state government. Proposals for and the ensuing struggle to achieve decentralization of the Ocean Hill-Brownsville district of New York City probably arose from the same parental aspirations as those mentioned earlier. Parents are demanding a share of control in and closer association with the schools. They are more than likely motivated by a desire to make teachers and administrators more responsive to the needs of the people they serve. Unless parents are taken into the educative process, a new and sadder alienation between home and school has begun.

[5]S. Weintraub, G. Della Piana, and H. Martin, "Reading Achievement and Maternal Behavior," *Reading Teacher* 20 (December 1966): 225-30.

[6]R. K. Sommers, "Effects of Material Attitudes upon Improvement of Articulation when Mothers are Trained to Assist in Speech Correction," *Journal of Speech and Hearing Disorders* 29 (May 1964): 126-32.

[7]Joseph E. Brzeinski, "Beginning Reading In Denver," *The Reading Teacher* 18 (1964): 22-26.

Concerned parents want to help their children. How can schools effectively coordinate the efforts of the home and the school? Wilson and Pfau suggest practical solutions.

PARENTS *CAN* HELP!

Robert M. Wilson
Donald W. Pfau

When faced with evidence that their child is failing in reading, parents are generally moved to action. They seldom heed warnings that unplanned parental assistance may be detrimental, nor do they doubt that their attention will improve the situation. Indeed, it is with confidence and determination that parents sense their obligation to alleviate the stumbling blocks which are impeding their child's reading progress.

"HANDS OFF!"

"Hands off! This is our problem," is no longer a justifiable response from the educator. Educators are aware that parents rightfully want to assist at home when their child has reading problems. Yet concern mounts when educators realize that the efforts of parents may be more harmful than helpful (Bond and Tinker, 1957; Harris, 1961) and that many parents are unsuited to work with their child in an instructional setting. The fact remains, however, that when a child falters in reading, the parents are usually compelled to find means to assist him (Gans, 1963).

Since it is realistic to assume parents are involved with helping their child overcome his reading difficulties, it becomes desirable to learn more about the role parents are playing. Specifically, it seems probable that educators could do a better job of helping parents provide assistance if they were more cognizant of the types of activities which parents provide for their children.

To better understand the nature of parental involvement, second- and fourth-grade teachers from selected middle-class suburban

From *The Reading Teacher* vol. 21, no. 8 (May 1968): 758-61. Reprinted with permission of Robert M. Wilson and the International Reading Association.

communities were asked to have the parents of the children in their classes respond to an eight-item questionnaire. It concerned the types of activities they employed when they tried to help the child overcome his reading problems. Each teacher divided her children into three groups according to reading performance (fast, average, and slow) so that tabulated responses would reflect the parental practices used with three types of reading achievers. The total sample included seventy-one children.

The results of the questionnaire indicated that nearly 100 percent of the parents questioned offered help to their child when he requested it. Further, it was discovered that the parents of "slow" readers were those most likely to be asked. Nearly all reported working in the development of word attack skills, comprehension skills, and building interest in reading. For teaching success to be achieved in these areas, a relatively sophisticated understanding of the reading process is typically required. Yet, parents reported conducting much of their work without information or cooperation from school personnel. All respondents, however, expressed a desire for some kind of cooperation from the classroom teacher that would be implemented by demonstration and specific assistance.

IMPLICATIONS

It seems necessary to discover the most effective means of stimulating parental involvement so that positive help for troubled readers is insured. In many instances past efforts to educate parents have been restricted to the lecture method; that is, the parents have been told what to do and what not to do. Telling parents "how to help" is ineffective as a means of insuring healthy teaching-learning situations at home, especially when one considers the degree of parental involvement that is suggested by this study. Several possibilities appear to be more promising.

First, educators should be interested in having parents realize that there are portions of instruction which need reinforcement by parents at home and other portions which are better left to the educator. Involving parents in areas where they can fruitfully assist may serve to disinvolve them from areas in which their help will prove less profitable.

Second, educators should make certain that parents not only be told which types of activities would benefit their child and which would not but also that they be shown the method involved. For example, a common area of suggestion for parents is that they listen to their child read. While most teachers agree that this is sound advice, it does not follow that parents understand precisely what makes a good listener, nor that they realize the benefits to be accrued from good listening.

Then too, when educators inform parents that it is often better to tell a child an unfamiliar or puzzling word so that he can get on with the story, would it not be better to demonstrate what happens to a child's understanding of the story when he struggles to apply weak word-attack skills in translating an excessive number of unfamiliar words? Demonstrating more adequately reveals than does telling the advantage of supplying words so that the child can experience continuity and pleasure in an uninterrupted flow of ideas.

Third, once a technique is demonstrated, parents should have an opportunity to practice the technique under the watchful eye of the educator. The total process here would allow the parents to learn what to do, to see how to do it, and to try it under observation.

Finally, educators should be interested in seeing that parents discover for themselves whether or not they are well-suited to work with their child. A supervised situation with positive educator reaction in which the parents work with their child allows for better self-evaluation. For those parents who are unable to establish the rapport necessary for effective learning to occur, the groundwork has been established for guiding them to other types of cooperative effort. When the parent cannot effectively control his frustration with the child or when the parent loses his emotional control, then it must be assumed that further efforts to assist will be of little value.

PROGRAMS

Whether it is the teacher or the clinician who is to work directly with the parents of the children who are having difficulty in reading, it would seem that effective programs could be developed. For the three to eight problem readers in any room, the teacher may choose an individual conference with the parents followed by group demonstrations of procedures and techniques which she feels will be helpful. She may choose to work with each child and his parents individually. In either case, effective parental cooperation can be achieved without excessive expenditures of time, and the teacher could feel more certain about the educational value of the reading techniques being used at home.

Several attempts have been made to help parents in a clinic setting. For example, parents of children at the University of Maryland Reading Center are provided situations in which parents are free to ask questions, to observe tutoring, to receive a thorough interpretation of testing results, to engage in training sessions, and to render a cooperative service in the interest of their child. Every effort is made to be certain that when a book is taken home, it will be read and discussed appropriately.

The New York City schools have also developed a carefully coordinated realistic approach to sound cooperation (Lloyd, 1965). Still another approach to parental involvement has been reported in the Denver Prereading Project in which parents are given instruction by way of television (McManus, 1964).

SUMMARY

Working with parents of troubled readers appears to be an area of concern for educators. If acceptable remedial maneuvers are shrouded in secrecy, it is hardly likely that much good is attained by asking parents to cooperate. Likewise, it is futile to tell parents they are not teachers and, therefore, should not help their child. Assisting children at home can no longer be considered "off-limits." Reading teachers the country over must be encouraged to take a fresh look at the possibilities of parental cooperation when working with problem readers. Cooperation is a two-way street. Educators will need to marshal every effort to make effective parental cooperation a reality. Regardless of the difficulties, this type of cooperative venture is possible, profitable, and necessary if children are to receive the best possible help when reading difficulties occur.

REFERENCES

Bond, G. L., and Tinker, M. A. *Reading Difficulties, Their Diagnosis and Correction,* pp. 108-09. New York: Appleton-Century-Crofts, 1957.

Casey, Sally L. *Ways You Can Help Your Child with Reading,* p. 2. New York: Row-Peterson, 1960.

Gans, Roma. *Common Sense in Teaching Reading,* p. 283 Indianapolis, Indiana: Bobbs-Merrill, 1963.

Harris, A. J. *How to Increase Reading Ability,* pp. 266-67. New York: David McKay, 1961.

Lloyd, Helene M. "New York City's Program for Developing the Role of Parents in Reading Progress." *The Reading Teachers* 18 (1965): 629-33.

McManus, Anastasia. "The Denver Prereading Project Conducted by WENH-TV." The Reading Teacher 1 (1964): 22-26.

Robinson, H. A., and Rauch, S. J. *Guiding the Reading Program,* p. 7. New York: Science Research Associates, 1965.

12

Professional Responsibilities and Roles

Competent teachers appear to be the crucial variable in providing optimum instruction, and in-service programs are designed to increase this competency, but ... why have reactions to in-service programs generally been negative? Waynant outlines strategies which appear to provide positive reactions and applications of techniques of methodology.

TEACHERS' STRENGTHS: BASIS FOR SUCCESSFUL IN-SERVICE EXPERIENCES

Louise F. Waynant

In-service teacher education is potentially one of the most important and effective means of helping teachers acquire current professional information and learn alternative teaching strategies. This paper is addressed to techniques designed to assure successful in-service programs.

From *Educational Leadership* vol. 28, no. 7 (April 1971): 710-13. Reprinted with permission of the Association for Supervision and Curriculum Development and Louise Waynant. Copyright © 1971 by the Association for Supervision and Curriculum Development.

THE PROBLEM

Traditional in-service programs often have been ineffective in spite of substantial investments of time, funds, and consultant services. In many instances, teachers have found in-service programs threatening, confusing, or irrelevant (Harris, 1966). Teachers who are threatened by in-service programs may feel that their approaches or techniques have been wrong and that their skills are inadequate. Teachers also may fear trying new teaching strategies because of past failures (Conlin, 1967; Williams, 1966).

Other teachers become confused by in-service programs which deal with techniques or methods that appear to be in conflict with current procedures. Teachers become uneasy about what they are doing, yet do not know what they might do differently (Harris, 1966). Confusion may result when information is presented without practical suggestions for its implementation. Conflicting testimony from consultants often adds another source of confusion.

Teachers are also critical of in-service programs which they feel are irrelevant to the problems confronting them and the children they teach. The problem of irrelevancy is intensified when consultants come to an in-service situation and attempt to *impose* upon teachers a particular method or technique.

A major reason for teachers' criticism of—or lack of response to —traditional in-service programs appears to be the emphasis placed on teachers' *deficiencies.* Too often administrators, supervisors, and consultants have looked for what is wrong, rather than what is right, with teachers and their teaching. Frequently teachers' interests, wishes, and teaching strengths have been ignored or overlooked when in-service programs are designed. Taken together, the problems make traditional in-service programs an intolerable threat to the security and professional well-being of many teachers.

The dilemma is intensified when those who plan and implement the in-service work are not held accountable for the results of the program. This lack of accountability may lead to lack of evaluation and to a perpetuation of the failure of in-service programs.

A SOLUTION

One solution to the problem of providing relevant, effective in-service programs might be found in looking for teachers' strengths and assets and in accepting teachers' own interests and concerns. Waetjen states, "If a person is accepted and valued and esteemed, he becomes an inquiring person and he actualizes himself" (Waetjen, 1965, p. 243). Raths emphasizes that ". . . if those around us have genuine respect for us, they will not want to remake us into images of themselves" (Raths, 1954, pp. 159-60).

Maximum involvement of teachers in planning the in-service program appears to be another solution to the problem. Harris advises that planning should be "undertaken cooperatively, with those persons to be affected by the in-service program systematically involved in all stages of the planning" (Harris, 1966, p. 260). Results of a study by DeCarlo and Cleland reflect the positive attitudes which teachers develop toward in-service programs which give them what they want and need (DeCarlo and Cleland, 1968).

The following guidelines based on teachers' strengths and providing for maximum teacher involvement may be useful in planning in-service work:

1. Identify teachers' strengths, interests, and concerns through observation and discussion.
2. Utilize teachers' strengths, interests, and concerns in planning and conducting the in-service program.
3. Provide a feedback system whereby teachers can inform consultants if information is useful, relevant, and clear enough for implementation.
4. Guarantee consulting results in performance terms.

PROJECT BONUS

Project Bonus, a Title I summer program in Carroll County, Maryland, serves as a model of an in-service program built on teachers' strengths, interests, and concerns and providing maximum involvement of teachers in planning and implementation.

Project Bonus involved two phases. Phase 1 involved a week of in-service training in reading for teachers, and Phase 2 consisted of six weeks of pupil instruction. Consultant assistance was available during both phases.

Planning

1. In the initial planning session, county administrators met with university personnel to discuss the general objectives and dimensions of the project. Following this, consultants visited the Title I Classrooms in Carroll County to meet the principals, teachers, and children who would be involved in

the project. During the initial visits, consultants noted materials and instructional techniques which teachers used well and asked principals the question, "What do you believe are the greatest professional strengths of the teachers and aides on your staff who will be working in Project Bonus?"

2. A planning meeting was arranged in which teachers, aides, and resource personnel met in small groups to discuss interests, strengths, and concerns. A checklist of objectives to guide the workshop was developed on the basis of the interests and concerns identified by the teachers.

3. A second series of school visits was scheduled during which each teacher involved in Project Bonus met with a consultant-resource teacher team to discuss the proposed objectives. Teachers were asked to indicate which of the objectives were of greatest interest to them and to add any objectives which they felt were important. Each teacher was asked to list at least one area in which he felt he could be of help to other teachers or aides. The consultants noted special abilities or expertise with techniques and materials which each teacher displayed.

4. A new set of objectives was formulated on the basis of teacher reaction to the original objectives. The new set of objectives, the Project Bonus Objectives Checklist, became the blueprint for the workshop and the basis for postworkshop evaluation. This list follows:

Project Bonus Objectives Checklist

(Check each one Yes or No)

1. Teachers will be able to use alternate strategies in teaching reading comprehension. For example:

    a. Teachers can stimulate peer questioning.
    b. Teachers can stimulate questioning beyond a literal level.
    c. Teachers can develop activities that allow children to work together.
    d. Teachers can develop activities that require manipulation of materials.

2. Teachers will be able to use the language experience approach and develop skills from it. For example:

    a. Teachers can draw a story from children.
    b. Teachers can use experience stories to develop sight vocabulary.

    c. Teachers can use experience stories to develop comprehension skills.

    d. Teachers can use experience stories to develop discrimination skills.

3. Teachers will be able to use alternate strategies to workbook type independent activities. For example:

    a. Teachers can use learning centers to stimulate creative writing.

    b. Teachers can help children use magazines, newspapers, and photographs in independent activities.

4. Teachers will be able to develop skills in book sharing. For example:

    a. Teachers can use role playing or creative dramatics for book sharing.

    b. Teachers can encourage the use of alternate endings or different titles for stories.

5. Teachers will be able to examine the performance of children to determine their strengths. For example:

    a. Teachers can diagnose strengths from oral reading.

    b. Teachers can use interest groups or skill groups.

Guarantee

The consultants guaranteed county administrative coordinators that at least 80 percent of the teachers would indicate that they had met all the objectives proposed for the workshop. Consultant pay was based upon that guarantee.

Implementation

Project Bonus was initiated by having teachers, aides, and resource teachers meet in groups of three to tell one another of their experiences, abilities, and teaching strengths. These were summarized, recorded, and immediately distributed to workshop participants, consultants, and visitors. The summary sheet helped workshop participants to use peers in consultant roles.

    Teachers who had previous experience with materials or techniques described at the workshop assisted other teachers in microteaching situations and frequently acted in a resource capacity. For example, teachers familiar with the language experience approach did peer teaching to demonstrate techniques such as recording stories. One teacher displayed pupil-made books and explained how independent activities could be developed from these books. A teacher interested in dramatics described ways to use creative dramatics in individualized reading programs.

The consultants guided the teachers in the development and reinforcement of new methods and techniques and demonstrated the use of techniques and materials. They also supplemented present knowledge with additional information, and encouraged teachers both to capitalize on their present teaching strengths and to begin using alternate strategies presented during the workshop.

Feedback

Feedback concerning the clarity, effectiveness, and utility of each day's session was provided through use of every-participant response techniques in which all participants responded to questions regarding methodology, materials, and ability to implement new procedures. If incorrect or negative responses were made, reteaching, further explanation, or demonstrations were offered.

Evaluation

Evidence of the success of Project Bonus was derived from workshop evaluation, teacher performance, pupil progress evaluation, and principals' reports of behavior change evidenced during the fall semester.

1. At the end of the workship, teachers evaluated their experience by means of the Project Bonus Objectives Checklist. All teachers (100 percent) rated favorably the five major areas included on the checklist, indicating that they could implement those particular skills immediately in the classroom. At the end of the teaching session, 97 percent of the teachers who reevaluated the behaviors on the checklist indicated they had actually practiced the behaviors in the classroom and planned to practice them during the fall.
2. Project Bonus teachers implemented with their pupils the techniques and skills discussed during the workshop. For example, learning centers were in almost every classroom.
3. Project Bonus teachers observed both a dramatic, positive change in the attitude and behavior of a majority of their pupils and a significant improvement in scores on a test of word recognition.

4. Reports from principals early in the fall semester indicated that Project Bonus teachers not only were using new techniques and skills in their regular school classrooms but also were sharing these ideas with colleagues.

It appeared that a major reason for the success of Project Bonus was the high amount of teacher involvement in its planning and implementation. Also helpful was the emphasis placed on identifying and utilizing teachers' strengths and interests rather than their weaknesses and deficiencies.

Likewise it appeared that the positive approach taken with teachers was reflected in the significant improvement in attitude and achievement among pupils in the summer session.

REFERENCES

Bowers, Norman D., and Soar, Robert S. "Studies in Human Relations in the Teaching-Learning Process." *V. Final Report: Evaluation of Laboratory Human Relations Training for Classroom Teachers.* Chapel Hill: University of North Carolina Press, 1961.

Conlin, Marcia R., and Haberman, Martin. "Supervising Teachers of the Disadvantaged." *Educational Leadership* vol. 24, no. 5 (February 1967): 393-98.

DeCarlo, Mary Rossini, and Cleland, Donald L. "A Reading In-Service Education Program for Teachers." *The Reading Teacher* 23 (November 1968): 163-69.

Harris, Ben M. "In-Service Growth—The Essential Requirement." *Educational Leadership* vol. 24, no. 3 (December 1966): 257-60.

Raths, Louis E. "How Children Build Meanings." *Childhood Education* 31 (December 1954): 159-60.

Waetjen, Walter B. "Facts about Learning." In *Readings in Curriculum* edited by Glen Hass and Kimball Wiles. Boston: Allyn and Bacon, 1965.

Williams, Lois. "The Consultant-Teacher Transaction." *Educational Leadership* vol. 23, no. 7 (April 1966): 541-44.

What is the role of the reading specialist? With whom, how, and where does the specialist discharge his professional obligations? Spicknall provides a challenge—and gives direction for meeting this challenge.

FROM READING SPECIALIST TO READING RESOURCE TEACHER

Stella P. Spicknall

The following case is presented for changing the role of the reading specialist to a reading resource teacher. The ideas included have been tried and tested in Prince George's County, Maryland.

The role of the reading specialist is changing. No longer does he maintain a self-contained reading room when he instructs groups of problem readers in isolation from their classmates. Instead, he assists these pupils as they work on academic tasks in the setting where the action is—the classroom. Under this arrangement, the reading specialist works both with pupils and with their classroom teachers. His reading room becomes a language arts instructional center and is used by teachers and pupils. The reading specialist thus becomes primarily a reading resource teacher and a member of the instructional team in the school. Although his responsibility is still to assist pupils with special reading needs, what he does and how he does it are changing.

For the past three years the personnel of the reading program of Prince George's County, Maryland, have been working to develop a Reading Resource Program that will provide schools with broader services for reading improvement. These broader services are defined within a six area framework of:

*Parent and Community Education with the school taking the
initiative in establishing communication and understanding be-

---

This article was written especially for this volume.

tween school, the home, and all the forces that are a part of the child's environment.

*Teacher Education with the need being continuous and ongoing for increasing competence in the teaching of reading at all levels.

*Identification and Diagnosis as a basis for appropriate instruction to meet the varied needs of individual pupils.

*Instruction based on diagnosis as an integral part of the language arts program in listening, speaking, reading, and writing.

*Resources which are available to each school to enable its staff to meet the reading needs of the school population.

*Research with its many implications for improved methods and techniques of helping pupils achieve in reading.

Under this framework, reading specialists are becoming reading resource teachers and are searching for ways to provide assistance to greater numbers of pupils in this rapidly growing school system.

THE PROBLEMS RELATED TO CHANGING THE ROLE OF THE READING TEACHER

The transition, however, has not been easy either for the reading resource teachers themselves or for the school staffs whom they serve. To be a resource teacher, the reading specialist must leave the security of the clinical set-up. Instead of using the diagnostic and instructional skills as learned in his graduate-level reading courses, he must both modify and adapt them to classroom situations. He now assists with a wider range of reading problems, not only of a remedial nature but also pertaining to developmental reading.

For the classroom teacher, this change has meant that pupils receive services in a different form. The classroom teacher is no longer relieved of the physical presence of his problem readers. Instead, the teacher must incorporate help for these pupils into the classroom set-up and within the classroom.

For the administrator this change has presented new and different problems. Not only must he have the special skills necessary to assist teachers in working cooperatively, but he must know how to modify schedules, how to provide planning time, and how to encourage and support classroom teachers, reading teachers, and other specialists as they venture to work cooperatively for the good of the pupils in the school.

All personnel concerned recognize that in any school situation the reading resource role may or may not be developed successfully. The tasks of reorganizing pupils with reading problems must be pursued simultaneously. Obtaining the necessary commitment and involvement of teachers, pupils, and parents will speed the development of teachers' cooperative efforts and promote effective learning in the classroom.

To give effective service, the reading program can never become highly structured and inflexible, but must develop from the strengths of the people involved. As new personnel are introduced the program must be expected to assume different characteristics in accordance with the strengths and background of experiences of the participants. At the local level, school personnel must clarify goals, specify roles, and develop procedures for involving newcomers, so that changes in participants will not cause setbacks to programs.

An acute and general problem arises from the training and educational experiences of the reading specialist. He is an experienced classroom teacher who has earned at least twelve graduate hours in a sequence of reading courses. Traditionally these courses have trained the teacher to become adept at remediation and in individual and small-group instruction and to serve as a clinician diagnosing severe reading problems.

It is a great disadvantage that many graduate courses for reading training continue to emphasize the clinical aspects of the job. It is encouraging to note that one local institution that trains a large number of the county reading are building resource role experiences into each of their graduate courses in reading. Their trainees will be more able to serve as reading resource teachers immediately rather than having to learn on-the-job.

THE COUNTY FRAMEWORK FOR CHANGES IN CURRICULUM

Because of the complexity of initiating and maintaining reading teachers as reading resource teachers, developing a successful reading resource program depends largely upon a continuing and effective in-service training within a framework which provides for change. Fortunately, the county curriculum office has provided a framework both for in-service training and for keeping the program abreast of the curriculum. The vehicle for overall curriculum change is the Instructional Council with its component Curriculum Committees.

The following dated main events summarize the changes affected by the Curriculum Committee for the Reading Resource Program:

1968 Polled principals to obtain descriptions of current reading programs and to make an assessment of needs. Made a study of the ways to make the reading program better meet the needs identified in the reports.

1969 Made recommendations to the Instructional Council (subsequently approved) citing the situation in the schools and stating the basic six-area framework for developing the program. Changed the name of the program from Reading and Study Skills to Reading Resource Program in order to better describe the services provided.

1970 Initiated a study of the different programs and the organizational patterns for reading instruction both within the county schools and in other school systems. Identified some aspects of the reading resource role in which reading teachers generally are successful.

The curriculum development of the Reading Resource Program can be stated as a four-step process that is ongoing, sequential, and is repeated year by year. This process involves reading teachers and utilizes other teachers and consultants as resource personnel. The steps may be described as follows:

1. Discussing the program, clarifying and restating its goals, and identifying successful procedures.
2. Developing the guidelines and writing curriculum materials broad enough to be used countywide, yet specific enough to assist personnel new to the program.
3. Introducing the program as developed in the Curriculum Committee and as expressed in the curriculum guides through workshops for teachers and through scheduled meetings of small groups of reading teachers.
4. Implementing the program within the schools; adjusting and modifying it to meet local needs; obtaining feedback from pupils and from teachers to effect further changes.

Trends in the program are indicated in a listing of the titles of curriculum guides developed in the summer sessions and used by reading teachers during the year.

1967 The Reading and Study Skills Program for Elementary Schools, Revised
The Reading and Study Skills Program for Secondary Schools, Revised

1968 The Reading and Study Skills Program—Kindergarten thru Grade 12
The Volunteer in Language Development

1969 The Reading Resource Program
The Reading Center Services
TESOL—Teaching English to Speakers of Other Languages

1970 The Reading Resource Program (Revised with supplement)
Parent Reading Discussion Groups

These guides have all been developed by writing teams of county reading specialists working with the staff of the Reading Resource Program during the summer months. In 1967, this writing was preceded by a weekend workshop for teachers (reading and classroom), supervisors, principals, and consultants from outside the county, working together to evaluate the program and to identify trends in pupil needs and to recommend changes in the guidelines. Since that time, each revision has been initiated by such an open discussion held over a period of several days with representative school staff members.

It was in 1967 that the words "corrective and "remedial" were deleted from the description of the reading program as being compressing and limiting.

In 1968, the elementary and secondary manuals were integrated into a single handbook. In 1969, the program became titled the Reading Resource Program. And in 1970, the resource role was more specifically defined.

IN-SERVICE TRAINING, THE INSTRUMENT OF CHANGE

Because reading resource teachers need to be cognizant of the assistance classroom teachers receive in the county-wide meetings, they are expected to participate in language-related-in-service meetings attended by classroom teachers. Meetings specific to the needs of reading resource teachers are not scheduled on the countywide in-service meeting dates. Monthly in-service meetings utilize varied grouping practices by areas, special interests, or special needs.

In addition to providing instruction about varied techniques, multi-level adaptations, and new materials, these monthly in-service meetings are the means of sharing information and exchanging ideas about the varied and developing role of the reading resource teacher.

The following summary of activities in these meetings indicates the trend toward the reading resource role:

1967–68　With the approval and support of the Director of Curriculum, indicating the reading resource role and encouraging reading specialists to broaden their services.

Encouraging school programs to develop on the basis of pupil need in consideration of the teacher's professional skills so that some schools maintain remedial-corrective programs and others adopt various aspects of a reading resource program.

Identifying successful activities when the reading resource teacher has extended his services to the classroom teacher.

Identifying successful experiences when the classroom teacher has worked with pupils within the classroom and has been invited to return.

Accepting the responsibility to oversee the programs for the pupils tested at the county Reading Clinic. Reading Clinic personnel make an intensive diagnosis and specific plan of instruction for pupils with severe reading problems. The reading teachers will assist the classroom teacher in the implementation of this plan within the classroom setting.

1968–69　Clarifying the role of the classroom teacher as the one responsible for the pupil's instruction, and the role of the reading teacher as one to provide additional help to pupils with special needs.

Establishing the role of the reading resource teacher as a service person within the curriculum.

Continuing to identify successes in serving as reading resource teachers.

Accepting the obligation of direct and continuing service to pupils with severe reading problems.

1969–70 Working to develop an understanding of how the two aspects of the reading resource role—help to pupils, help to teachers—can both be implemented and successfully intermixed.

Sharing ideas and visiting other reading teachers to gain feedback on being a resource to another reading teacher and on using another reading teacher as a resource.

Working with special consultants to learn of other possible ways of assisting pupils and teachers.

1970-   Getting feedback from principals and supervisors with
(spring   regard to the current functioning of the reading pro-
and   gram in the school, current pupil needs, and immedi-
summer ate steps to be taken in continuing the service in the
to   school.
Date)
Summarizing and categorizing the multitude of effective activities reported by reading teachers.

Working with consultants and with classroom teachers to develop a program suited to a specific group of pupils.

Developing as a supplement to the handbook, the first draft of a section that more precisely identified the resource role.

GUIDELINES FOR READING TEACHERS FUNCTIONING IN A RESOURCE CAPACITY

Many of the problems of internal organization are resolved, and the reading resource teacher's role within the six-area framework has now been clarified. Even now, reading resource teachers are involved with classroom teachers in modifying content area programs, in developing new programs, and in building preventive programs. At this time, special attention is being paid to identifying children with potential reading problems early in their school experience and in planning for these children. Secondary reading teachers are helping to keep potential dropouts in school by assisting classroom teachers as they adjust the curriculum so that these pupils may function successfully as learners.

SUMMARY

It is our hope that you profit from our stages of development. The program as described, is extremely exciting and the results very rewarding.